MANAGERIAL CONTROL AND ORGANIZATIONAL DEMOCRACY

MANAGERIAL CONTROL AND ORGANIZATIONAL DEMOCRACY

EDITORS

Bert King
Office of Naval Research

Siegfried Streufert
University of Bielefeld
Federal Republic of Germany

Fred E. Fiedler
University of Washington

1978

V. H. WINSTON & SONS
Washington, D.C.

A HALSTED PRESS BOOK

JOHN WILEY & SONS
New York   Toronto   London   Sydney

V. H. Winston & Sons, a Division of Scripta Technica, Inc., Publishers
1511 K St. N.W., Washington, D.C. 20005

Distributed solely by Halsted Press, a Division of John Wiley & Sons, Inc.

Library of Congress Cataloging in Publication Data
Main entry under title:

Managerial control and organizational democracy.

Selected papers from a conference held in Munich, July 25–30, 1976.
"A Halsted Press book."
Includes bibliographical references and indexes.
1. Industrial management—Addresses, essays, lectures.
2. Employee's representation in management—Addresses, essays, lectures. 3. Leadership—Addresses, essays, lectures. 4. Decision-making—Addresses, essays, lectures. 5. Organizational behavior—Addresses, essays, lectures. I. King, Bert T. II. Streufert, Siegfried. III. Fiedler, Fred Edward.
HD31.M29393   658.4   77-13200
ISBN 0-470-99323-5

Composition by **Marie A. Maddalena**, Scripta Technica, Inc.

DEDICATION

This book is gratefully dedicated to our colleagues in the social, behavioral, and management sciences who, by their professional endeavors, have contributed to international understanding and cooperation.

CONTENTS

PART 1. MANAGERIAL CONTROL UNDER DEMOCRATIC CONDITIONS

PART 2. THEORIES OF LEADERSHIP AND ORGANIZATIONAL CONTROL

PART 3. CONSTRAINTS ON DECISION MAKERS

LIST OF CONTRIBUTORS

Axelsson, Runo. University of Bradford, Bradford, England.

Bass, Bernard M., Ph.D. Graduate School of Management, University of Rochester, Rochester, New York.

Beach, Lee Roy, Ph.D. Department of Psychology, University of Washington, Seattle, Washington.

Blood, Milton R., Ph.D. College of Industrial Management, Georgia Institute of Technology, Atlanta, Georgia.

Butler, Richard J. Management Centre, University of Bradford, Bradford, England.

Castore, Carl H., Ph.D. Department of Psychology, Purdue University, Lafayette, Indiana.

Cummings, L. L., Ph.D. University of Wisconsin-Madison, Center for the Study of Organizational Performance, Madison, Wisconsin.

Dachler, H. Peter, Ph.D. International Institute of Management, Berlin, Federal Republic of Germany, and University of Maryland, College Park, Maryland.

Drake, Bruce. University of Washington, Seattle, Washington.

Fiedler, Fred E., Ph.D. Department of Psychology, University of Washington, Seattle, Washington.

Gunderson, E. K. Eric, Ph.D. Environmental and Social Medicine Division, U.S. Naval Health Research Center, San Diego, California.

Hackman, J. Richard, Ph.D. Administrative Sciences, Yale University, New Haven, Connecticut.

Hickson, David J., Ph.D. Management Centre, University of Bradford, Bradford, England.

Huber, George, Ph.D. Graduate School of Business, University of Wisconsin, Madison, Wisconsin.

Katz, Ralph, Ph.D. Organizational Studies and Management, Massachusetts Institute of Technology, Cambridge, Massachusetts.

Mitchell, Terence R., Ph.D. University of Washington, Seattle, Washington.

O'Connell, Michael J., Ph.D. United States Air Force Academy, Colorado Springs, Colorado.

Partridge, B. E. Management Centre, University of Aston, Birmingham, England.

Rosenstein, Eliezer, Ph.D. Technion-Israel Institute of Technology, Israel.

Streufert, Siegfried, Ph.D. University of Bielefeld, Bielefeld, Federal Republic of Germany.

Suedfeld, Peter, Ph.D. Department of Psychology, University of British Columbia, Vancouver, British Columbia, Canada.

Vroom, Victor H., Ph.D. School of Organization and Management, Yale University, New Haven, Connecticut.

Wilson, David. University of Bradford, Bradford, England.

Yetton, Philip W., Ph.D. Manchester Business School, Manchester, England.

PREFACE

A number of large-scale research and/or social action programs have been initiated recently in an attempt to provide alternatives to classical managerial control systems. These programs have highlighted participation in decision-making, industrial democracy, the quality of working life, power equalization, worker management, democratic leadership, and related concepts. They have proliferated to such an extent that one observer (Raskin, 1976*) heralded the "Outlines of a New Industrial Society" emerging.

In general, such programs have attempted to increase job productivity and the quality of working life by striving for accommodation based on peaceful social change rather than labor-management confrontation. The common denominator of such efforts has been an alteration of power relationships in the direction of giving a greater voice to workers with respect to decisions involving working conditions and even, in some cases, to how the entire organization would be managed. To the extent that such innovations occur,

*Raskin, A. H. Outlines of a new industrial society begin to emerge in West Europe. *International Herald Tribune*, July 23, 1976, p. 6.

they should alter leadership behavior and philosophies, the degree of participation by workers, and decision-making practices. In this volume, we examine a number of developments at the frontiers of research which pertain to designing and evaluating new, more democratic systems for managing organizations and leading work groups.

In Part I of this volume appear chapters that consider how control is, or should be, exerted under democratic (or autonomous) conditions. Bass and Rosenstein review the European experiments on industrial democracy and the American programs involving participative management. They point out that in considering which approach to use, or in evaluating the impact of such programs, it is necessary to take into account national differences, situational factors, occupational levels, etc. Integration of the industrial democracy and participative management models can come about, they maintain, through increased emphasis on self-planning and self-control at different levels in the organizational hierarchy.

Dachler finds it difficult to interpret the results of research on participation because of the prevailing lack of explicit recognition of the different underlying theoretical or ideological bases of the various experiments and programs. He recommends a very broad view of participation which takes into account the kinds of *questions* and assumptions implicit in democratic theory, socialism, the human growth and development approach and in the productivity (or efficiency) viewpoint of participation. He shows that an organizational control system must be analyzed with respect to the total social context in which it occurs and can best be understood when one combines the viewpoints of the several scientific disciplines which deal with participation and management.

Hickson and his colleagues regard organizations as governed by interest units. A coalition of interest units (both within and outside the organization) shapes organizational decision making and determines, for instance, the autonomy of decision making, its pace, and its "scan" (or information utilization). In this chapter we see substantial progress toward the objective of welding such concepts into a theory of power and decision making in organizations.

Gunderson examines the naval organization with its prescribed formal structure and its universal system of regulations designed to control its personnel from above. In spite of this centralized authority, he finds a wide range of differences among organizational subunits with respect to coordination and control problems and management practices. At the level of Navy ship divisions (where heterogeneity of tasks, personnel and environments is common), different leadership practices and control techniques prevail. In certain types of divisions, personnel report substantial autonomy or self-control in performing their jobs. Hence, Gunderson finds it useful to analyze managerial control and worker autonomy within the context of a social systems model which includes relationships among organizational structure and context, social processes, the physical environment, and the organizational climate.

Continuing the concern with control processes, Hackman describes his Job Characteristics Theory, which provides a design and instruments for creating self-managing (or autonomous) work groups. In his chapter, he analyzes those factors most critical to the success of self-managing work groups: how to staff them, how to structure their work, what norms to encourage, etc. In addition to considering how to design work groups, he devotes attention to issues involved in managing them.

The managerial control studies mentioned above have brought us from the level of national differences and ideology (Bass and Rosenstein; Dachler) through the level of the organization and its relationships to environmental factors (Hickson et al.; Gunderson) to the group level. The last study examines factors at the individual level. Blood presents a conceptual approach that appears unusual, if not unique, in the organizational field. He draws on the behavioral self-control and cognitive behavior-control fields in order to create a model which provides for exerting organizational control via the use of self rewards. His self-reward model has important implications for the practice of management including goal-setting, job description, and job redesign.

In Part II we turn to a consideration of leadership processes and their implications for organizational control. Fred Fiedler echoes the concern that was frequently expressed in the chapters referred to above: the need to identify the situational and environmental variables that determine the effectiveness of managerial control and leadership. In this latest statement of his contingency approach to leadership, Fiedler focuses on factors in the immediate situation that, together with leadership style, influence performance in work groups. Furthermore, he moves from a static concern with what characterizes the leader and his group at a particular point in time to a dynamic or longitudinal viewpoint. This shift helps him to explain what happens to leadership processes when changes occur in the organizational environment. Since organizations, even the most conservative ones, typically do change, a dynamic approach like this should enable us to make better predictions of organizational phenomena than his earlier, more static model. Fiedler's most recent data furnish support for his position that we can "improve organizational performance by teaching the leader how to diagnose and modify situational control in order to maintain an optimal match between leadership style and situation in a continuously changing organizational environment" (p. 130).

The Yetton-Vroom chapter covers the latest developments with respect to their descriptive and normative models of leadership. In common with a number of the other authors in this volume (e.g., Fiedler, Dachler, Gunderson, Bass, and Rosenstein), they focus on situational variables, or contingencies, which determine leadership effectiveness. In contrast to Fiedler (who also makes considerable use of situational factors), Vroom and Yetton find that a leader's behavior shifts not only over the long run but even within a single day. In addition, they would reject the classical dichotomy of participative vs. autocratic leaders in favor of the recognition that there are participative vs. autocratic *problems*.

Through the use of multivariate statistical procedures, Yetton and Vroom show that their model accounts for more variance in leadership decision-making than does the participation variable alone. In addition, by focusing on decision-making they foreshadow some of the concerns in Part III of this volume, which deals exclusively with that process and the factors that influence it.

Like Dachler and Hickson et al., Butler espouses a largely sociological approach which involves the thesis that leaders are made great by the organization in which they work and that the organization, in turn, is influenced by the environment and the social context in which it is embedded. In that way, of course, he had adopted a contingency approach, as did Fiedler and Yetton and Vroom, for example. The difference is, however, that Butler goes beyond the immediate task, personality, and work group factors that Fiedler or Yetton and Vroom focus on and analyzes the larger oranizational and social world.

Another noteworthy aspect of Butler's approach is his concern with power. He makes this variable more explicit and more central than do Fiedler or Yetton and Vroom. The power variable, for some reason, has not received as much attention as it deserves, and Butler helps to rectify that situation.

Katz reports that extant leadership studies have ignored the "complex set of interrelationships transpiring among all of the group members" (p. 165). His own theory of the leadership process accordingly centers around the state of conflict (or disequilibrium) in the group with respect to either task factors or affective relationships and the effects of different leadership styles under each of those conflict conditions. He speculates that future managers will have to pay more attention to the particular individuals in the group, the ways that they interact, and the conflicts that arise within the group. This would, of course, require the manager to make successful diagnoses as to the level and kind of conflict within his group and to be able to alter his leadership behavior in accordance with such diagnoses.

Partridge provides us with an unusual vantage point with respect to our central concern with managerial control and organizational democracy. In this study of shop stewards and the union members they represent, we certainly have an instance of democracy in an organizational work setting. But as with democracy in general, it is necessary to consider issues of power with respect to what the leader can accomplish. In the case of the steward, his power stems from deciding what norms to associate with a given union member's grievance and (as with leaders in any setting) feeding back appropriate information to the group.

In underscoring the importance of power factors and situational influences, Partridge agrees in principle with Fiedler, Butler, and Hickson et al. To the extent that he stresses the decision-making aspects of organizational control, his approach has elements in common with Yetton and Vroom and with the authors in Part III of this volume (which examines various aspects of the decision-making process).

We might note also that Partridge has conducted what so many recommend, but so few actually undertake: a field study utilizing a data-gathering technique not restricted to a survey. In sum, his sociological approach, his research design and his selection of subjects provide a refreshing counterbalance to the laboratory locus, the psychological orientation, and the questionnaire approach that characterize so much of the research in this field.

As we have seen, one of the common themes in Part I on managerial control and Part II on leadership deals with decision making. The manager or leader must continually make decisions with respect to recruitment, task assignments, promotions, rewards/punishments, etc. In addition, we saw there that a number of situational constraints affect such decision making. In Part III we turn to an intensive analysis of decision making in groups and organizations, the factors that determine how many and what kinds of decisions are made, and the impact of the decisions on the work group, on productivity, and on the decision maker himself.

Suedfeld considers the ways in which the characteristics of the decision maker and the environment determine the kinds of decisions made and their degree of effectiveness. In analyzing decision making in a number of international crises, he found certain kinds of managerial control tended to facilitate *complex* decision making and complex decision making in turn seemed to characterize those crises that did not result in war. On the other hand, several international confrontations that ended up in war were characterized by a significantly lower level of complexity during the group decision-making and communication processes that preceded the outbreak of hostilities.

Nevertheless, Suedfeld resists the temptation to recommend a particular kind of managerial control or leadership decision making. Rather, he advocates a more individualized attempt on the part of management to match the personalities of the decision makers and the organizational context in which the decisions are made to the particular kinds of decisions that are demanded.

Streufert's chapter represents the culmination of a decade of research by himself and several colleagues on the topic of decision making. He takes into account both the characteristics of the environment and of the decision maker as they affect the decisions made.

There is, of course, a close relationship between the Streufert and Suedfeld chapters. Suedfeld deals with the entire range of information load conditions while Streufert deals with what essentially constitutes the middle of Suedfeld's continuum. Within that middle range, their views generally agree.

Streufert focuses on the structure of decision making and includes in his purview both long-term strategic decisions and more rapid decisions made in a tactical context. Like Suedfeld (and so many of the other authors in this volume), he thinks in terms of a contingency approach. This leads him to anticipate a future time at which it would be possible for us to match the organizational (or environmental) situation with the characteristics of the manager or decision maker so as to optimize managerial decision making.

Cummings et al. present a study under controlled laboratory conditions of the effects of both organizational structure and the organizational environment on decision processes and outcomes. Using as their vehicle the tactical and negotiations game developed by Streufert, they examined the effects of the information load for work groups experimentally organized in either a hierarchical or a loosely structured (committee) manner. The loosely structured group represents some of the conditions often recommended by those who advocate more participation in decision making and more democracy in work groups. The tightly structured hierarchical groups placed the burden of decision making on the leader.

Their results echo the theme found in many of the studies in this volume: the complexity of outcomes involving the satisfaction and effectiveness of groups organized along different lines. Even the decision maker's level of satisfaction depends on a number of variables, so that it is difficult to defend a prescription involving any one variable, they maintain. In fact, Cummings and his colleagues specifically state that we must look critically at the numerous current prescriptions calling for decentralized organizational structures, loose structures, or less of an emphasis on hierarchical work groups. They find that under some conditions hierarchy and tight structure result in satisfaction and organizational effectiveness. Since the results of relatively simple laboratory experiments like theirs give rise to complex interactions, they see the need for a good deal of caution in generalizing about real life organizations where, of course, conditions are far more complex than in the laboratory.

Like Cummings et al., Beach and his colleagues believe that the great complexity in real-life organizations makes it difficult to analyze causal relationships there. Consequently, they advocate using laboratory research to examine many of the important organizational issues. In their paper in this volume they have selected for laboratory experimentation three different issues: (1) the effect of different power relationships within a work group on the task satisfaction of the group; (2) the credibility of sources who supply information (in this case, on job applicants); and (3) the effects of the structure of information and the recipient's ability to control the rate of incoming information on both the accuracy of his judgments and his confidence in them.

One of the more interesting aspects of this research is its attempt to bring to bear on decision making the large body of social psychological literature on communication and persuasion in which source credibility has been confirmed as a critical variable. Such cross-fertilization among the areas of leadership, management, participation, and decision making would seem to offer exciting prospects for future research.

In the course of analyzing decision making in groups and organizations, Castore has identified a number of gaps in the literature. He indicates that managers (especially upper level managers) typically have to make decisions about issues for which no clear-cut criteria are available. However, the available research data mostly deal with those situations in which such criteria are available. In addition, he shows that we lack adequate information as to what variables come to bear once the group or organization has made a decision. That is, we need more data on the process of implementing decisions in organizational contexts and on what happens when the decision-making group receives feedback about the outcomes of decisions made earlier. Filling in such gaps in our understanding will help us to understand more fully the decision-making process in organizations.

The history of this volume goes back to 1973 when Lyman Porter, Fred Fiedler, and Bert King began discussing possible ways of integrating research in the fields of leadership and management. That led to a letter to the Human Factors Division of the North Atlantic Treaty Organization (NATO) by Fiedler in November, 1973, proposing an international conference. In 1974, King and Fiedler submitted a formal conference proposal which NATO agreed in December, 1974, to support under the title "Coordination and Control of Group and Organizational Performance." NATO designated King as the U.S. Co-Director and Siegfried Streufert as the European Co-Director for this Conference.

This volume contains less than half of the papers from that Conference, which was held in Munich, Federal Republic of Germany, on July 25–30, 1976. Appreciation is hereby expressed to Dr. B. A. Bayraktar of the NATO Human Factors Division for his continued help with respect to the Conference and to Dr. Pieter J. D. Drenth of the Free University of Amsterdam who represented NATO at the Conference and delivered a stimulating welcome address there.

We would also like to express our gratitude to the members of the Conference Scientific Advisory Committee. They reviewed all papers submitted for the Conference and provided highly useful advice as to which should be presented there. In addition to the editors of this volume, the Committee included the following scientists: Pieter Drenth, Dr. Frank Heller of the Tavistock Institute of Human Relations, Dean Lyman Porter of the University of California at Irvine, and Dr. Bernhard Wilpert of the International Institute of Management in Berlin. However, blame for any shortcomings in this volume can legitimately be attributed only to its editors since they made the final decisions on its content and format.

We would also like to express our appreciation to those who served as session discussants or as chairmen or rapporteurs for informal working groups, and to those who chaired the paper sessions at the Munich Conference. The discussants consisted of Dr. Val Cervin of the University of Windsor in Ontario, Canada; Dr. Carl Castore of Purdue University; Dean Lyman Porter, Dr. L. L. Cummings of the University of Wisconsin; and Dr. Susan Vinnicombe of the Imperial College of Science and Technology in London. The session chairmen included Mr. S. E. Poppleton of Middlesex Polytechnic in Enfield, England; Dr. Frank Heller; Dr. Carson Eoyang of the Naval Postgraduate School in Monterey, California; Dr. Donald Walizer of the U.S. Army Research Institute in Heidelberg, West Germany; Mr. A. Godwin of the Ministry of Defence, London; and Dr. Peter Weissenberg of the State University of New York at Binghampton.

Dr. Gerald A. Randell of the University of Bradford in England served as chairmen and rapporteur for the informal working group on Leadership. Dr. Frank Friedlander of Case Western Reserve University and Dr. Agnes Koopman-Iwema of the University of Amsterdam did the same for the working group on Participation. Pieter Drenth performed as chairman and rapporteur for the work group that discussed Industrial Democracy.

The Office of Naval Research provided partial financial support for the research reported herein by Bass and Rosenstein; Beach, Mitchell, and Drake; Blood; Hackman; Streufert; and Yetton and Vroom.

Mrs. Kathy Duncan and Ms. Elizabeth Wolter contributed immeasurably to this volume by assisting with correspondence, administrative arrangements, and editing of the papers.

PART 1

MANAGERIAL CONTROL UNDER DEMOCRATIC CONDITIONS

INTEGRATION OF INDUSTRIAL DEMOCRACY AND PARTICIPATIVE MANAGEMENT: U.S. AND EUROPEAN PERSPECTIVES[1]

Bernard M. Bass
University of Rochester

Eliezer Rosenstein
Technion-Israel Institute of Technology

The post-World War II era has seen the distinct growth of two trends in management-worker relations: industrial democracy and participative management.

If we begin in the country, Sweden, in which the earliest and probably the most progress towards industrial democracy and participation was made, we readily see the need for clarifying what we mean by industrial democracy and participative management before we can intelligently discuss how to integrate the two approaches.

> People started talking about participation in Sweden 50 years ago. They called it industrial democracy. But here, as elsewhere, it remained talk. Now, suddenly, experiments of all kinds, in and outside the business world, are popping up overnight.

---

[1] Paper presented at the NATO Conference on Coordination and Control in Groups and Organizations, Munich, July 25-31, 1976.

1

Worker say-so. Decision-sharing. Employee influence. Self-govern-
ing groups. On-the-job democracy . . . So far, the interpretations are
as varied as the trials.

In 1946, employer and employee organizations agreed that in
firms with over 50 employees works councils, with representatives
from both sides, would meet regularly to solve problems and
exchange information. These have worked well or badly, but without
enhancing the average employee's sense of fulfillment. Subsequently,
these organizations, through their mutual Development Council for
Collaboration Questions, initiated a number of projects in firms of
various sizes to provide channels for employee influence. Others have
sprung up in government firms and departments, or at the
spontaneous initiative of employees. [Link, 1971, p. 36]

So we now may see in Swedish industry employee participation in job
design, local councils of employees, profit sharing after one year's
employment through loans to buy shares with full voting rights, production
groups, changes to hourly pay from piece rates, job enrichment, job rotation,
scrapping of the assembly line, increased employee autonomy co-op
organization, self-activation, suggestions systems, and information exchanges
about investment decisions (Link, 1971).

To confuse matters, in the U.S. many of these same practices have been
introduced simply as progressive personnel practices by managements who also
can still view "industrial democracy" as a movement threatening management
decision-making prerogatives and a "socialist takeover."

The Different Approaches

For purposes of defining the issues more carefully, it may be helpful to
differentiate among approaches, then show how they might be integrated.

Approaches may be direct or indirect. Workers may participate directly or
through representatives. That is, they may participate in decisions with their
own boss or through representatives on management councils. Approaches
may also be formal or informal. Periodic MBO sessions may be formally
organized for managers and their subordinates. Or, as a consequence of
education, personality and interest, as they see fit, managers may discuss
objectives with their subordinates and their success in attaining them.

The formal approaches may be independent of legal sanction or supported
by national or local legislation. The Dutch *werkoverleg* is a formally
constituted consultative work group which carries no particular legal support.
On the other hand, the West German co-determination law, which became
operative in 800 large German corporations, July 1, 1976, requiring worker
representation at the highest management levels, is an approach which began

during the military occupation after World War II—and evidently had a lot of inspiration from the U.S. military government (Raskin, 1976).

Again, industrial democracy or worker participation may involve sharing by workers in the *consequences* of the decision-making. They may share in the profits or in the savings from reduced costs of production in which they have been involved, say, as in the Scanlon Plan (Lesieur, 1958). Or, they may participate in tax-benefited pension plans for Employee Stock Ownership Programs (Drucker, 1976).

Industrial democracy also may be seen in collective bargaining between representatives of employee unions and management. Approaches other than collective bargaining often are seen by unions as anti-union efforts.

Two Distinct Trends

For purposes of discussion, what we see are two initially distinct major trends: One is structural; the other is behavioral.

The structural approach is formally organized industrial democracy, increasing the equalization of power, by joint decision-making through direct representation or elected representation on *ad hoc* or permanent committees, councils, and boards at various levels of management decision-making. Often this is connected with formalization of the distribution of extra benefits to workers through sharing of profits, through disbursing of stock ownership, and through sharing of cost-reduction gains in the paycheck and in the pension. At the highest level, elected worker representatives sit on the Board of Directors of the firm or agency. It is now commonplace in European capitalist economies such as West Germany, and in socialist economies such as Yugoslavia. Joint-consultation bodies, joint management boards, and self-government are the major institutionalized arrangements of the industrial democracy model. Such mechanisms have been seen as "integrative" in that one formal structure is established for representatives of both management and workers.[2] In the U.S. and to a lesser extent elsewhere, industrial

[2] Industrial democracy has also been associated with collective bargaining—a form of "disjunctive" participation. Workers form an organization counter to that of management for the purpose of interacting with it from outside (Walker, 1970, 1974). But for the purposes of our analysis here only integrative participation will be considered as an approach to industrial democracy although there are obvious contributions to influencing management through bargaining pressure. Nevertheless, bargaining is distinctly different in form and effect from collaboration. Collective bargaining is a formal process of accommodation to resolve conflicting interests of equal parties. Joint consultation assumes management and labor share common objectives that can provide the basis for cooperation between the two. Integrative bodies are formal mechanisms for the elaboration and expression of common interests. In practice the border between the two may be blurred, since collective bargaining as well as the integrative mechanisms include elements of both cooperation and conflict (Rosenstein, 1976; Tannenbaum, 1974).

democracy has come to several hundred firms who voluntarily instituted the Scanlon Plan where committees of workers and managers share in cost-reduction planning as well as in the subsequent benefits (Lesieur, 1958). Increasingly, we are likely to see more worker representation on Boards of Directors through their stock ownership. Stock is being purchased by worker pension plans and through profit-sharing plans some of which are now encouraged through an investment tax credit.

The behavioral approach is participative management. It is face-to-face, informal, sharing of decision-making at the work place. It is "shop floor democracy." It is an informal arrangement between a manager and his immediate subordinates where the manager through inclination, indoctrination, training, organizational policy, social pressure or other personal reasons involves his subordinates in consensual decision-making with him about matters of consequence to all concerned. Arrangements can be institutionalized to some degree for participative management making use of such mechanisms as consultation on a regular basis with individual subordinates alone or in groups or formally delegating responsibilities to them (Ritchie, 1974; Strauss, 1963; Strauss & Rosenstein, 1970). And an organizational climate of trust is needed. But it is as a style of management that participation has been most promoted in the United States by such theorists as Likert (1961) and McGregor (1960). Nevertheless, participative management is by no means commonplace in either the United States or elsewhere. In PROFILE studies we have completed in the U.S., the modal style of relating between middle managers and subordinates seems to be *consultation*. The manager obtains information and opinion from his subordinates before he, the manager, makes his decision of consequence to all concerned (Bass, Valenzi, Farrow, & Solomon, 1975). According to corresponding studies we have completed in Spain for higher level managers in smaller firms, consultation likewise seems to be the model way of relating to subordinates. However, manipulation and authoritarian direction are much more frequently observed in Spanish than in U.S. managers.

Participative management has been expected to increase satisfaction, involvement, and commitment as well as to improve performance. However, it has been easier to show the effects on attitudes and feelings than on performance. We are just beginning to learn the conditions under which participation is likely to be counterproductive. Personality, task, organization, and culture make the difference (Ritchie, 1974; Sashkin, 1976; Singer, 1974).

Participative Management and Satisfaction as a Function of Culture and Organization

Cascio (1974) noted that among 272 managers[3] who played subordinate

[3]Data came from the International Research Groups on Management data bank now housed at the State University of New York at Binghamton.

Table 1. Reported Satisfaction of Subordinates Following Decision-Making with Participative, Persuasive, and Directive Supervisors

N	Culture	Percent of subordinates who were most satisfied in decision-making meetings with participative supervisor
65	Dutch-Flemish ($N = 116$)	64.7
50	Nordic: Danish, Norwegian, Swedish, Austrian, West German, German Swiss ($N = 202$)	56.4
202	Anglo-Americans: British-Northern Irish, American, Australian	53.1
179	Latin: Brazilian, Columbian, French, Italian, Spanish, French Swiss, Walloon	52.6
28	Japanese	50.0
37	East Indian	29.4

$\chi^2 = 12.306$ ($p < .05$).   From Cascio (1974), p. 599.

roles in Exercise Supervise (Bass, 1967), whether or not participants were most satisfied in decision-making meetings with participative supervisors depended on their national identity.

Table 1 shows that among Europeans and Japanese, at least 50% were most satisfied with participative supervisors. But for India, the figure dropped to 29.4%. In turn, 75% of Indian managers preferred uninterested, uninvolved subordinates when making decisions while Americans, Europeans, and Japanese preferred active, involved subordinates. Function made a difference as well. While 57% of managers from Personnel preferred participative supervisors, only 50% from Sales and 44.4% from Finance did so.

Participative Management and Productivity as a Function of Organization

Recent analyses we have completed with our PROFILE (Bass, 1976, in press) point to organizational and task elements which alter the frequency with which participative management will be employed and its subsequent effectiveness. According to survey data from 277 U.S. subordinates, participative management is most frequent when organizational policies are clear, the organizational climate is warm and trusting, the manager has long-term objectives, tasks are complex and subordinates have more information about the decision than does the manager. Effectiveness of work unit operations is enhanced by participative management when organizational policies are clear, tasks are complex, and subordinates have more discretionary opportunities on how to complete their jobs.

Possible Relations Between Industrial Democracy and Participative Management

Despite the major differences between industrial democracy and participative management in format and organizational locus of interaction, they both share the same objectives: to increase workers' understanding, acceptance, satisfaction, commitment, and ownership of decisions, and as a consequence to produce greater operational effectiveness.

Traditionally, management is conceived as planning, direction, and control. Participation modifies management to incorporate self-planning, self-direction, and self-control. The idea of worker participation, in all its forms, is widespread today over many countries, countries differing in economic development and political system. However, there is a considerable gap between the ideological acceptance of the idea on the one hand and its actual implementation on the other (Derber, 1970; Walker, 1974). This gap constitutes a source of disappointment to those ardent advocates of participation who find it difficult to illustrate, on a wide scale, the positive impact of participatory programs. Nevertheless, it seems that participation of workers in decision-making is far from being a marginal issue in contemporary management (Gold, 1976; Roach, 1973).

Origins

Despite their general appeal and common objectives, participative management and industrial democracy have developed independently. The promotion of one is somehow associated with the neglect of the other. Thus, in the U.S., worker participation is associated with the participative style of management and, on occasion, with collective bargaining. In Europe, on the other hand, worker participation is mainly associated with industrial democracy.

Cross-Atlantic Influences. But there is a continuing flow of influences across the Atlantic in both directions. There has been a considerable transfer of participative management practices from the U.S. to Europe. European management has been under the influence of American management education in the post-World War II era. This has been due to U.S. multinational corporate investment in European industry as well as U.S. private foundation and university support for European management education.

At the same time, we are beginning to see the first signs of the transfer of European industrial democracy to the U.S.

After the U.S. Chrysler Corporation offered its workers in Britain two seats on the British Board of Directors, U.S. United Auto Workers' President Leonard Woodcock wondered if Chrysler was ready to make the same offer in the U.S. but he regarded the matter as "a philosophical thought," not a big demand.

But industrial democracy has not been totally absent in the U.S. In the 1920's, the government model of an elected body of worker representatives with relatively little real power legislating arrangements appeared in paternalistic companies. More recently, as a counterbalance to the adversary and crisis character of labor-management collective bargaining, the steel industry formed a joint labor-management committee which was to work together as a study group on a more continuing basis on problems of common interest. Jamestown, New York, is involved in a total community effort involving industry and labor representatives to revive the local economy. Rushton management and its miners are practicing a form of industrial democracy as is Eaton Corporation (Recent Initiatives, 1976).

Nevertheless, the two major models have thus been almost mutually exclusive. Labor apologists such as Gomberg (1957) have seen participative management and the human relations movement in general as management ploys to avoid sharing power with employees. Only through collective bargaining can employees exert real influence. At the same time, participative management was on much more fertile soil in the U.S. with its traditions of democracy and individualism than it was in more class-conscious Europe. But, we now see the prospects brightening for a merger of the two models. There is more than one alternative for the relationships between these two models. Industrial democracy and participative management can be *compensatory*, i.e., if you have one, you don't need another. Or, one approach can *complement* the other. A third possibility is one of *differential application*, i.e., each can be applied to different aspects of worker-management relations. Let us look at each of these alternatives.

COMPENSATORY RELATIONSHIP

The argument here is, if you have one, you don't need the other. With industrial democracy, properly practiced, workers can vote for policy changes through their elected representatives. They can make their feelings known about organization-wide matters by communicating with their elected representatives. The major weakness of this argument is, of course, the limited degree, or the complete lack, of relevancy of the participation-at-the-top-of-the-organizational-hierarchy for the employee at the place where the work is performed (Emery & Thorsrud, 1969). Another weakness is the exclusion of the lower and middle management from the participatory process. These managers, often ignored and eliminated from the mechanisms of industrial democracy, disassociate themselves from the participatory process and undermine its potential effectiveness. On the other hand, with participative management, the argument is that no formal organizational mechanisms are needed to permit workers to share their grievances and suggestions with their immediate superiors. Regular organizational channels are used if Likert's linking pin Systems 4 structure is operative (Likert, 1967). What they discuss is likely to be more relevant to their immediate workplace than to organization-wide matters, per se. However, the danger of concentrating on participative management measures of all kinds (including socio-technical programs at the shop level) while ignoring participation at the top is that when the crucial and strategic decisions are made unilaterally by management, participation at the bottom of the hierarchy will be gradually limited to most marginal issues. Consequently, participative management measures will lose their meaningfulness.

COMPLEMENTARY RELATIONSHIP

Each approach can reinforce the other. Democracy, or better yet, consensual decision-making, is practiced within the immediate face-to-face work group as well as in the democratic election of representatives of that work group to higher management councils. It may very well be that to have substance industrial democracy must operate side-by-side with face-to-face participative management. Rus (1970) and Obradovic (1975) have well documented the degree to which, despite the formalities of worker council decision-making about organization-wide issues in Yugoslavia, in fact it is the managers, bankers, technocrats, Communist party members and other key people who initiate the decisions of consequence. Workers may feel no real ownership of decisions in an industrial democracy where immediate manager-worker relationships are traditional and authoritarian. Similarly, Wilpert (1975) and Rosenstein (1976) have drawn attention to the phenomenon of "double loyalty" and other internal problems of integrative mechanisms in West Germany and Israel, respectively.

Thus, participative management and industrial democracy measures each have their relative advantages and disadvantages as participatory mechanisms. Overall, we see more useful complementarity between the two rather than compensation between the two. The key to the mutual support between participative management and industrial democracy lies in the extent that participative management results in self-planning in the organization for the worker no longer supplies much of the energy for industrial production. He decreases in his role as guider of tools. As technology advances, increasingly the worker becomes the regulator of an industrial process, the adjuster, the monitor and diagnostician dealing with unprogrammed, unpredictable fluctuations in the system (Davis, 1971). For this kind of effort, the worker must have an *understanding* of that part of the system for which he is responsible. This understanding should be based on broad rather than narrow training. The worker should be ready to react without necessary consultation with higher authority. He must be adaptable and committed to his role in the organization (Bass, 1972). And for this, self-planning at all levels in the organization is likely to be most efficacious.

Self-Planning as the Key to Complementarity of Participative Management and Industrial Democracy

While several approaches can be suggested for promoting understanding, responsibility, adaptability and commitment, the single most effective means is to promote participative processes of the planning function. This in turn will have positive influences on the maintenance of an effective industrial democracy.

For a total of 1,417 managers from 12 nationalities (North American, British, Irish, Danish, German, Dutch, Belgian, Swiss, French, Italian, Colombian, and Japanese) engaged in a simulation to contrast the effects of self-planning with executing plans developed by others, both productivity and satisfaction were generally increased by self-planning. Several reasons can be suggested for this.

First, sense of accomplishment may be more when executing one's own plan rather than an assigned plan. Second, there may be more of a tendency to try to confirm the validity of a plan by executing it successfully and more confidence that it can be done. Third, there may be more commitment to see that the plan works well. Fourth, there may be perceived more flexibility, more room for modification and initiative to make improvements in an assigned plan. Fifth, understanding of the plan is likely to be greater. Sixth, human resources may be better utilized. Seventh, there are likely to be fewer communication problems and consequent errors and distortions in pursuing instructions. Eighth, competitive feelings aroused between planners and those who must execute the plans are avoided because planners and doers are the same persons.

Although not everyone prefers (see Hackman, pp. 61-91) or thrives with self-planning, for the average participant performance is superior and commitment and satisfaction are greater with self-planning (Bass & Leavitt, 1963; Bass, in press).

Situational Considerations

Self-planning may be contraindicated in certain situations.

Planning may require special knowledge, information and facilities ordinarily unavailable to the doers. Time required to plan may make it impossible for those who must execute the plans to engage in developing them. There are individual differences in performance and satisfaction with self-planning as well as national differences.

Nationality. In our study of the 1,417 managers, objective efficiency differences favoring self-planning failed to materialize for our German sample who did just as well working on others' plans as their own although, subjectively, they were like other nationalities in preferring to work on their own plan, feeling more committed and responsible for it and thinking it a better plan. Managers from the United States profited most from self-planning, while relative to other nationalities Northern European managers seemed to gain the least advantage from self-planning. Efficiency[4] differences favoring self-planning by nationalities were in this order: North Americans, 13.7; Irish, 12.8; French, 11.8; Colombians, 8.8; British, 8.5; Italians, 8.0; Japanese, 7.9; Belgians, 6.1; Dutch, 5.5; Swiss, 5.2; Danes, 1.1, and West Germans, −2.0. That is, others' plans were operated slightly more efficiently by the West Germans.

Occupational Level. Self-planning clearly constitutes a meaningful means of participation for professionals due to their strong identification with their occupation and their expectations for intrinsic rewards. In most cases they expect to take part in the planning phase of their work. Self-planning by professionals may help to moderate the potential conflict between the professional and the organization, since it will enable him to utilize his own internalized, normative system to influence the choice of methods used to solve his problems (see Hall, 1975, pp. 81–84). But the importance and meaningfulness of self-planning as a component of the job has also surfaced for blue collar and white collar employees as a consequence of the growing interest in job enrichment (Davis & Cherns, 1975; Walton, 1973).

Policy Considerations

Many individuals prefer to leave planning to others. Ideally, opportunities for self-planning should be an optional attribute of a job assignment. There are great efficiencies in standardized programs and plans such as blueprints or available computer routines and the conditions for self-planning are surely constrained by these already available structures for laying out the procedures

---

[4]Efficiency was calculated by measuring the amount of assemblies completed less a correction for excess production for inventory.

for getting work done. Nevertheless, there still remains much unprogrammed work now planned by higher authority or by staff specialists whose plans are reviewed by higher authority before they are implemented. It is in these unprogrammed and particularly unprogrammable areas that self-planning can be introduced with profit. Existing jobs are being redesigned, but a fundamental policy change is required if self-planning is to be encouraged. As long as planning is seen as a management prerogative, self-planning will be in conflict with the organization's authority and decision structure. Many other changes may be required also if self-planning is to be encouraged, changes more suited to an industrial democracy than a traditional top-down organization, suggesting that participative management and industrial democracy are more likely to complement each other.

Risks. Higher authority will be required to take more risks with operating personnel, allocating more responsibility and autonomy to them to promote self-planning and self-control. At the same time, organizational developmental efforts need to be encouraged to reduce worker suspiciousness about management's motivation as opportunities for worker self-planning are increased.

Coordination. If self-planning is instituted, coordination requirements within the "doer" group are likely to increase. More attention will have to be paid to horizontal communications—characteristic of democratic rather than autocratic government. As self-planning results in more varied methods and in greater self-control, more closed feedback loops will be necessary in comparison to what is required when planning is centralized (Bass, 1970).

Training. If planners are now needed because special knowledge is required to do adequate planning and if self-planning is of sufficient value, then operators need to be provided special training in how to plan. The democratic aspect here is the likely general upgrading of the status and general skill level of the whole "citizenry." Staff planners need to become teachers and consultants on how to plan. Many of the skills we ordinarily think must be present or learned by supervisors, such as planning, are skills that are needed by operators if self-planning is to be encouraged. Special training may be usefully provided to operators on objective-setting, scheduling, evaluating plans and measuring progress towards achieving planning goals. Supervisors can serve as the consultants to operators. Instead of providing plans and schedules, they can help operators to plan and schedule for themselves.

Complementarity of industrial democracy and participative management is also seen if operator self-planning requires fuller understanding of organizational processes and policies outside the immediate working area of the operator. Again, broader training of operators is likely to be required. This, in turn, is likely to make operators more readily available for transfer and promotion, more alert to systems problems and ready and able to communicate such discoveries horizontally and upwards.

Self-direction. Self-planning goes hand-in-hand with self-direction and self-control. It becomes increasingly necessary to self-plan if adequate self-direction and self-control are to be expected, for the latter will require high degrees of understanding, commitment and felt responsibility which are most likely to develop under self-planning. In turn, such understanding, commitment and felt responsibility are ideals to be sought in the good worker citizens of an industrial democracy.

DIFFERENTIAL APPLICATIONS

While we have seen so far the general utility of a mutually supportive participative management within a democratically-organized industry, further examination suggests that while many issues call for both as we have already indicated, different issues may call for one without the other, or for neither.

We can sort issues into: (a) those likely to be better handled by means of democratically elected worker representatives; (b) those better handled by face-to-face participative management; (c) those where both approaches are likely to be appropriate; (d) those where neither is desirable and it is advisable to reserve decisions exclusively for management (assuming them to be responsible to all constituencies including employees, shareholders, customers, and community). The following list illustrates these four possibilities and our reasons for the choice of approach:

	Industrial democracy	Participative management	Reason
A. Pay and benefits	X		Principles of equity, company finances, need to avoid maximizing self-interest.
B. Job satisfaction		X	Participative management will directly improve.
C. Career development	X	X	Broad policies need to be set at higher levels, but career planning is best as self-planning.
D. Working conditions: workload and socio-technical issues	X	X	Plant-wide problems and community affairs are best dealt with by council and staff. On the other hand, improvements at the local level may be instituted

E. Job security	X	X	and implemented best through participation in the decision process at the local level. Market conditions and finance of the firm as a whole require organization-wide attention. Yet some commitment to strategies such as sharing reductions in hours can be best accomplished at local levels of participative endeavor.
F. Financing marketing capital investment			Optimal strategies here should be sought by a management responsible to its various constituuencies. To the degree to which best solutions are matters of mathematics, legal constraints or market demands rather than debate, decisions should be reached without necessary worker involvement.

This list is far, of course, from being exhaustive. It rather suggests some examples as a basis for further study and examination. The important point seems to be that the nature of the subject may determine the extent to which industrial democracy and/or participative management measures can be effectively used. It is dangerous to talk, though, in universal terms since this may vary in various countries depending on structural variables and on the value system of the particular society.

* * * * *

We examined the relationships between two models of worker participation: industrial democracy and participative management. These models, which have gained considerable popularity during the last 40 years or so, have developed independently. Often emphasis on one was associated with the neglect of the other. However, from a conceptual and a practical point of view, there is neither need nor justification to view these models as mutually exclusive.

Moreover, since both models are based on the assumption that those at the bottom of an organizational hierarchy take part in the authority and managerial functions, they may reinforce and augment the favorable effects of each other (see also Patchen, 1972).

Although the two types of worker participation must be simultaneously developed and integrated, there is also an optimal division of labor among these in terms of organizational and personnel issues to be dealt with. Moreover, cultural and national differences must also be taken into account. Nevertheless, a major contribution to the effectiveness of industrial democracy will be due to the extent it fosters the side-by-side development and implementation of participative management styles in the face-to-face interaction between superior and subordinates.

REFERENCES

Bass, B. M. Combining management training and research. *Training and Development Journal*, 1967, **21**, 2–7.

Bass, B. M. When planning for others. *Journal of Applied Behavioral Science*, 1970, **6**, 151–171.

Bass, B. M. *Greater productivity and satisfaction through self-planning.* First International Sociological Conference on Participation and Self-Management, Dubrovnik, Yugoslavia, December 13–16, 1972.

Bass, B. M. A systems survey research and feedback procedure for management and organizational development. *Journal of Applied Behavioral Science*, 1976, **12**(2), 215–229.

Bass, B. M. Utility of self-planning in a counterbalanced experiment replicated in twelve countries. *Journal of Applied Psychology*, in press.

Bass, B. M., & Leavitt, H. J. Some experiments in planning and operating. *Management Science*, 1963, 574–585.

Bass, B. M., Valenzi, E. R., Farrow, D. L., & Solomon, R. J. Management styles associated with organizational, task, personal and interpersonal contingencies. *Journal of Applied Psychology*, 1975, **60**, 720–729.

Cascio, W. F. Functional specialization, culture, and preference for participative management. *Personnel Psychology*, 1974, **27**, 593–603.

Davis, L. E. The coming crises for production management: Technology and organization. *International Journal of Production Research*, 1971, **9**, 65–82.

Davis, L. E., & Cherns, A. B. (Eds.). *The quality of working life.* New York: Free Press, 1975.

Derber, M. Cross-currents in workers participation. *Industrial Relations*, 1970, **9**, 123–136.

Drucker, P. *The unseen revolution: How pension fund socialism came to America.* New York: Harper & Row, 1976.

Emery, F. E., & Thorsrud, E. *The form and content in industrial democracy.* London: Tavistock, 1969.

Gold, C. *Employer-employee committees and worker participation.* Key Issues No. 20, New York State School of Industrial and Labor Relations, Cornell University, 1976.

Gomberg, W. The use of psychology in industry: A trade union point of view. *Management Science,* 1957, **3**, 348–370.

Hall, R. H. *Occupations and the social structure.* Englewood Cliffs: Prentice-Hall, 1975.

Lesieur, F. (Ed.). *The Scanlon plan.* New York: Wiley, 1958.

Likert, R. *New patterns of management.* New York: McGraw-Hill, 1961.

Likert, R. *Human organization.* New York: McGraw-Hill, 1967.

Link, R. Alienation. *Sweden Now.* June 1971, 36–40.

McGregor, D. *The human side of enterprise.* New York: McGraw-Hill, 1960.

Obradovic, J. Workers' participation: Who participates? *Industrial Relations,* 1975, **14**(1), 32–44.

Patchen, M. *Participation, achievement and involvement on the job.* Englewood Cliffs: Prentice-Hall, 1972.

Raskin, A. H. The workers' voice in German companies. *New York Times,* June 11, 1976.

Recent initiatives in labor-management cooperation. National Center for Productivity and Quality of Working Life. Washington, D.C., February 1976.

Ritchie, J. B. Supervision. In G. Strauss et al. (Eds.), *Organizational behavioral research and issues.* U.S. Industrial Relations Research Association Series, 1974, 51–76.

Roach, J. M. *Workers' participation: New voices in management.* A Report from the Conference Board, New York, 1973.

Rosenstein, E. *Workers' participation in management: Problematic issues in the Isareli system.* Systems research working paper series, School of Management, State University of New York at Binghamton, 1976 (mimeo).

Rus, V. Influence structure in Yugoslav enterprize. *Industrial Relations,* 1970, **9**, 148–160.

Sashkin, M. Participation in organizations: Types, effects, contingencies and change. School of Business Administration, Wayne State University, 1976 (mimeo, 43 p.).

Singer, J. N. Participative decision-making about work—An overdue look at variables which mediate its effects. *Sociology of Work and Occupations,* 1974, **1**(4), 347–371.

Strauss, G. Some notes on power-equalization. In H. J. Leavitt (Ed.), *The social science of organizations: Four perspectives.* Englewood Cliffs: Prentice-Hall, 1963, 41–84.

Strauss, G., & Rosenstein, E. Workers' participation: A critical view. *Industrial Relations,* 1970, **9**, 197–214.

Tannenbaum, A. S. Systems of formal participation. In G. Strauss et al. (Eds.), *Organizational behavior research and issues.* U.S. Industrial Relations Research Association Series, 1974, 77–105.

Walker, K. *Workers' participation in management: Concepts and reality.* Synthesis report presented at the second World Congress of the International Industrial Relations Association, Geneva, 1970.

Walker, K. Workers' participation in management-problems, practice and prospects. *Bulletin of International Institute of Labor Studies*, 1974, **12**, 3–35.

Walton, R. E. Quality of working life: What is it? *Sloan Management Review*, Fall 1973, 11–12.

Wilpert, B. Research on industrial democracy: The German case. *Industrial Relations Journal*, 1975, **6**, 53–64.

THE PROBLEM NATURE OF PARTICIPATION IN ORGANIZATIONS: A CONCEPTUAL EVALUATION [1]

H. Peter Dachler
*International Institute of Management,
Berlin, and University of Maryland*

The international literature on participation in decision-making, industrial democracy, power equalization, worker management, democratic leadership, and similar topic issues is diffuse in meaning and purpose, involves frequent contradictions, harbors a plethora of undefined terms, is plagued by ambiguous theoretical underpinnings, and provides a few useful statements for the policy makers. Even a cursory review of this literature quickly leads to the depressing conclusion that there is yet no clear set of questions regarding the issues of participation, let alone a set of answers which begins to define the nature of this phenomenon and its determinants and consequences.

The major problem underlying participation research is the fact that it is nearly impossible to determine what participation entails. It means different things to different investigators; the issue originates in different value systems;

[1] This paper is based on an earlier and longer version by the author and Bernhard Wilpert of the International Institute of Management in Berlin. Helpful comments were provided by Roger Dunbar, Walter Goldberg, J. Richard Hackman, and Benjamin Schneider.

it is grounded in psychological, sociological, economic, political, and legal paradigms; it transcends micro and macro issues regarding individuals, organizations, and whole societies, from individual motivation and ability considerations, through leadership and group dynamic issues, to organizational factors and socio-political structures and processes within and between societies; and it originates as a research problem in both basic and applied social science theory and research.

Such a state of affairs could well indicate an active, healthy, and rapidly developing social science research area, provided that the heterogeneity in approaches, purposes, origins of questions, and research results indicated some process of convergence—a crucial requirement for the development of a conceptualization of participation in decision-making. Unfortunately, such convergence is not apparent in the participation literature and one is left with terms, such as participation in decision-making or industrial democracy, which seem to refer to important aspects of organized activities, but which are devoid of any theoretical significance, beyond pointing to various common sense notions in need of research.

Thus, it is questions, not answers, that participation research currently needs most. Existing statements regarding participation in decision-making too often obscure the questions which gave rise to them, making a cumulative understanding of this phenomenon difficult, if not impossible. A search for questions necessitates a reexamination of the *problem nature* of participation, i.e., what questions for consideration or solution does the participation phenomenon require or imply? Within the limited space available, this chapter briefly outlines the major problem dimensions of participation, their interdependencies, and some of the resulting sets of conceptual and research questions, in an effort to rethink the ways in which participation in decision-making within organizations can be conceptualized and researched.

Participation appears to include three broad interdependent dimensions. One refers to the various theories or ideologies underlying participation and the various implied goals and objectives which participation is supposed to accomplish. A second dimension is concerned with the contextual boundaries within which participation occurs and which limit the potential of participation in terms of its processes and outcomes. The final problem dimension involves different possible structural forms or types of participation, as well as different qualitative properties which can characterize a given type of participation structure within an organization.

Theories and Goals Underlying Participation

The theoretical or ideological foundations of participation can be classified into two broad categories. Within the first category, participation is viewed as a general social phenomenon, which is affected by, and, in turn, affects the general society, its institutions or organizations, and its individuals. Within the other category of theories, participation is thought of as an organizational treatment phenomenon, a management or organizational design technique which helps to alleviate a number of dysfunctional problems within organizations. The first two schools of thought, to be outlined below, fall into the former category; the second set of theories belongs to the latter category. There are at least five broad questions of importance regarding participation, to which each theoretical orientation explicitly or implicitly addresses itself: (1) The basic origin of concern with participation; (2) the assumptions made about people; (3) the context in which participation is to occur; (4) the characteristics of participatory social arrangements; and (5) the societal outcomes derived from participation. We will only summarize each theory's major arguments on each of these issues, realizing the necessary over-simplification from a large and often diffuse literature, containing numerous elaborations and different emphases (cf. Greenberg, 1975; Pateman, 1970; Strauss & Rosenstein, 1970; Walker, 1974).

Democratic Theory. The origin of concern for participation lies in the ideals of self-governance and the overwhelming obstacles created for it by centuries of thinking about governance and social decision-making in terms of various forms of autocracy and elitism. Arguments for self-determination by ordinary citizens have been based on the belief that the vast potential capacity of human nature represents a basis for wise and effective self-government. This potential capacity of people is seen in terms of the inherent collective wisdom and intelligence of society's members, as well as in terms of individuals' potential to be responsible, interested in civic matters, informed, rational, and cooperative.

Recently, scholars of the democratic process have questioned most of these assumptions, citing social science research and theory, which has found people to be apathetic, unknowledgeable, irrational, and too easily swayed by the technology of mass influence (cf. Dahl, 1956; Eckstein, 1966; Haller, 1972; Pateman, 1970). The debate about what characteristics of people are necessary for an effective participatory democracy and which assumptions about people are reasonable in the light of social science research, indicates a central aspect of the participation phenomenon. This issue, however, rests heavily on the context in which participatory social arrangements occur.

Early works on democratic theory emphasized the *potential* of human nature, arguing that the democratic process not only uses the inherent capacities of participants, but it also progressively develops those capacities, giving the democratic process further impetus and direction for improving decision outcomes. The predicted educative and developing nature of the democratic process implies that, since individuals are affected by all organizations of which they are part, participatory democracy cannot be confined to the political process alone, but must exist and properly function in all relevant social, economic, and political organizations (cf. Pateman, 1970). More recent analysts of democracy have pointed to the constraints which are put on participatory social systems by such contextual factors as the complexity of issues to be resolved in modern industrial societies, the requirements for, and power base of, specialized expertise, the problem of conflicting interests, and apparently existing limitations of human nature emerging from social science research (cf. Bachrach, 1967; Eckstein, 1966; Mulder & Wilke, 1970; Naschold, 1969; Scharpf, 1970).

The arguments among democratic theorists regarding characteristics of participating people and the context in which participatory systems should, or do, exist, are also reflected in the debates about what characteristics participatory social systems themselves can or should have. Traditional democratic theory envisages a society in which ordinary citizens directly participate in every aspect of social decision making. Against this ideal model or moral standard, recent critics have pitted a variety of less intensive and more restricted participation schemes, which include various forms of indirect or representative participation, and which emphasize leadership functions of elite subgroups under the control of some electoral process as well as various conflict resolution schemes (cf. Bachrach, 1967; Thompson, 1970).

The societal outcomes which democratic theories strive for depend upon what values are emphasized. Primary concern with the health and development of human personality and the ideal of a truly democratic and free society characterize the arguments of participatory democrats, whereas other variants of democratic theory put greater emphasis on the stability and efficiency of social systems, which is argued to conflict with the realization of a totally democratic society (cf. Sartori, 1962).

Socialism. The interest in participation in industrial organizations within the socialistic tradition originated in Marx's concern about the debilitating effects of the capitalistic system and its social and economic order on human personality and freedoms, and finds current expression in the disaffection of the New Left with centralized, bureaucratic, Soviet-style socialism.

Socialism gives work and the production process a central role in explaining human personality and social processes. Alienation of producers is assumed to be a result of the dialectical relationship between capital and labor, the high degree of specialization and division of labor which characterizes the capitalistic production system, and the consequent powerlessness and apathy of workers. The potential of people to become economically liberated (Vanek, 1975), by actively and creatively participating in, and ultimately controlling the production process, is a central assumption in the various existing brands of socialism. These assumptions, however, are again tied to the context of worker participation.

Participation is argued to accomplish both the progressive increase in control of the production process by members of the working class, and the education and development of workers, which are necessary for workers to perform the tasks originally carried out by managers as representatives of capital. The prevailing capitalistic value frameworks and conditions in Western, industrial nations as obstacles to socialist revolutionary change, and the necessity for developing class consciousness and confidence through worker participation is an important issue in the more recent socialist literature (cf. Gorz, 1973). This concern also shows up in socialist arguments that participation should originate from the workers themselves as a result of political struggle.

Although there is a considerable debate in the socialist literature on what characteristics participatory systems ought to have, different forms of workers' councils as a starting point for progressively greater participation, at increasingly higher levels of economic activity, seem to underlie many of the writings on this issue. Another dimension of importance here is the interaction between participatory systems within industrial organizations and the revolutionary political party (cf. Gorz, 1973; Vanek, 1971).

The societal outcomes which socialism expects from participation involve a revolutionary change in the total societal system and the creation of a proletarian culture characterized by a cooperative, non-elitist production and social system in which the human personality can develop optimally and mundane considerations cease.

Human Growth and Development. The origin of the issue of participation within the human growth and development tradition is part of a more general concern with the apparent contradiction between what is traditionally thought to be necessary for efficient and stable organizations and requirements posited by recent personality, motivation, and attitude theories regarding personality growth and development of individual potential and mental health (cf. Argyris, 1964; Herzberg, 1966; Likert, 1967; Maslow, 1954; McGregor, 1960). Based upon acceptance of a basic human need hierarchy, which culminates in self-actualizing needs (Alderfer, 1972; Maslow, 1954), human growth and development theorists assume that in situations where needs lower in the hierarchy are more or less fulfilled, people seek self-actualization. Although the definition and meaning of this state of self-actualization are by no means clear, it implies that people can be mature and seek to exercise a certain amount of autonomy and independence, and that they must be allowed to adopt a long-range time perspective and to develop their special capacities and skills.

The growth and development assumptions about people interact with the context of organized behavior, including participation. Traditional theories of organization, in search of stability and efficiency, have stressed division of labor and rational coordination of activities, which imply job specialization and repetitive tasks, as well as direction and control through a unified chain of command, close supervision, and a reward structure based primarily on extrinsic factors. Although growth and development theories clearly emphasize the need for organizational efficiency and preserving the stability of organizations existing in the current social and economic order, they do, however, argue for assigning greater importance to the intrinsic motivational properties of work itself (e.g., job enrichment, management by objectives) as well as for allowing greater worker influence, autonomy, and responsibility (e.g., participation, delegation, employee-oriented supervision). Recent psychological research and theory have added still further contextual dimensions which involve radically new interpersonal and organizational rules and cultures (cf. Argyris, 1969, 1975, 1976; Deutsch, 1973; Israel & Tajfel, 1972).

There are no specific statements within the growth and development theories regarding the characteristics which participatory social arrangements in organizations should have. It is clear, however, that participation is viewed as limited to issues surrounding the work itself (i.e., the actual tasks to be accomplished and the relevant interpersonal relationships) rather than the broad spectrum of organizational issues to be resolved. More importantly, human growth and development theories speak about participation not only with respect to decision-making as such, but also with respect to processes that involve such "growth treatments" as sharing of ideas and feelings, joint ownership of organizational change programs, and sharing of information, knowledge, and other resources.

Since growth and development theories use as their unit of analysis individuals in the context of organizations (mainly work organizations), and since participation is only one issue within the more general concern for matching people and organizations to the benefit of both, there is no explicit concern with societal outcomes from participation. Implicit, however, is the emphasis on the stability and efficiency of existing organizations, on acceptance of the existing general social and economic order, and on the reduction of social costs incurred by mental ill-health.

Productivity and Efficiency. Contrary to the theoretical orientations discussed so far, in which organizational productivity and efficiency are implicit goals, or are explicit among a number of additional humanistic objectives, this last rationale for participation has productivity and efficiency as its primary, or even sole, focus. The origin of concern for participation lies in the existing problem of wide-spread dissatisfaction within the work force, as well as in what are thought to be the costly and efficiency-reducing consequences of dissatisfaction and alienation (namely, reduced quality and quantity of production, absenteeism, turnover, sabotage, and labor unrest).

Basically, the assumption is made that participation increases general satisfaction, morale, or group cohension; that it enhances commitment toward issues on which people are allowed to participate (Coch & French, 1948); and that it enlarges the amount and accuracy of relevant information concerning the issue under consideration (cf. Lawler & Hackman, 1969; Lowin, 1968; Strauss, 1963). Whether these effects of participation change organizational outcome variables is seen to depend, in part, on the context in which participation occurs. Thus, participation is expected to increase effectiveness to the extent that: (a) The issues around which participation occurs are relevant to the work itself; (b) people, by participating, get more accurate information about an organizational context which *in fact* allows real and meaningful positive outcomes to result from effective performance; and (c) effective performance is *not* largely beyond the control of the worker (cf. Blumberg, 1969; Hackman, 1976; Lowin, 1968).

Participation within this point of view is limited in scope and intensity. It is restricted to issues surrounding task accomplishment, and is characteristically under the complete control of management, with no intended challenge to the basic power prerogatives of business leaders.

The productivity and efficiency rationale for participation does not explicitly espouse particular societal values or outcomes which participation as such is to serve. Within the larger systemic view, participation is a relatively minor means of insuring the stability of the current social and economic order, of increasing industrial productivity, and of avoiding disruptive labor unrest.

Summary. Each of the theoretical points of view, although different in emphasis, in value-orientations, and in explicitness, addresses itself to a number of important questions regarding the participation phenomenon. The lack of explicit recognition of the underlying theoretical or ideological bases in much of the research on participation is one important reason for the difficulty in interpreting the vast research on this topic. Since the nature of participatory social arrangements in organizations is in principle different within the different theoretical orientations (and within the various combinations of them), we may have to start thinking of various (although related) participation phenomena, rather than trying to define one relatively homogeneous and readily delimited phenomenon.

On the other hand, it seems important to recognize that, at least with respect to *general* characteristics of participation, the four theoretical bases are not really competing theories of participation, but represent complementary points of view. In other words, a view of participation which incorporates the major *kinds* of questions contained in all the theoretical orientations provides a more complete or realistic problem definition of participation than do the questions of any one theoretical school of thought alone. This argument will find further elaboration in the following brief summaries of the remaining problem dimensions of participation.

Contextual Boundaries and Potential of Participation

The combined arguments contained in the various theoretical orientations lead to the conclusion that, although the majority of current research tends to view participation within organizations as a rather limited organizational phenomenon or intervention issue, it is, in fact, a systems problem of the most complex and far reaching variety. One can think of the *systemic* nature of participation, its structures and processes, in terms of an interacting set of five broad categories of factors:

(1) Societal characteristics such as social, economic, and political frameworks, legal structures and processes, norm, value, and interest structures (e.g., Nord, 1974; Tannenbaum, Kavcic, Rosner, Vianello, & Wieser, 1974; Vanek, 1975).

(2) Characteristics of relevant other organizations such as congruence between participation-relevant *intra*-organizational factors and *inter*-organizational factors (cf. Clegg, 1960; Eckstein, 1966; Naschold, 1969; Nord, 1974; Vanek, 1975).

(3) Characteristics of the focal organization including technology and task characteristics, management policies, reward systems, information and control systems, selection, training, and promotion systems (e.g., Blumberg, 1969; Hackman, 1976; Patchen, 1970).

(4) Group characteristics like leadership, cohesion, conflict, coalition-formation, decision-making processes, and interpersonal relations (e.g., Janis, 1972; Lowin, 1968; Mulder & Wilke, 1970; Peterson, 1968; Vroom & Yetton, 1973).

(5) Individual characteristics such as motives, intelligence, education, experience, interpersonal skills, available resources and information, and attitudes (e.g., Adizes, 1971; Lammers, 1967; Tabb & Goldfarb, 1970).

These factors both affect the nature of participation in organizations and *are affected* by a given participatory arrangement. The boundaries and potential of participation are then circumscribed by this *systemic* configuration of variables. While each of the theoretical orientations differs with respect to which of these categories of factors it concentrates on, and which factors within a given category are given greatest theoretical weight, the systemic nature of participation involves *all categories* of factors. This seems true, even though different *configurations* of factors may define different participation phenomena. In this sense, the theoretical orientations are complementary rather than competing views of participation.

Space limitations do not allow a systematic review of the available research literature to document these arguments. But a few examples may help in at least outlining the conceptual issues of concern. Clearly, both democratic and socialist theorists view participation in organizations as part of a more general societal phenomenon from which it cannot be separated. Within these two theoretical points of view, participation is embedded in societal characteristics on the basis of the underlying social values and goals, which in turn imply societal structures and processes which are necessary to achieve these values and goals. However, democratic and socialist theories largely neglect to systematically question under what organizational, group, and individual conditions participation can in fact achieve the desired societal outcomes and values (cf. Adizes, 1971; Haller, 1972).

On the other hand, human growth and development theorists as well as the productivity and efficiency views of participation focus on a limited set of intra-organizational factors without systematically questioning what organizational, group, and individual characteristics fit, support, and are congruent with an intended participatory decision-making arrangement *and* with the values and goals this participatory arrangement is to serve. Thus the problem of participation within these latter two theoretical points of view requires questions regarding the individual, group, and organizational characteristics which, together with a congruent kind and quality of participatory arrangement, can achieve the values and goals inherent in these two theories. Moreover, research on participation within the human growth and development tradition, or within the productivity and efficiency tradition, has completely neglected to question whether the individual, group, and organizational conditions which might be necessary for participation to achieve the intended values and goals, require corresponding changes in societal characteristics. The alternative question, whether the inherent values and goals underlying these two theoretical orientations of participation are viable within the existing societal characteristics, is equally ignored.

Although participation needs to be understood in terms of the underlying values and ideologies, from which outcome and process criteria for research have to be explicitly derived, a systems conception of participation does not in general allow a direct linear effect of participation with respect to these outcome and process criteria—a lesson so often ignored in participation research. Rather, the effects of participation are moderated by a large set of interacting variables at the individual, group, organizational, inter-organizational, and societal level, which affect the type and quality of participatory arrangements, and which in turn are affected by the participatory arrangements in organizations.

Types and Properties of Participation

Although terms like participation in decision-making or industrial democracy are often used as if they referred to some agreed upon social decision-making arrangement, a bewildering variety of participation schemes seems to exist, requiring a multidimensional analysis, rather than being identifiable along any one continuum. Participatory social arrangements differ along a number of structural dimensions, as well as along different dimensions which make up what one might call the "qualitative character" of participation (see also Walker, 1974).

Structurally, participatory arrangements differ at least with respect to (1) direct versus indirect participation, where the distinction refers to immediate, personal involvement of organization members in decision-making, as opposed to their mediated involvement through some form of representation (Lammers, 1967), and (2) formal versus informal participation, where the basis of legitimation rests either in formal prescriptions and agreements which are imposed on the organization, or in an informal consensus emerging among interdependent partners. The qualitative character of participation can vary along such dimensions as *intensity*, which reflects some "influence—power—sharing continuum" (cf. Heller, 1971; Vroom & Yetton, 1973), *social range*, which differentiates the range of participating individuals, and the *complexity* and *importance* of *decisions* involved in the participation process.

In practice, of course, these properties of participation schemes are mixed in varying and often intricate patterns, serving different purposes. For example, within the German participation system, the institution of a works assembly, which involves quarterly meetings of all employees, has only information exchange and consultative functions, while the works council and supervisory board representatives are vested with certain decision authority. The Yugoslav workers' collective, on the other hand, together with the institution of the workers' referendum, has far reaching decision rights beyond mere information exchange functions.

Although there are continuing debates in the literature regarding the most "desirable" participatory arrangement (e.g., Strauss & Rosenstein, 1970), it seems futile to argue about different participatory social arrangements in organizations, as if there existed some finite number of reasonably differentiated participation models, from which one had merely to choose the one which best accomplishes some intended purposes. Such debates in principle deny the systems nature of participation, where the kind and quality of participation has to be understood not only in terms of the basic underlying values and ideologies, but also in terms of the individual, group, organizational, interorganizational, and societal variables which determine the participatory arrangements, set limits to the values and goals which participation can serve, and which ultimately are also affected by the participation schemes existing in organizations.

CONCLUSION

Although space constraints did not allow discussion of many important issues, and often made it necessary to oversimplify in the interest of giving a broad summary, the various sets of questions for consideration, which appear to make up the participation problem, lead to the conclusion that it is perhaps misleading to speak of, or think about, participation as one relatively unified, relatively homogeneous phenomenon. The various levels and ideologies underlying participation, which have too often been ignored in the participation literature, and the different systemic characteristics of participation implied by the different theoretical points of view, make it more reasonable to think of various phenomena which, currently at least, fit under ill-defined terms like participation in decision-making or industrial democracy.

However, even with respect to different participation phenomena, the analysis presented in this chapter militates against the conceptualization of any participation phenomenon as an isolated, relatively independent, non-systemic issue. Whether the focus of the underlying theoretical rationale for participation is limited or broad, specific or general, on societal, organizational, or sub-unit levels, the systemic nature of participation phenomena can no longer be ignored. Just as it is impossible to adequately describe participation only in terms of societal issues, without analyzing the corresponding organizational, group, and individual characteristics, a conceptualization of participation as solely an intra-organizational phenomenon, which fails to consider the prevailing social-economic-political characteristics of the society, is likely to lead to superficial, if not misleading, results.

Finally, it is important to note that within all theoretical schools of thought, concern with the issue of participation originated as a "real world problem," rather than from some pre-existing *discipline* paradigm. As a "real world problem," participation transcends a variety of disciplines, including political science, law, economics, sociology, and psychology. This fact has not been sufficiently recognized in ongoing participation research. The fragmentary treatment of participation is perhaps in part due to the practice of studying it within the boundaries of a given discipline. A systems conception of participation derived from the real world manifestation of the many relevant issues requires much greater efforts in attempting to integrate the knowledge and methods available in the various relevant discipline paradigms (cf. Vanek, 1970, 1971).

REFERENCES

Adizes, I. *Industrial democracy: Yugoslav style.* New York: Free Press, 1971.

Alderfer, C. P. *Existence, relatedness, and growth: Human needs in organizational settings.* New York: Free Press, 1972.

Argyris, C. *Integrating the individual and the organization.* New York: Wiley, 1964.

Argyris, C. *Organization and innovation.* Homewood, Ill.: Dorsey Press, 1965.

Argyris, C. The incompleteness of social psychological theory. *American Psychologist*, 1969, **24**, 893–908.

Argyris, C. Dangers in applying results from experimental social psychology. *American Psychologist*, 1975, **30**, 369–485.

Argyris, C. Theories of action that inhibit individual learning. *American Psychologist*, 1976, **68**, 265–274.

Bachrach, P. *The theory of democratic elitism.* Boston: Little, Brown, 1967.

Blumberg, P. *Industrial democracy: The sociology of participation.* New York: Schocken Books, 1969.

Clegg, H. *A new approach to industrial democracy.* London: Blackwell, 1960.

Coch, L., & French, J. R. P., Jr. Overcoming resistance to change. *Human Relations*, 1948, **1**, 512–532.

Dahl, R. A. *Preface to democratic theory.* Chicago: University of Chicago Press, 1956.

Deutsch, M. *The resolution of conflict: Constructive and destructive processes.* New Haven, Conn.: Yale University Press, 1973.

Eckstein, H. *A theory of stable democracy.* Princeton, N.J.: Princeton University Press, 1966.

Greenberg, E. S. The consequences of worker participation: A clarification of the theoretical literature. *Social Science Quarterly*, 1975, **56**, 191–209.

Gorz, A. *Socialism and revolution.* Garden City: Anchor/Doubleday, 1973.

Hackman, J. R. Group influences on individuals. In Marvin D. Dunnette (Ed.), *Handbook of industrial and organizational psychology.* Chicago: Rand McNally, 1976.

Haller, W. Grenzen der direkten Demokratie. *Schweizerische Juristen Zeitung*, 1972.

Heller, F. A. *Managerial decision making.* London: Tavistock Publishers, 1971.

Herzberg, F. *Work and the nature of man.* Cleveland: World, 1966.

Israel, J., & Tajfel, H. (Eds.). *The context of social psychology: A critical assessment.* New York: Academic Press, 1972.

Janis, I. L. *Victims of groupthink: A psychological study of foreign policy decisions and fiascos.* Boston: Houghton Mifflin, 1972.

Lammers, C. J. Power and participation in decision-making in formal organizations. *American Journal of Sociology*, 1967, **2**, 201–217.

Lawler, E. E., & Hackman, J. R. Impact of employee participation in the development of pay incentive plans: A field experiment. *Journal of Applied Psychology*, 1969, **53**, 467–471.

Likert, R. *The human organization: Its management and value.* New York: McGraw-Hill, 1967.

Lowin, A. Participative decision-making: A model, literature critique, and prescriptions for research. *Organizational Behavior and Human Performance*, 1968, **3**, 68–106.

Maslow, A. *Motivation and personality.* New York: Harper & Row, 1954.

McGregor, D. *The human side of enterprise.* New York: McGraw-Hill, 1960.

Mulder, M., & Wilke, H. Participation and power equalization. *Organizational Behavior and Human Performance*, 1970, **5**, 417–429.

Naschold, F. *Organisation und Demokratie.* Stuttgart, 1969.

Nord, W. R. The failure of current applied behavioral science: A marxian perspective. *Applied Behavioral Science*, 1974, **10**, 557–578.

Patchen, M. *Participation, achievement, and involvement on the job.* Englewood Cliffs, N.J.: Prentice-Hall, 1970.

Pateman, C. *Participation and democratic theory.* London: Cambridge University Press, 1970.

Peterson, R. B. The swedish experience with industrial democracy. *The British Journal of Industrial Relations*, 1968, **6**, 193–210.

Sartori, G. *Democratic theory.* Detroit: Wayne State University Press, 1962.

Scharpf, F. *Demokratie Theorie zwischen Utopie und Anpassung.* Constance: Universitäts Verlag, 1970.

Strauss, G. Some notes on power-equalization. In Harold J. Leavitt (Ed.), *The social science of organization.* Englewood Cliffs, N.J.: Prentice-Hall, 1963.

Strauss, G., & Rosenstein, E. Workers' participation: A critical point of view. *Industrial Relations*, 1970, **9**, 197–214.

Tabb, J. Y., & Goldfarb, A. *Workers' participation in management.* London: Pergamon, 1970.

Tannenbaum, A. S., Kavcic, B., Rosner, M., Vianello, M., & Wieser, G. *Hierarchy in organizations.* San Francisco: Jossey-Bass, 1974.

Thompson, D. *The democratic citizen.* London: Cambridge University Press, 1970.

Vanek, J. *The general theory of labor managed market economies.* Ithaca, N.Y.: Cornell University Press, 1970.

Vanek, J. *The participatory economy: An evolutionary hypothesis and a strategy for development.* Ithaca, N.Y.: Cornell University Press, 1971.

Vanek, J. *The self-management: Economic liberation of man.* Harmondsworth: Penguin, 1975.

Vroom, V. H., & Yetton, P. W. *Leadership and decision-making.* Pittsburgh: University of Pittsburgh Press, 1973.

Walker, K. F. Workers' participation in management: Problems, practice and prospect. *International Institute for Labor Studies (IILS) Bulletin,* 1974, **12**, 3–35.

DECISIVE COALITIONS

David J. Hickson, Richard J. Butler,
Runo Axelsson, and David Wilson
University of Bradford, England

Organizations of Today

It is often said that today we live in "organizational societies." The organizations of our age are said to stand astride society like colossi. So they do. Yet the image conveyed by such descriptions is of something altogether more purposeful, more forceful, than is the case. These colossi are not "single minded," they do not have autonomous "free will," they are not "motivated" by a single steely drive (if these psychologically tinged adjectives can be abused by using them in this way). Rather, these organizations are fumbling, tugged to and fro by pressures this way and pressures that way from powerful interests, turning from side to side as decision-making priorities wax and wane, stumbling into blind alleys because there is not enough information on what lies ahead.

This is what life is like, as far as we can tell, in two sharply contrasted organizations which we have been studying. One, quiet and stable, is an electricity utility; the other, more bustling and turbulent, is a university. Both are in Britain. The effects of ownership have been controlled by selecting both from the publicly owned sector of the economy. In both cases, data have been collected since 1974 by interviews held with top executives, administrators and department heads, and analyses of agendas and minutes of meetings. Some internal meetings have been attended, and some interviews conducted with executives or administrators of main external organizations.

The two organizations are described below, the electricity board first.

An Electricity Board (XEB)

XEB is an example of an organization dominated by the power of other organized interests. It is a creature of the state that sets the rules under which it operates, being one of 14 such autonomous boards in England and Wales (Scotland differs), constituted by the Electricity Act of 1947. The Act charges all boards with the duty "to acquire from the Generating Board bulk supplies of electricity and to plan and carry out an efficient and economical distribution of those supplies to persons in their area who require them." That is, the boards transmit and sell electricity, a separate Central Electricity Generating Board (CEGB) being responsible for the production of the electric current. Like the other boards, XEB gets supplies of current from the "national grid" network of bulk supply cables radiating from the CEGB's generating stations.

XEB sells to industrial, commercial, and domestic consumers, but cannot export. In line with the other electricity boards, XEB cannot sell electricity outside its own area, but it has a legal and de facto monopoly within its own area. XEB also sells domestic electrical appliances in its numerous showrooms.

The state retains control of its nominally autonomous creation through its monopoly of capital supply. This comes via a filtering process in a national body called the Electricity Council. XEB, the other electricity boards, and the CEGB are all represented on the Council. The Council's main function is to coordinate forecasts of electrical energy consumption prepared by its own staff, by the CEGB, and by the boards; and to arrive at a consensus among these parties on what funds each requires to meet the forecast demand. Funds are then allocated by the state. So, like British universities (see the XU case described below), XEB has its relationship with the state mediated by a national council/committee. In its case, the Electricity Council brings together many of the powerful outside interests that surround it.

This is well illustrated by the issue of pricing policy. In theory, XEB could choose between alternative price strategies and, for example, substitute for the capital it gets from the state by extracting more money from consumers. But in practice, the price for electricity has to be agreed upon in the Electricity Council, and even this has to work within government policy. In the period in question, the government held prices down. This was done partly through the

Council and partly through a national Prices Commission which also controlled appliance prices. So on prices, XEB was effectively immobilized.

In any case, Electricity Council price decisions are heavily influenced by the CEGB's position. There is no practicable alternative to CEGB for the supply of current, for though XEB and the others are nominally empowered to have their own generating facilities, the capital cost and CEGB opposition prevent that. Thus CEGB has as great or greater power over prices as does the government, since what it charges XEB largely determines what XEB can charge. Indeed, XEB's annual report admits that it exercises direct control over less than 10% of its own costs.

Moreover, XEB has effectively no marketing alternatives and no marketing decisions to make. The Act (quoted above) requires it to provide a service to any consumer who can pay for it, and determines which consumers and how many by defining XEB's area boundaries. Large industrial consumers, and local governments who buy in bulk for street lighting, etc., press in upon XEB and closely watch its reliability and pricing. Even in the sales of domestic appliances, the rules of "unfair competition" constrain XEB from selling more than a range of goods related to electricity consumption. Protests would arise from private firms and political interests if XEB were suspected of taking advantage of its monopoly position in electricity supply to extend into different retail markets.

In brief, XEB's choices are negligible. It has no real outputs alternatives: The state constituted it to supply electricity only, and in any case large national coal, gas, and oil utilities would prevent it moving into other forms of energy. It has no real prices alternatives: Government and Prices Commission dominate pricing and so does the Central Electricity Generating Board. Through the Electricity Council, the other electricity boards ensure that XEB keeps in step with them on all matters of any consequence.

Here is an organization immobilized by a balance of power tipped sharply in favor of external interests.

Internally, XEB appears unruffled. Its activities are divided between four functions—Engineering, Commercial, Accounting and Secretarial. Engineering is in the influential position of being responsible for the primary activity of moving electricity through cables from the points of distribution at generating stations to the consumers' premises, from point A to point B. Commercial runs the shops. Accounting records each consumer's consumption, sends the bills, and collects the cash. And Secretarial does everything else: principally purchasing, all personnel functions, and the legal and estate management aspects of activities which involve owning large numbers of sites for electrical stations and cables and infinite complexities in laying cables in and over the land of others.

Internal meetings are anything but a jostling for power. Function committees are occupied with the minutiae of routinely running an organization which has few alternatives, and in which the possibility of alternatives seems not to be raised. There is no suggestion of politicking, competing for resources, or pushing new activities.

In contrast to this, the second case, XU, is agitated by the power of its own faculties and departments.

A University (XU)

XU is a middle-sized, "non-Oxbridge," provincial university with about 8,000 students, one of Britain's approximately 50 state-financed university institutions. Like each of the others, it is established by Royal Charter, a form of incorporation which vests it with a certain legal autonomy from the Queen's ministers, i.e., from government.

Like the other universities, XU depends overwhelmingly on the state for money. But in Britain its distribution from the exchequer is filtered through a body composed mainly of nominated academics called the University Grants Committee (UGC). The national Department of Education and Science arranges with UGC the national total of funds to be available. The UGC then allocates the total among universities. It provides more than 80% of XU's income. But UGC is an institution controlled by academics, and not influenced by a single dominant supplier as is the Electricity Council to which XEB belongs.

And XU has a substantially free hand in the way it spends its money, the UGC merely earmarking certain relatively small proportions for, say, medicine, and possibly expressing a view that some particular department should desirably be expanded (or contracted). Eustace and Moodie (1974) survey British universities' organization and financing and stress their freedom from government interference. The money is simply awarded as a block grant with no breakdown of intended use. Although in practice the commitment to salaries of tenured staff forms the bulk of expenditure so there is only a marginal flexibility at any one time, what shall be done with this margin is open to decision.

What is done arises from XU being a degree awarding body, which means that its charter gives it the freedom to develop new "product lines," i.e., programs. While XEB is only allowed to distribute electricity and sell appliances, XU can offer whatever education it pleases.

XU operates in a more open market than does XEB. In developing new programs, it has to consider its position relative to other universities and polytechnics with whom it has to compete nationally for students. It has no geographically defined monopoly as does XEB. This sense of competition is heightened for XU by the "rule" that calculates its revenue from the UGC directly in terms of student numbers. Success in the competition with other universities to obtain funds from the state via the UGC is overwhelmingly a matter of numbers as correlations between student totals and funds allocated have shown (Dunworth & Cook, 1974). More students means an entitlement to more teaching staff which sooner or later, depending on current economic conditions, means more money allocated to establish faculty. Like all British universities, XU controls its own admissions and does not take in all those who apply.

This means that XU, by comparison to XEB, is not hemmed in by large external interest units which restrict its choices of students, programs, etc. While XEB is surrounded by the Central Electricity Generating Board, by the territories of other similar distribution Boards, by monopolistic or oligopolistic suppliers of alternative energies (coal, gas, oil), by large manufacturers as suppliers or customers, and so on, the only large external organization directly influencing XU is the University Grants Committee, and that has a comparatively light touch. XU has a wide range of choices open to it: It can develop courses to appeal to the many, and frequently transient, wishes of students; it can set out to cater for the fads and foibles of educational change; it can develop undergraduate, graduate or post experience courses; it can develop a research potential or set out to gain contract research money from industry; it can utilize halls of residence for summer courses and for conferences; it can deliberately aim to attract more overseas students. By contrast, XEB is confined to worrying about whether or not it can sell pocket electric calculators or electric showers.

The problem XU faces is more one of selection. For there are limitations on resources and each department has its competing claims. It is just because the system and its rules are set in such a way as to make it reasonable for a department to put in a claim for resources that here decision-making processes do involve a high degree of jostling for power. In this organization, comparatively greater power resides in internal interests.

The internal structure consists of nine faculties (Arts, Science, Engineering, etc.) which are loose assemblies of "production" departments. Each department protects and advocates its own "product" of teaching and research in certain subjects. Faculty meetings tend to have much discussion on "product" range and demand, whether a new course or program is likely to appeal to students and who should teach it and so be conceded a claim on resources. There are also concerns about "quality control," that is, the examination system, and whether student Jones should pass or fail.

As Baldridge (1971) and Blau (1973) have shown with data from American universities, Western universities are a form of organization that is a loosely coordinated set of "production" subunits jostling for "production" resources. Because each department has its own "product(s)," departments are not sequentially interdependent with one another in the sense defined by

Thompson (1967) as feeding work from one to the next. There is merely the exchange of service teaching. University departments share only the pooled interdependence of drawing upon a common pool of resources. Indeed, Thompson (1967) wonders how such an organization can get anything done except infighting (!), and hypothesizes the necessity of an "inner circle."

University organization has to the full the character portrayed so vividly by Cohen, March, and Olsen (1972) and by Cohen and March (1974). As they put it:

> A key to understanding the processes within organizations is to view a choice opportunity as a garbage can into which various problems and solutions are dumped by participants. The mix of garbage in a single can depends partly on the labels attached to the alternative cans; but it also depends on what garbage is being produced at the moment, on the mix of cans available, and on the speed with which garbage is collected and removed from the scene [Cohen and March, 1974:81].

Those from university organizations who read this colorful characterization may think wryly that the garbage seems to clog up committee processes for an interminable time before it is removed! Be that as it may, into XU's garbage can drop possibilities for new "markets" or different "customers" or whatever. Each internal subunit has its own preferences for programs, courses, new teaching methods, research projects, etc. which are offered as solutions to the problems that such possibilities bring with them. As Cohen and March (1974; p. 81) again put it so aptly, XU is a "collection of choices looking for problems"; it has "solutions looking for issues" and "decision makers looking for work." They go so far as to call universities organized anarchies:

> The properties of universities as organized anarchies make the garbage can idea particularly appropriate to an understanding of organizational choice within higher education. Although a college or university operates within the metaphor of a political system or a hierarchical bureaucracy, the actual operation of either is considerably attenuated by the ambiguity of college goals, by the lack of clarity in educational technology, and by the transient character of many participants.

Organizational Coalitions

In short, decision-making in XU is subjected to the interests of internal subunits, whereas, comparatively speaking, decision-making in XEB is subjected to the interests of other organizations external to it. So organizations can be seen to be subject to the power of both.

The study of subunits has grown gradually but fruitfully and a theory of subunit power has emerged from it. Landsberger (1961), for example, deduced from the histories of three British firms that when a resource was scarce the subunit responsible for obtaining that resource was in a powerful position. On the single issue of product innovation in two American food-processing units, Lawrence and Lorsch (1967) found that subunits ranked as facing the most uncertain sub-environment were also ranked as most influential. Crozier's (1964) study of French tobacco plants brought out the hypothesis that power is related to "the kind of uncertainty upon which depends the life of the organization" (Crozier, 1964, p. 164). This work was drawn together by Hickson, Hinings, Lee, Schneck, and Pennings (1971) into a strategic contingencies theory hypothesizing that the power of a subunit ensued from its control of contingencies for other subunits, this control being yielded by a combination of three main variables, coping with uncertainty, centrality, and non-substitutability. Hinings, Hickson, Pennings, and Schneck (1974) reaffirmed the theory operationally on North American brewing and container manufacturing organizations.

Theory about the power of what we shall call "organizations-in-contact," those organizations related to a particular focal organization, is not so readily summarized despite Marrett's (1971) efforts. Benson (1975) synthesizes many concepts, though he examines the characteristics of interorganizational networks in their own right and not as linkages radiating from a focal organization. But his clear thinking may well be seminal for either point of view as he sees interactions between organizations as ultimately explainable by the needs for resources of the organizations involved. The primary needs are for money and for recognized domains of activity. Then particular organizations may gain power over others because they provide those others with vital services and because they have centrality in the interaction between organizations. Over and above this, an organization's power rests on the ability to mobilize in its support groups ranked highly in the surrounding society.

Benson's analysis is influenced by the exchange framework of Levine and White (1961), a framework supported independently by the experimental work of Burgess and Nielsen (1974) who produce convincing evidence that "inequitable" exchange continues because alternatives open to the losing party are worse. This must be a common state of affairs in society, including interorganizational relationships. It has been in some degree operationalized by Pugh, Hickson, Hinings, and Turner (1969) in their measure of an organization's dependence which summarizes a series of variables such as its reliance on others for money (ownership) and specialist services, and the dominance of it by large suppliers and customers, or of them by it (see also Mindlin & Aldrich, 1975). Jacobs (1974, p. 53) agrees: "Organizations are controlled by those who comprise or control the organization's most problematic dependence."

Benson (1975) points out the close resemblance of that part of his analysis which is concerned with power to intraorganizational subunit analysis. Both stress uncertainty of resources, coping with that uncertainty, centrality of position, and the availability or substitutability of alternatives. This encourages us to explore the potentialities of uniting the two: intraorganizational *and* interorganizational power.

We therefore need a view of organizations which is capable of combining intraorganizational and interorganizational analysis at a nonindividual level of analysis. We do not deny the importance of people but acknowledge the usefulness of understanding the conditions that enable a social (or collective) unit to be powerful, or at least, to be a powerful base for individuals to utilize. This may offer some corrective to the long-standing emphasis on individual influence alone. As Perrow (1970, p. 84) wrote of the difficulties in defining power:

> Part of the problem, I suspect, stems from the persistent attempt to define power in terms of individuals and as a social-psychological phenomenon . . . . Even sociological studies tend to measure power by asking about an individual.

We propose to use a model of an organization as comprising a *coalition of interest-units*, where interest-units are identifiable collectivities internal and external to the organization. This is neither an intraorganizational nor an interorganizational perspective alone.

These interest-units are defined by, and have in common, an interest in that organization. Taken all together, it is their *coalition of interests* that sustains (or destroys) that organization. This does not mean coalition in the sense of particular alliances or of common policies or even of direct relationships between coalition interest-units, but in the sense advanced by Cyert and March (1963). They write of the total coalition of managers, workers, stockholders, suppliers, customers, lawyers, regulatory agencies, etc., all of whom have some interest in a business organization. Within this overall coalition, "sub-coalitions" can form to further particular joint interests.

By an interest we mean that the interest-unit as a whole derives some benefit or value from coalition membership—Blau and Scott's (1962) concept of benefit. This might be a necessary resource for a customer unit, a market for a supplier, or in the case of a university, some political benefit for a state funding agency or better facilities for a students' union.

Though they restrict themselves to the political economy of public organizations, Wamsley and Zald (1973) recognize that there are both external and internal interest-units for organizations. They see an external political system of interest groups, competing public organizations, legislative committees, and control agencies; and an internal one of subunits with differing interests. In a private firm, Pettigrew (1973) reveals something of how these systems function. He traces the power of two subunits, computer programming and systems analysis, in a decision within a company to purchase a computer. "Kenny" (the Head of Management Services) stands advantageously between the internal interests concerned and the several competing computer manufacturers, and the two subunits vie with each other in advocating the award of the contract to one manufacturer rather than to another.

The concept of *contract* helps to define further what an interest is, and to identify interest-units. External organizations such as materials supplier companies may have sales contracts *formalized in legal documents* (legal contract), wholesalers or customer organizations will have *verbal* offer-acceptance contracts (common law contract), and government departments put on the focal organization an *obligation* to cooperate (social contract). Internal departments have *"bureaucratic"* contracts for the performance of their functions, enforced by organizational sanctions. Of the several forms of "contract," this last requires an extra word of explanation. It means, for example, that a training department can be regarded as having a contract with its focal organization to train that organization's members, or a local government surveyor's department can be regarded as having a contract to undertake mapping and planning functions for its organization.

The notion of a coalition of interests does not imply only cooperation between them. Within a coalition there will frequently be conflicting interests, as, for example, when a benefit for one interest-unit means less benefit for another. Moreover, interest-units take differing views as to the reason for the existence of the organization. An environmentalist society might say that General Motors *should* exist for the benefit of America, an investment company for the benefit of their dividends, and a trade union for the benefit of employees. As the customers, environmentalists, shareholders and employees do not, in the main, consist of the same people, a conflict of interest becomes likely.

Coalition and Decision

The vivid contrast between XU and XEB which prompts us to take this view of organizations then takes us a further step. The decision-making in XU and XEB is constrained, respectively, more by internal interest units or by external interest units. Thus the coalition model should be a fruitful source of explanation for organizational decision-making.

Variables of both are required, as follows:

```
┌─────────────────────┐       ┌─────────────────────┐
│ Coalition variables │ ────► │ Organizational decision- │
│                     │       │    making variables  │
└─────────────────────┘       └─────────────────────┘
```

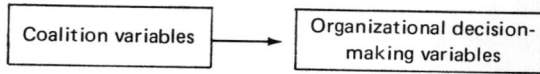

The time is long overdue for the translation of sweeping descriptions of decision-making characteristics, such as "uncertainty avoidance" or "problemistic search" (Cyert & March, 1963), into meaningful variables, i.e., variables which have theoretical interest and operational relevance.

In research terms, the first question must be to ask what it is that any given organization unit has to decide, that is, what autonomy does it have? This has been operationalized by Pugh, Hickson, Hinings, and Turner (1968) as the number of decisions that can be made by and within an organization as distinct from those that are made for it from without. Their lead in measuring this against a standard list of decisions can be followed here. The measurement of autonomy achieves two things at once. It is a first indication of the power of external interests in the form of the range of decision-making they allow to the organization in question; and it provides a basis for exploring how far their power, or the power of internal subunits, affects what is done within that range of autonomy.

How does this power distribution affect the speed and effectiveness of decision-making? Does a coalition dominated by external organizations result in restricted but fast decision-making (as XEB could imply)? Does a coalition dominated by internal subunits result in widely scanning but slow decision-making (as XU could imply)? Scan (information utilization) and pace may be useful kinds of variables for investigation, as Hage (1975), too, has recently argued.

Characteristics of the coalition which might explain decision-making have already been implicitly referred to. First and foremost is the power distribution among interest-units. The sheer number of interest-units may also be relevant. XU and XEB differ sharply here, XU having an almost uncountable number of internal subunits as against four for XEB, while XEB has many more external organizations-in-contact. Interdependence should be crucial, that is, dependence on sole suppliers (as XEB on the Central Electricity Generating Board), cross-links between external units (as in the Electricity Council and XEB), reliance on crucial departments (as XU on its powerful medical faculty).

These variables can be summarized as follows:

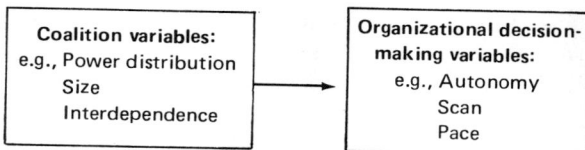

```
┌────────────────────────┐       ┌────────────────────────┐
│ Coalition variables:   │       │ Organizational decision- │
│ e.g., Power distribution│ ────► │ making variables:      │
│      Size              │       │    e.g., Autonomy      │
│      Interdependence   │       │         Scan           │
│                        │       │         Pace           │
└────────────────────────┘       └────────────────────────┘
```

Fresh fieldwork is under way beyond the two preliminary cases described here: We are endeavoring to elucidate more, and more interesting, concepts and to weld them into a theory of power and decision-making.

REFERENCES

Baldridge, J. *Power and conflict in the university.* New York: Wiley, 1971.

Benson, J. K. The interorganizational network as a political economy. *Administrative Science Quarterly*, 1975, **20**, 229–249.

Blau, P. M., & Scott, W. R. *Formal organizations.* London: Routledge & Kegan Paul, 1962.

Blau, P. M. *The organization of academic work.* New York: Wiley, 1973.

Burgess, R. L., & Nielsen, J. M. An experimental analysis of some structural determinants of equitable and inequitable exchange relations. *American Sociological Review*, 1974, **39**, 427–443.

Cohen, M. D., & March, J. G. *Leadership and ambiguity: The American college president.* New York: McGraw-Hill, 1974.

Cohen, M. D., March, J. G., & Olsen, J. P. A garbage can model of organizational choice. *Administrative Science Quarterly*, 1972, **17**(1), 1–25.

Crozier, M. *The bureaucratic phenomenon.* London: Tavistock, 1964.

Cyert, R. M., & March, J. G. *A behavioral theory of the firm.* Englewood Cliffs: Prentice-Hall, 1963.

Dunworth, J. E., & Cook, W. R. *Incentives to the efficient use of resources in universities.* University of Bradford, Schools of Social Sciences Research Report, 1974.

Eustace, R., & Moodie, G. C. *Power and authority in British universities.* London: Allen & Unwin, 1974.

Hage, J. *Frontier problems in organization theory: Issues, analytical units, and variables.* Paper presented to American Sociological Association, August 1975.

Hickson, D. J., Hinings, C. R., Lee, C. A., Schneck, R. E., & Pennings, J. M. A strategic contingencies theory of intraorganizational power. *Administrative Science Quarterly*, 1971, **6**(2), 216–229.

Hinings, C. R., Hickson, D. J., Pennings, J. M., & Schneck, R. E. Structural conditions of intraorganizational power. *Administrative Science Quarterly*, 1974, **19**(1), 22–43.

Jacobs, D. Dependency and vulnerability: An exchange approach to the control of organizations. *Administrative Science Quarterly*, 1974, **19**(1), 45–59.

Landsberger, H. A. The horizontal dimension in bureaucracy. *Administrative Science Quarterly*, 1961, **6**, 299–332.

Lawrence, P. R., & Lorsch, J. W. *Organization and environment.* Cambridge: Graduate School of Business Administration, Harvard University, 1967.

Levine, S., & White, P. E. Exchange as a conceptual framework for the study of interorganizational relationships. *Administrative Science Quarterly*, 1961, **5**, 583–601.

Marrett, C. B. On the specification of interorganizational dimensions. *Sociology and Social Research*, 1971/2, **56**, 83–99.

Mindlin, S., & Aldrich, H. Interorganizational dependence. *Administrative Science Quarterly*, 1975, **20**(3), 382–392.

Perrow, C. Departmental power and perspectives in industrial firms. In M. N. Zald (Ed.), *Power in organizations.* Nashville: Vanderbilt University Press, 1970.

Pettigrew, A. *The politics of organizational decision-making.* London: Tavistock, 1973.

Pugh, D. S., Hickson, D. J., Hinings, C. R., & Turner, C. Dimensions of organization structure. *Administrative Science Quarterly*, 1968, **13**(1), 65–105.

Pugh, D. S., Hickson, D. J., Hinings, C. R., & Turner, C. The context of organization structures. *Administrative Science Quarterly*, 1969, **14**(1), 91–114.

Thompson, J. D. *Organizations in action.* New York: McGraw-Hill, 1967.

Wamsley, G., & Zald, M. N. The political economy of public organizations. *Public Administration Review*, 1973, **33**, 62–73.

ORGANIZATIONAL AND ENVIRONMENTAL INFLUENCES ON HEALTH AND PERFORMANCE [1]

E. K. Eric Gunderson
Naval Health Research Center
San Diego, California

Organizational coordination and control must be viewed in the context of existing technology, prevailing social values, and degree of environmental hazard. The modern navy is a technologically advanced segment of the national society and also is a self-contained institution with a unique history and traditions. Meaningful analysis of naval organizations requires an appreciation of the sociocultural and political context in which the modern naval establishment operates. The problems of coordination and control aboard navy ships offer a fertile field for research on managerial practices and group performance. Because the ship is a closed and isolated ecological system

[1] Report Number 76–39, supported by Naval Medical Research and Development Command, Department of the Navy, under Research Work Unit MF51.524.002–4019. The views presented are those of the author. No endorsement by the Department of the Navy has been given or should be inferred.

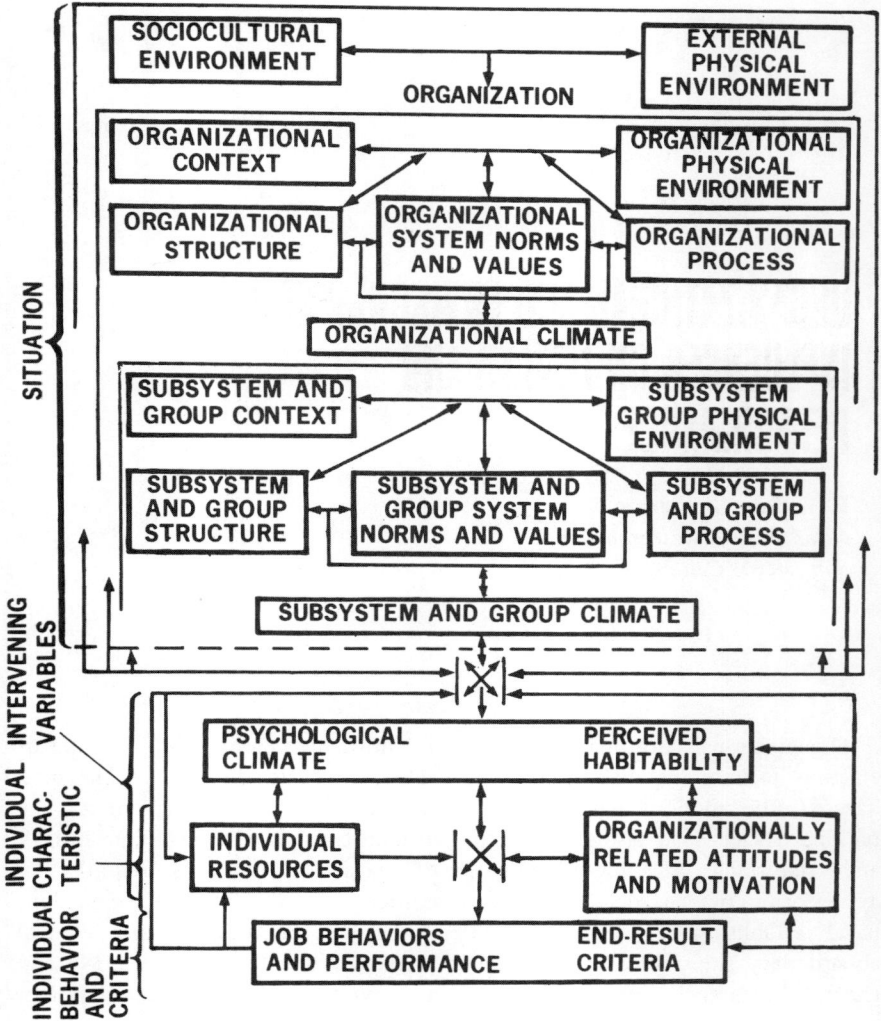

Fig. 1. Social system model.

while at sea, organizational and environmental contraints and leader behaviors have an impact on all aspects of the sailor's day-to-day life experience.

The study to be described is part of a larger research program concerned with the development of a social system, or integrating, model which encompasses a wide range of environmental, organizational, and individual characteristics and provides a framework for analyzing relationships between the individual and his organizational environment and also for evaluating the effectiveness of individuals, organizational subsystems, and the organization as a whole in achieving organizational objectives. The term integrating model refers to an attempt to represent both the characteristics of persons and the properties of organizational settings as well as their interactions.

The model represents organizations at several levels: external environment, total organization (ship), major subsystems (departments and divisions), work groups, and individuals. In a recent paper James, Jones, Bruni, Hornick, and Sells (1974) have explicated the model in detail and reported a series of empirical analyses designed to examine relationships among its major components. Some of these relationships are exemplified in Figure 1, where each organizational level (total organization, subsystem, work group) has its own context, structure, process, physical environment, and climate components and is embedded within the next larger subsystem or level. Interconnecting arrows represent interrelated events and interactions of the type proposed by integrating models. In the present study, relationships between selected components of the social systems model and subsystem performance and safety are examined, and the possible relationships of coordination and control processes to these components are explored. Aboard Navy ships, it will be shown that the division is the most important organizational level for assessing the influences of organizational climate and physical environment and examining problems of coordination and control. Primary attention is given to the variable domains of organizational climate and physical environment because these domains have important influences on performance and health (safety) (James, Jones, Bruni, Hornick, & Sells, 1974; Pugh, Erickson, & Jones, 1976).

Problems of coordination and control are central concerns in the operation of any organization. Coordination is defined here as the division of labor and the structuring of work activities. Control system refers to procedures for monitoring, evaluating, and changing job behaviors to conform to management objectives. Thus, coordination and control are viewed as management initiated processes to regulate work behavior. Organizational control systems are primarily designed to achieve and maintain satisfactory levels of performance; coordination and control efforts also may have important secondary effects on worker satisfaction and retention. Finally, coordination and control processes have significant implications for workers' health and safety.

Table 1. Climate Components and Defining Variables with Highest Loadings[a]

I.	*Conflict and ambiguity*
	Subsystem conflict: degree to which subsystem goals, policies, and actions conflict. .66
	Ambiguity of structure: degree to which role definition, lines of authority, responsibility, and communication channels are undefined or unclear. .66
	Interdepartmental cooperation: degree of cooperative action, communication, and mutual help among departments. −.57
	Communication—down: degree to which information is communicated to subordinates on matters affecting their work, status, and well-being. −.55
II.	*Job challenge, importance and variety*
	Job challenge: degree to which individuals receive opportunities to make full use of their abilities, skills, and knowledge. .75
	Job importance: degree of importance of job to organization. .68
	Job variety: range of types of tasks, equipment, and behaviors involved in jobs. .67
	Job isolation: degree to which job restricts opportunities to interact with other persons. −.54
III.	*Leader facilitation and support*
	Work facilitation: degree to which leaders provide resources, guidance, problem solutions, and aid subordinates in achieving planned goals. .80
	Interaction facilitation: degree to which leaders encourage development of close, cohesive work groups. .77
	Leader support: degree to which leaders are aware of and are responsive to needs of subordinates and show consideration for their feelings of personal worth. .72
	Goal emphasis: degree to which leaders stimulate subordinates' involvement in meeting organizational goals. .72
IV.	*Workgroup cooperation, friendliness and warmth*
	Cooperation: existence of an atmosphere of cooperation to carry out difficult tasks; evidence of mutuality of goals and sharing of reward for success. .75
	Reputation for effectiveness: degree to which work group enjoys a record of effective performance and is expected to perform well by peers as well as supervisors. .72
	Friendliness and warmth: degree to which warm, friendly relations, trust and mutual liking prevail. .64
	Esprit: degree to which members show pride in their group, their fellow members, and their record as a group. .59

[a]The four composites with highest loadings are described for each component; only three composites had loadings of .40 or greater for the Job Standards component.

Table 1. (cont'd)

V.	*Professional and organizational esprit*	
	Professional esprit: degree to which individuals believe that their profession has a good image to outsiders and provides opportunities for growth and advancement.	.79
	Organizational esprit: degree to which individuals believe that the organization performs an important function and offers them opportunities for growth and reward.	.66
	Openness of expression: degree to which organizational atmosphere fosters expression of ideas, dissent, criticism, opinions, suggestions, and other information upward.	.64
	Confidence and trust—up: degree of confidence and trust of members in their superiors.	.61
VI.	*Job standards*	
	Job standards: degree to which exacting standards of quality and accuracy are required in job performance.	.54
	Job pressure: adequacy of time, information, and resources to complete assignments and degree of threat implied for substandard performance.	.40
	Confidence and trust—down: degree of confidence and trust of superiors in their subordinates.	−.40

METHOD

The study to be described sampled 20 U.S. Navy ships operating in the Atlantic and Pacific Oceans during the latter half of 1973. Eighteen of the 20 ships were destroyer-types: 4 destroyers or DDs (crew size about 225); 6 destroyer escorts or DEs (crew size about 250); 5 guided missile destroyers or DDGs (crew size about 280); and 3 missile frigates or DLGs (crew size about 360). The remaining two ships were attack aircraft carriers which represented major differences in size, mission, and organizational structure. The social system of primary interest was the crew of a small destroyer-type naval ship (crew size 225 to 360 men) and its principal subsystems, namely, departments and divisions.

Each destroyer-type ship had at least four departments: Weapons, Supply, Engineering, and Operations. In addition, frigates (DLGs) had Communications Departments and approximately one-third of the ships had separate Navigation Departments. The four major departments generally were made up of divisions as follows: (a) Weapons Department—Deck, Ordnance (Guns), Fire Control, and Anti-Submarine Warfare divisions for all ships and Missile divisions for the DDGs and DLGs; (b) Supply Department—one Supply division; (c) Engineering Department—Boilers, Machinery, Repair, Electrical, and Auxiliary divisions; and (d) Operations Department—Navigation, Communications, Electronics, and Intelligence divisions. The numbers of possible subsystems available for study were 105 departments and 281 divisions.

The primary test instrument used in the study was a 400-item questionnaire, the Habitability and Shipboard Climate Questionnaire, which contained biographical and service history data, 145 items pertaining to organizational and job characteristics, and a set of environmental dimensions describing work and living conditions. Crew members rated their working areas, messing (eating) areas, berthing (sleeping) areas, heads (sanitary facilities), and the entire ship on 11 environmental dimensions: temperature, ventilation, cleanliness, odor, size, number of people, lighting, color, privacy, noise, and safety. This questionnaire was administered to ships' crews near the beginning of 7- to 8-month overseas deployments.

Organizational climate measures were constructed by grouping the 145 questionnaire items into 35 composites reflecting salient job, leadership, division, work group, and total organization variables, and subjecting these composites to principal components analysis in a sample of 4,315 Navy enlisted men. The analysis yielded six higher order climate components, which are described in Table 1. The derivation of these components is described in detail in James et al. (1974) and, in addition, the relationships among division context, structure, climate, and other oganizational variables are presented.

Eight dimensions of division performance, derived from 24 descriptive statements designed to be applicable to all divisions, were evaluated by each department head for the divisions in his department. The 24 items were presented to raters in a "mixed-standard" format (Arvey & Hoyle, 1974); these items defined the following dimensions: (a) quality of work; (b) completion of planned maintenance schedule; (c) readiness to fulfill commitments; (d) performance under pressure;·(e) efficiency; (f) cooperation with other divisions; (g) leadership; and (h) safety. The safety rating was dropped from the present analysis because it did not pertain directly to performance and did not correlate substantially with other criteria.

Additional division performance criteria were ratings by division heads concerning: (a) the use of drugs and alcohol ("nonexistent" to "frequent"), and (b) the frequency of requests for transfer out of the division.

Illness and accident data were collected on all ships by recording individual dispensary visits throughout the overseas deployments. Records of disciplinary offenses were obtained for seven of the Pacific ships and provided a basis for an analysis of the correlates of disciplinary rates.

RESULTS

Physical Environment. Crew members' perceptions of the physical characteristics of their work environments are shown in Figures 2 and 3. Mean ratings on five environmental scales were derived by departments and by divisions within department. The highly correlated temperature and ventilation dimensions were combined into one scale, as were cleanliness and odor and size and number of people (crowding). Noise and safety were treated as separate dimensions; lighting, color, and privacy were omitted from this analysis.

In Figure 2, mean standardized values for each scale were plotted to provide work area profiles for four departments—Navigation, Communications, Weapons, and Engineering. Values above the mid-line represent favorable environmental conditions, and values below the mid-line represent unfavorable conditions. In Figure 3, mean values for divisions within two departments—Weapons and Engineering—are shown for each environmental dimension separately.

When environmental ratings were aggregated at the department level, large differences in perceived working conditions were apparent (Fig. 2). Navigation, Communications, and Weapons personnel, although differing somewhat on all environmental dimensions, generally reported their working conditions as relatively favorable, while Engineering Department personnel experienced very unfavorable environmental conditions.

In Figure 3, working conditions were compared among divisions within two departments—Weapons and Engineering—and it can be seen that divisions within departments varied markedly in environmental conditions. The most striking example was that the Boilers and Machinery divisions of the Engineering Department differed considerably from the Repair and Electrical divisions of the same department on almost all dimensions. Boilers and Machinery work areas were reported to be extremely hot, dirty, noisy, and unsafe compared to other divisions.

These results clearly demonstrated two important points that have relevance not only for performance and safety but also for problems of coordination and control: (a) Physical work environments vary markedly among major ship subsystems (departments and divisions), and (b) much of this variance can only be accounted for at the division level.

Organizational Climate. Not only do divisions aboard ship vary considerably in work environment characteristics, but division types also vary widely in structure, staffing, equipment, technology, and functions or tasks. A multiple discriminant analysis was conducted to classify average profiles of climate scores for 223 divisions into a meaningful typology of division climate. Twelve functional types were enumerated, and this number was reduced to seven by means of a hierarchical grouping procedure (Jones & James, 1976).

Climate profiles for the seven division types are shown in Table 2 in terms of deviations of more than one-half standard deviation from the grand mean for each of the six climate components. Thus, salient climate characteristics of

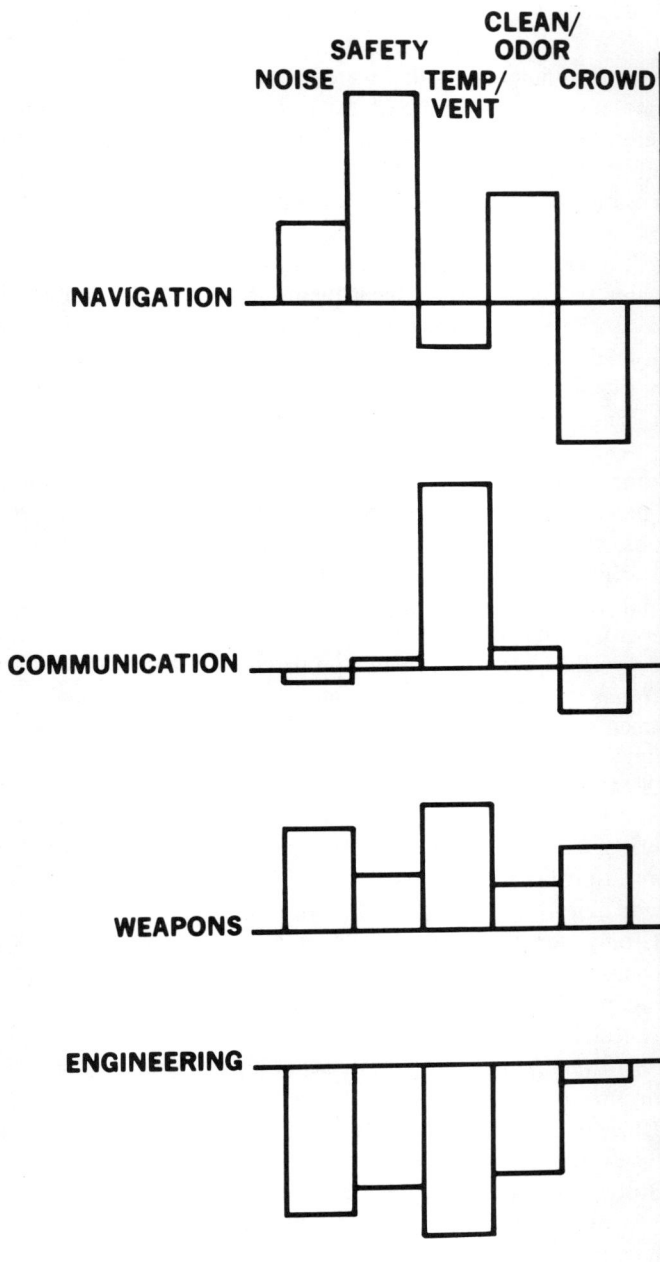

NOISE SAFETY TEMP/VENT CLEAN/ODOR CROWD

NAVIGATION

COMMUNICATION

WEAPONS

ENGINEERING

*HIGH SCORES REPRESENT FAVORABLE HABITABILITY

Fig. 2. Differences in perceived work environments by department.

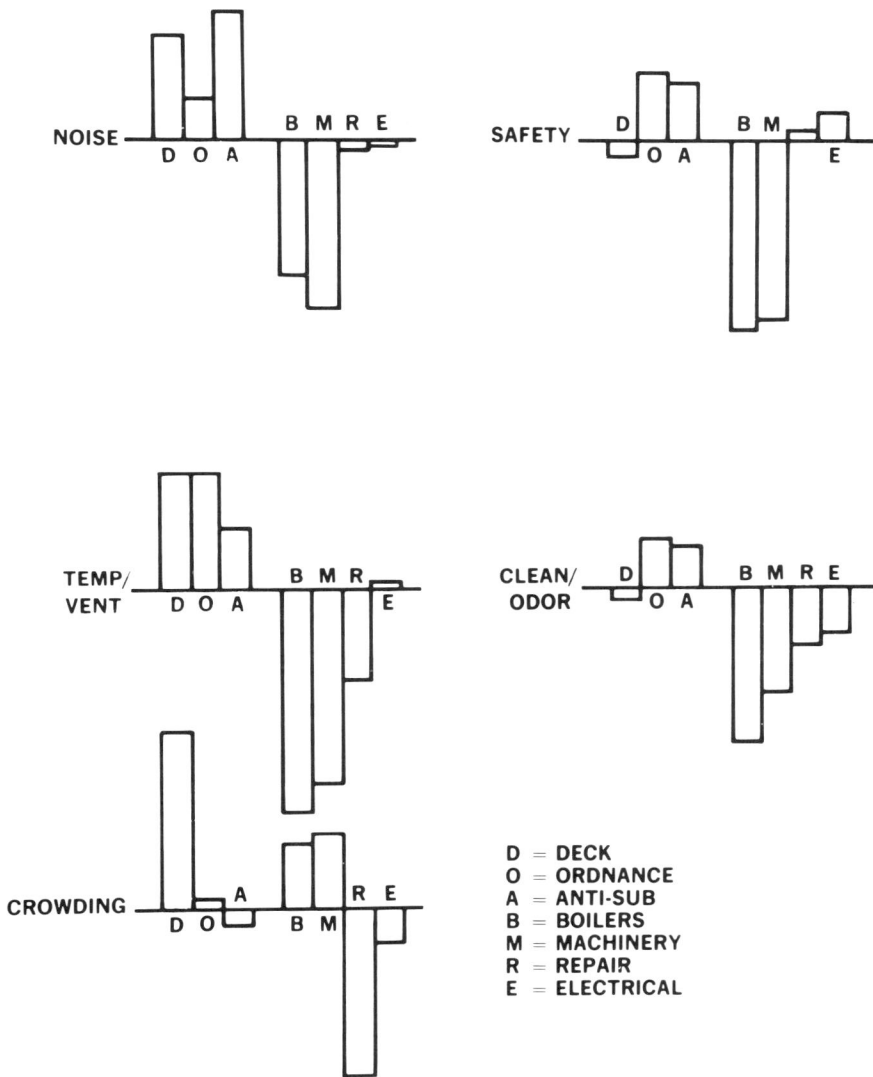

Fig. 3. Differences in perceived work environments by division within Weapons (deck, ordnance, anti-submarine) and Engineering (boilers, machinery, repair, electrical) departments.

Table 2. Differences in Climate Profiles by Division Type[a]

Division type	Conflict, ambiguity	Job challenge	Leader support	Workgroup cooperation	Professional esprit	Job standards
				Climate components		
I. Navigation, Anti-Submarine Warfare, Guns				+		
II. Missiles, Fire Control, Nuclear, Auxiliary, Repair, Electrical	+					
III. Communications, Intelligence					–	+
IV. Boilers, Machinery				–		
V. Deck		– –	–	– –		
VI. Electronics	++			+	–	
VII. Supply					+	–

[a] ++ Indicates that the division type mean was one standard deviation or more above the mean for all divisions.
+ Indicates that the division type mean was one-half of a standard deviation above the overall mean; – indicates one-half standard deviation below the overall mean; and – – indicates one standard deviation or more below the overall mean.

Table 3. Correlations between Organizational Variables and Division Performance[a]

Organizational variables	Division performance criteria								
	Quality	Maintenance	Readiness	Pressure	Efficiency	Cooperation	Leadership	Transfer	Drugs
Division context:									
Condition of equipment	19*	24**	29**	14	16*	11	15	−17*	−22**
Division structure:									
Size of division	−16*	−11	−08	01	−11	−10	−13	28**	37**
Specialization	−14	−19*	−12	−22**	−22**	−02	−07	−06	08
Number of levels	−06	−05	−03	01	−05	08	−06	16**	24**
Span of control	01	07	14	02	06	03	00	−33**	−31**
Division climate:									
Job challenge	−01	12	06	03	07	−06	01	−29**	−26**
Leader support	05	14	02	15	18*	13	22**	−18*	−07
Workgroup cooperation	33**	37**	33**	22**	24**	24**	24**	−44**	−42**
Professional esprit	05	01	05	00	05	25*	−02	05	00
Personnel resources:									
Time in Navy	06	10	11	03	07	11	−01	−36**	−31**
Advanced training	32**	30**	29**	28**	23**	21**	24**	−33**	−33**
Years of education	19*	13	18*	21**	21**	15	12	−44**	−30**
Intellectual aptitude	20**	26**	20**	17*	19*	08	20*	−43**	−34**
Quality of personnel	29**	26**	29**	35**	32**	29**	43**	−23**	−27**

*p = .05.
**p = .01.
[a]Decimals are omitted; n = 160.

53

each division type are indicated. For example, the Navigation, Anti-Submarine Warfare, and Guns cluster of divisions are above average in cooperative, friendly, and warm work group relations. Deck divisions, on the other hand, report a very low level of work group cooperation, friendliness, and warmth, a very low level of job challenge, importance, and variety, and a low level of leader facilitation and support.

Organizational Correlates of Division Performance. Analysis of the organizational variables that predict division performance might yield useful clues as to coordination and control practices that are consistent with effective performance. Correlations between selected organizational variables and division performance ratings are shown in Table 3. Variables considered to have possible relevance for coordination and control activities were included.

Correlations generally were low to moderate, but the overall pattern of relationships was suggestive. Quality of personnel resources, as indicated by average years of education, average intellectual aptitude score, amount of advanced training, and division officers' ratings of personnel quality, appeared to have a powerful effect on division performance. Among the climate dimensions, Workgroup Cooperation, Friendliness, and Warmth had special importance for predicting division effectiveness in that all correlations with the criterion measures were highly significant. Condition of work equipment was significantly correlated with six of the criteria, but generally this variable was less important than quality of personnel resources or work group relations.

Division structure variables appeared to have minor influence on performance, but the trends were interesting from the perspective that increasing division size and complexity might make coordination and control more difficult. Size of division, specialization (diversity of job types), and number of job levels all tended to correlate negatively with performance, although few of the correlations achieved significance for all divisions taken together. A small span of control, that is, close supervision, was associated with low frequency of transfer requests and drug and alcohol use.

Correlations between Organizational Variables and Division Effectiveness by Division Type. It is clear that large differences exist among divisions in physical characteristics of work environments and in organizational climate. This raises the question of whether patterns of organizational predictor-criterion relationships are similar in different types of divisions or whether there are important differences in the organizational variables that predict performance by division type. If the latter were the case, it would suggest that coordination and control processes also might vary in type and effectiveness. In order to test this proposition, two clusters of divisions were formed, representing a relatively high technical level and a low to intermediate technical level. The clusters included: (a) *High Technical*—Navigation, Guns,

Table 4. Correlations between Organizational Variables and Division Effectiveness by Division Type[a]

| | Effectiveness Criteria | | | | | |
| | Quality | | Maintenance | | Drugs | |
Organizational variables	High Technical[b]	Low Technical[c]	High Technical	Low Technical	High Technical	Low Technical
Division structure:						
Division size	−03	−27*	−17	−22	44**	31*
Specialization (job diversity)	−45**	13	−35*	12	−17	15
Span of control	−26	27*	04	28*	−28	−38**
Division climate:						
Workgroup cooperation, friendliness and warmth	38**	38**	40**	36**	−23	−31**
Personnel resources:						
Time in Navy	−17	31*	08	08	−19	−44*
Advanced training	49**	27*	51**	17	−15	−23
Quality of personnel	37*	11	53**	05	−28	−23

[a] Decimals are omitted.

[b] High Technical divisions ($n = 44$) —Guns, Fire Control, Missiles, Anti-Submarine Warfare, and Navigation.

[c] Low Technical divisions ($n = 55$) —Deck, Supply, Boilers, and Machinery.

and Anti-Submarine Warfare (Type I in Table 2) and Missiles and Fire Control (Type II); and (b) *Low Technical*—Boilers and Machinery (Type IV in Table 2), Deck (Type V), and Supply (Type VII). Combining divisions from the various types was necessary to provide sufficiently large *n*'s to conduct correlational analyses and comparisons. Results are shown in Table 4.

Division size correlated positively with drug and alcohol use for both High and Low divisions.

Specialization (diversity of jobs) had a negative impact on performance in the High divisions, but no effect in the Low divisions. This result suggests that division complexity had an adverse effect on performance in the High divisions.

A smaller span of control (closer supervision) had a beneficial effect on performance for Low Technical divisions but not for High divisions. This is consistent with the proposition that less technical, more routinized, more standardized jobs need more coordination and control than technical, nonroutinized, nonstandardized jobs.

Cooperative, friendly work group climate was positively related to effectiveness for both division types. It seems plausible that warm and friendly peer group relations would universally facilitate coordination and control efforts.

Time in the Navy was positively correlated with quality of performance and negatively correlated with drug and alcohol use for Low divisions only. This variable had no effect on the maintenance criterion.

Both the advanced training and quality of personnel variables had substantial correlations with performance for the High divisions; correlations were much lower for the Low divisions.

Thus, in High divisions, division effectiveness was primarily dependent upon superior technical skills and abilities, low specialization (Low division complexity), and work group cooperativeness. In Low divisions, division effectiveness depended to some extent upon division size, small span of control, Navy experience, and work group cooperativeness. These different patterns of correlation between organizational variables and division effectiveness criteria for diverse types of divisions suggest that coordination and control problems and practices also may vary in such a manner as to be consistent with division structure, climate, and personnel resources.

Manpower Utilization and Division Performance and Safety. A recent study of the relationships of division manning levels of division performance and injury rates (Dean, Harvey, Pugh, & Gunderson, 1976) provides a more direct example of the influence of coordination and control practices on organizational effectiveness. The Manpower Utilization scale was designed to measure the efficiency of personnel utilization within divisions. The scale was composed of four questionnaire items reflecting: (a) division members'

Table 5. Correlations of Manning Level and Perceived Manpower Utilization with Division Performance and Injury Rate[a]

Division performance criteria:	Percent Manning[b]	Manpower Utilization[c]
Quality	09	19*
Maintenance	−07	24**
Readiness	06	11
Pressure	06	09
Efficiency	03	18*
Cooperation	11	13
Leadership	14	00
Injury Rate	−04	−31**

*$p < .05$.
**$p < .01$.
$n = 123$.
[a] Decimal points have been omitted.
[b] The Percent Manning is the authorized number of division personnel divided by the actual number.
[c] The Manpower Utilization scale is the sum of the responses to four questionnaire items.

perceptions of work activity coordination; (b) division members' feelings that they did a whole piece of work as opposed to doing part of a job which was finished by someone else; (c) division members' feelings that they were helped by their co-workers; and (d) division members' perceptions of their workloads.

In Table 5 it can be seen that the Manpower Utilization scale was a predictor of division performance and injury rate while the objective measure of manning level (the ratio of authorized to actual personnel) was not. Manning level did not correlate with any of the performance criteria or with injury rate while the Manpower Utilization scale correlated significantly with four of the criterion measures. Thus, merely having sufficient manpower was not an important determinant of division performance or accident rate, but how personnel were utilized or coordinated in their work activities was related to division effectiveness and safety.

Injury Rates by Division. Differences among divisions in perceptions of work area safety and in injury rates are shown in Figure 4. Boilers and Machinery division personnel perceive their work environments as unsafe and experience relatively high injury rates. This relationship suggests that injuries are primarily the result of hazardous environmental conditions in these divisions. Deck division personnel do not perceive their work environments as

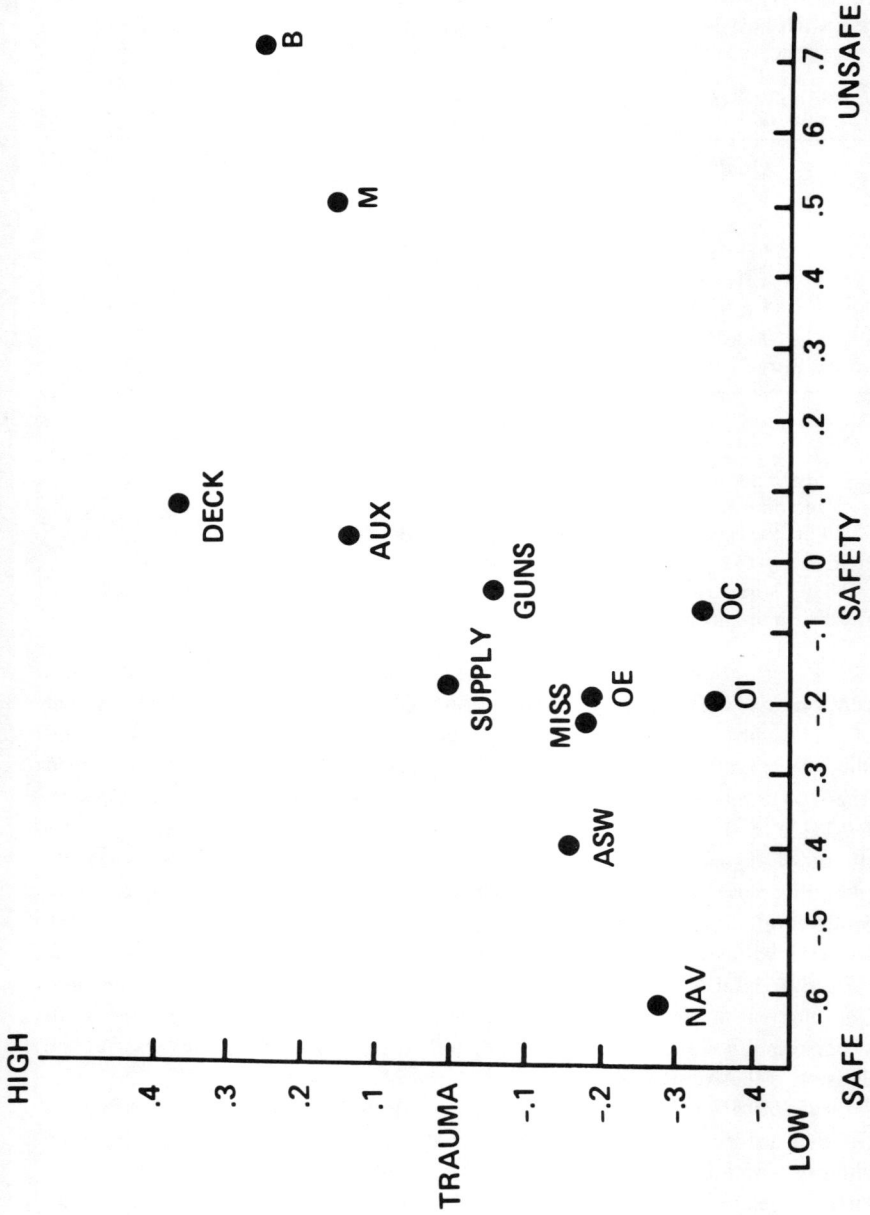

Fig. 4. Safety perceptions and injury rates by division.

particularly unsafe but nevertheless incur the highest injury rate of any division. The climate profile for Deck divisions (see Table 2) indicates a very unfavorable work climate—very low job challenge, very low work group cooperation, and low leader support—which suggests severe difficulties in coordination and control. In any case, the relatively high injury rates for Boilers, Machinery, and Deck divisions affirm the need for more effective control efforts in these divisions to prevent accidents.

DISCUSSION

The naval organization as a whole has a prescribed formal structure and a universal system of regulations and reward-punishment procedures designed to control the behavior of its members. At the ship subsystem level, organizational units (divisions) vary markedly in personnel resources, physical environments, division structures, and work climates. Coordination and control problems and effective management practices would be expected to vary in accordance with the characteristics of these heterogeneous division types.

Organizational variables that correlated with division performance appeared to have implications with respect to degree and types of coordination and control problems. Smaller division size with less complexity (less specialization and fewer hierarchical levels) would be expected to result in less difficult coordination and control problems (Lawler, 1976); high quality of personnel in terms of intellectual aptitudes, education, advanced training, and job experience should make coordination and control easier; a work group climate of cooperation, friendliness, and warmth should facilitate coordination and control efforts, and divisions with high levels of job challenge and leader support and a low degree of role ambiguity and conflict should be expected to have minimal coordination and control problems.

In the present study, Boilers, Machinery, and Deck divisions not only had hazardous work environments but unfavorable work climates as well. Coordination and control under these conditions would appear to be particularly difficult. It is noteworthy that not only are injury rates highest in these divisions, but on a subsample of seven ships with disciplinary data general illness rates, job dissatisfaction, and disciplinary rates also were found to be exceptionally high for these divisions. A greater degree of management control obviously is needed in hostile or hazardous work environments to protect workers' health and safety, but can stricter regulation with additional deprivations and frustrations be imposed without adversely affecting cooperation and motivation?

The objective of a combat ship is to be in a state of operational readiness at all times to meet any emergency. This need for a rapid and reliable response capability places many constraints on organizational operations, and coordination and control systems must be designed to fit this primary aim. Accordingly, control systems for the ship as a whole are authoritarian or autocratic in character, particularly under emergency conditions. However, at the division level, where heterogeneity of tasks, personnel, and environments is the rule, different leadership styles and control techniques may prove effective within a general framework of traditional authority. For example, in small divisions with advanced technology and highly trained personnel, division members reported considerable autonomy or self-control in carrying out their jobs. At the same time, these personnel are subject to certain ship-wide controls and to the same Navy-wide controls with respect to standards of conduct, promotion opportunities, etc., as are all other sailors. Thus, it seems useful to view coordination and control within the context of a social systems model in which relationships among context, structure, process, physical environment, and climate components can be analyzed at each level separately and integrated over several organizational levels. Such efforts are in progress at the Naval Health Research Center, San Diego.

REFERENCES

Arvey, R. D., & Hoyle, J. C. A Guttman approach to the development of behaviorally based rating scales for systems analysts and programmer analysts. *Journal of Applied Psychology*, 1974, **59**, 61–68.

Dean, L. M., Harvey, R. A., Pugh, W. M., & Gunderson, E. K. E. *Manning levels, organizational effectiveness, and health* (Report No. 76–16). San Diego, Calif.: Naval Health Research Center, 1976.

James, L. R., Jones, A. P., Bruni, J. R., Hornick, C. W., & Sells, S. B. *Relationships among subsystem context, structure, climate and performance from the perspective of an integrating model* (Tech. Rep. 75–4). Fort Worth, Texas: Texas Christian University, Institute of Behavioral Research, 1974.

Jones, A. P., & James, L. R. *Psychological and organizational climate: Dimensions and relationships* (Tech. Rep. 76–4). Fort Worth, Texas: Texas Christian University, Institute of Behavioral Research, 1976.

Lawler, E. E. Control systems in organizations. In M. D. Dunnette (Ed.), *Handbook of industrial and organizational psychology*. Chicago: Rand McNally, 1976.

Pugh, W. M., Erickson, J. M., & Jones, A. P. *Workers' perceptions of safety as a predictor of injury* (Report No. 76–75). San Diego, Calif.: Naval Health Research Center, 1976.

THE DESIGN OF SELF-MANAGING WORK GROUPS[1]

J. Richard Hackman
Yale University

In a provocative article titled "Suppose we took groups seriously . . . ," Leavitt (1975) raises the possibility that it might be better to design and manage organizations using groups rather than individuals as the basic building blocks. Among the advantages Leavitt sees as possible from such an approach are the following:

— Groups seem to be good for people, in that they can provide members with important social satisfactions, support under stress, enriched opportunities for learning, and a wider range of activities than might be available to individuals.

[1] This report was prepared in connection with research supported by the Office of Naval Research (Organizational Effectiveness Research Program, Contract No. N00014-75C-0269, NR 170-744). The author expresses appreciation to the numerous colleagues who commented on the earlier version of the paper, presented at the NATO Conference on Group and Organizational Control, Munich, July, 1976. Portions of this paper are based on a study by Hackman and Morris (1975).

— Groups can be good at finding problems, and at promoting innovation.

— Groups make better decisions than individuals on some kinds of tasks.

— Groups can be good tools for implementation in organizations, in that group decisions to which members are committed will be carried out willingly.

— Groups can control the behavior of individual members more effectively than often is possible using formal organizational controls.

— Groups can help fend off the negative consequences of large organizational size, by keeping communication lines short and hierarchies relatively flat.

Given possible benefits such as these, one could view work groups as a panacea for organizational problems, which assuredly they are not. For one thing, groups can turn sour: They can enforce norms of low rather than high work effectiveness (Whyte, 1955); at times they make notoriously bad decisions (Janis, 1972); they can fall into patterns of destructive conflict with other groups (Alderfer, 1977); and sometimes they exploit and stress group members rather than aid in their growth and personal well-being (Hackman, 1976). Moreover, despite the increasing number of organizations that are designing work to be done by interacting groups, there are still major gaps in our understanding of the reasons why some such groups function effectively—and why others turn out to be a source of continual difficulty and dismay for both group members and organizational management. These gaps currently place severe limits on our ability to develop and utilize groups as fully as possible in carrying out the work of organizations.

This chapter is intended to further understanding of what is required to create self-managing work groups and to maintain them at high levels of effectiveness.[2] Toward this end, the chapter attempts to identify those factors that are most critical to the design of self-managing work groups—including how such groups should be staffed, how their tasks should be structured, what kinds of norms regarding internal performance processes should be encouraged, etc. Although the chapter deals mainly with the *design* of self-managing work groups, attention also is given to questions about the management of such groups, and about the circumstances under which it is feasible and potentially advantageous to design work for groups rather than for individuals.

---

[2] For present purposes, a work group is considered effective if it meets the following criteria: (a) Group task performance meets or exceeds acceptable levels of quantity and quality; (b) group experience serves more to satisfy than to frustrate the personal needs of group members; and (c) social processes used in carrying out the work maintain or enhance the capability of members to work interdependen.. on subsequent group tasks.

EXISTING STRANDS OF RESEARCH AND THEORY

The notion of the "autonomous work group," developed by theorists and practitioners from the sociotechnical systems approach to organizational design, provides an excellent point of departure for thought about self-managing work groups. When autonomous work groups are formed, members of a small team (less than 20 members) are given major responsibility for planning and executing a whole and meaningful piece of work, and are encouraged to develop close ties with one another in carrying out the work activities. The idea is that the group provides a setting in which the social (i.e., interpersonal) and the technical (i.e., task technology) aspects of the workplace can be integrated and support one another (Emery & Trist, 1969; Trist, Higgin, Murray, & Pollock, 1963).

Specific arrangements in autonomous work groups (such as how the group task itself is designed, the composition of the work group, the nature of pay systems, and aspects of the organizational context) have varied from case to case in reported studies.[3] In general, however, the following seem to be core attributes of effective autonomous work groups:

1. A "whole" task for the group—i.e., one in which the mission of the group is sufficiently identifiable and significant that members find the work of the group meaningful.

2. Workers who each have a number of the skills required for completion of the group task, thereby increasing the flexibility of the group in carrying out the task. When individuals do not have a robust repertoire of skills initially, procedures are developed to encourage cross-training among members.

3. Autonomy for the group to make decisions about methods for carrying out the work, scheduling various activities, assigning different individuals to different tasks, and (sometimes) deciding which individuals will be permitted to join the group as new members.

4. Compensation and feedback about performance based on the accomplishment of the group as a whole, rather than on the individual contributions of group members.

Published reports suggest that autonomous work groups are being used frequently and successfully as part of organizational change activities involving the redesign of work. Sociotechnical systems theory is incomplete, however, in at least three respects that bear on the design and maintenance of interacting work groups in organizations.

[3] See, for example, Bucklow, 1966; Davis, 1966, p. 44; Davis & Trist, 1974; Gulowsen, 1972; Trist et al., 1963. An informative and succinct statement of the principles of sociotechnical design on which such applications are based is provided by Cherns (1976).

First, the theory does not specify the attributes of group tasks that are required for creation of effective autonomous work groups. Simple prescriptions about providing groups with autonomy and creating "whole" tasks do not provide the kind of operational specificity that is needed to guide applications of the theory. Also, because key task attributes are not specified, it is not possible to devise measures of those attributes for use in theory guided diagnoses of work systems prior to change, in evaluations of the effects of changes on the work, or in tests of the conceptual adequacy of the theory itself.

Secondly, individual differences among people are not explicitly dealt with in the sociotechnical approach. While it is recognized that individuals are social beings, and that social relationships must be carefully attended to in the design or change of any work system, the theory does not deal with the fact that social needs vary in strength among people. Such differences may affect whether individuals seek out or resist opportunities to participate in an autonomous work group. Moreover, the theory fails to deal with *other* human needs that may be salient for individuals in organizations, some of which (e.g., needs for personal growth) appear to affect how people react to their work and their work groups.

Finally, the theory does not address the internal dynamics that occur among members of work groups, or offer guidance about how such groups could be designed to increase the chances that they will achieve *internal* health and effectiveness. The assumption, apparently, is that members of autonomous work groups will develop on their own satisfactory ways of working together, and that they will be able to adjust their internal dynamics appropriately in changing task or organizational circumstances. Given the substantial evidence about ways that groups can go "sour," the validity of that assumption must be considered questionable.

The incompleteness of sociotechnical systems theory makes it difficult to translate from the general (and doubtless correct) tenets of the theory to either a set of testable propositions about the conditions under which autonomous work groups will and will not be effective, or to the specific action steps that should be taken to create and maintain such groups in different organizational settings. In particular, it appears necessary to flesh out the principles of sociotechnical systems design in the following three areas: (a) characteristics of jobs and tasks that prompt effective work behavior, (b) individual differences among people that affect reactions to work and to work groups, and (c) internal social processes that occur among members of work groups.

In the pages to follow, research and theory that may be useful in this regard are reviewed. Then, in the following section, these research streams are integrated in an attempt to specify the ingredients that are most critical to the design and maintenance of effective self-managing work groups.

Job Characteristics Theory

An approach to the design of work for individuals that provides considerable specificity about the characteristics of tasks and jobs has been proposed by Hackman and Oldham (1976), based on earlier studies of task attributes by Turner and Lawrence (1965) and Hackman and Lawler (1971).

The theory, which is summarized in Figure 1, proposes that both work effectiveness and personal satisfaction are enhanced when all three of the following psychological conditions are present: (a) The work is experienced as personally *meaningful*, (b) the jobholder feels personally *responsible* for the work outcomes, and (c) the jobholder has *knowledge of the results* of the work activities that have been carried out. Under such circumstances, a person feels an internal motivational "kick" when he or she does well, and experiences personal dismay when performance is poor—thereby creating an internal motivational impetus to perform as well as possible.

The theory also specifies the measurable characteristics of jobs that create the three psychological states described above. Knowledge of results is obtained through regular and trustworthy *feedback* from the job. Experienced responsibility is created when the job provides the employee with high *autonomy* to make decisions about planning and carrying out the work. And experienced meaningfulness is enhanced when any of three job characteristics are present: (a) *skill variety*, the degree to which the job requires use of a number of valued skills and abilities in carrying out the work; (b) *task identity*, the degree to which the job involves completion of a whole piece of work with a visible outcome; and (c) *task significance*, the degree to which the job has a substantial impact on the lives or work of other people.

It is possible to combine the five job characteristics into a single index that reflects the overall "motivating potential" of a job—i.e., the degree to which a job will prompt high *internal* work motivation on the part of job incumbents. This index, called the Motivating Potential Score (MPS) is computed as follows:[4]

$$MPS = \frac{[Skill\ Variety + Task\ Identity + Task\ Significance]}{3} \times Autonomy \times Job\ Feedback$$

Finally, job characteristics theory acknowledges that not all people will respond positively to a job that is high in motivating potential. Specifically, three individual difference moderators are specified and shown in Figure 1.

[4] Scores on the job characteristics can be obtained using the Job Diagnostic Survey (Hackman & Oldham, 1975), an instrument designed specifically to measure the concepts in job characteristics theory. The JDS scores for each characteristic range from 1 to 7; therefore, the MPS of a job can range from 1 to 343.

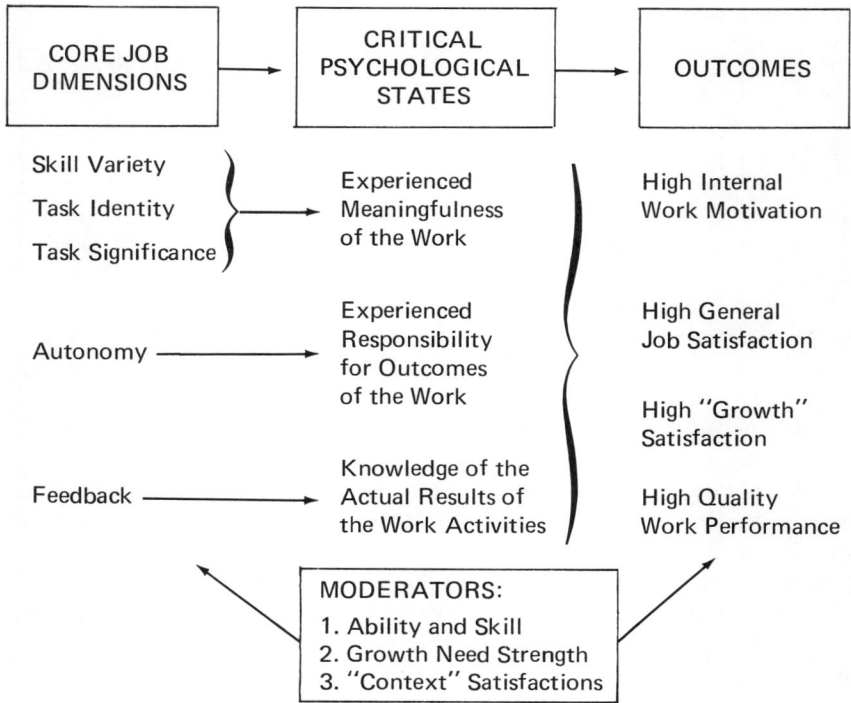

Fig. 1. The Job characteristics theory of work motivation.

1. The task-relevant *knowledge and skill* of the job incumbent. Consider a person working on a job high in MPS who does not have the skill required to perform the job successfully. Because of the motivating characteristics of the job, the person will care a great deal about doing well on it. And because the person does not have the skill needed to succeed, greater effort on the job will lead only to greater frustration at doing poorly. At some point, the person would be expected to cease trying to perform effectively, and either psychologically or behaviorally withdraw from the job.

2. The level of *growth need strength* of the job incumbent. Only if a person values personal growth and accomplishment to some degree would he or she be expected to respond with enthusiasm to the chance to work on a complex and challenging job, or to be personally motivated by the kinds of internal rewards that good performance on such a job can bring. In general, research evidence supports the proposition that growth need strength is one factor that determines who will—and who will not—respond positively to a job

that is high in motivating potential (for a review of this literature, see Hackman, 1977).

3. The level of *satisfaction with the work context* experienced by the job incumbent. If an employee is chronically and seriously dissatisfied with aspects of the work context such as pay, job security, supervision, or relations with co-workers, then that person is unlikely to respond positively to the opportunities for personal development offered by a complex, challenging job (Oldham, Hackman, & Pearce, 1976).

Research tests of job characteristics theory (e.g., Evans, Kiggundu, & House, 1976; Hackman & Oldham, 1976) have been generally supportive of theory-specified propositions. In addition, the theory has proven useful in guiding and evaluating organizational change programs involving work redesign, because it specifies (and facilitates measurement of) both job characteristics and individual differences among people, and shows how these two factors *interact* in determining how people react to their jobs.

Yet, like the similar theory of Herzberg (Herzberg, 1966; Herzberg, Mausner, & Snyderman, 1959), job characteristics theory is framed to apply exclusively to jobs that are done more or less independently by individuals. It offers no guidelines for the design of tasks to be done by interacting groups, nor does it address either the social needs of employees nor the social characteristics of jobs. And, because the theory is essentially a theory of individual work motivation, it offers no guidance in understanding how the interpersonal relationships that develop among members of an interacting work group influence the overall effectiveness of that group.

Individual Differences Theory and Practice

Not all jobs are well suited to a given person, nor are all people well suited for a given job. A great deal of research energy has been expended over the last several decades to generate theories of individual differences, and to devise strategies for measuring them so that good "matches" can be made between the capabilities of people and the requirements of their jobs.

These research efforts have led to some rather sophisticated technologies for assessing differences among people in their task-relevant knowledge and skill, and for assigning organization members to specific jobs for which they are fully qualified (Dunnette, 1966; Schneider, 1976). If an organization decides it wishes to identify the skill requirements of its jobs, and to develop measures for assessing individuals on those skills, the theory and technology needed to do so are available.

Less well developed are measurement devices and placement strategies that deal with the *interpersonal* skills of individuals, and with the needs people have to obtain social satisfactions in the workplace. This gap in research knowledge is of consequence for the design and staffing of self-managing work groups, because the social dynamics that occur in such groups may be as important as the task-relevant skills of individual group members in determining how well the work of the group gets done.

Moreover, very little is known about how the characteristics of individuals *combine* to influence the effectiveness of groups in which members work interdependently on a group task. Although there is a considerable social psychological literature on the consequences of homogeneity vs. heterogeneity of group membership (Haythorn, 1968; Hill, 1975; Schutz, 1958; Steiner, 1972), research on the topic has not yet proven useful in making decisions about the composition of interacting work teams in organizations. Indeed, it remains unclear exactly what characteristics of people are crucial (and what characteristics safely can be ignored) when interacting work teams are composed.

In sum, individual differences and their measurement are relatively advanced in a number of areas (particularly those having to do with the selection and placement of people based on measures of their knowledge and skill). Yet there presently is little understanding about some of the "softer" aspects of people (particularly those having to do with social skills, needs, and relationships) that can be applied directly to the design and composition of self-managing work groups. In some applications of autonomous work groups, these problems are circumvented simply by asking existing groups to make decisions about membership in the group—including who is selected to join, and whose membership is terminated. The practice is intriguing and worthy of systematic evaluation—but it also highlights the absence of any measurement procedures that could be used *a priori* to predict the likely "fit" between individuals and their work groups.

Group Interaction Process

The role of the interaction process that takes place among group members in affecting performance outcomes is complex and, at present, unclear (Hackman & Morris, 1975). Yet within the considerable literature on the topic is a body of research and theory that may be particularly relevant to the design and maintenance of self-managing work groups—namely, studies of interventions that are explicitly designed to help work groups improve the task-appropriateness of their internal processes. Such interventions can be sorted into two categories: (a) structured techniques that specify in some detail how members optimally should proceed with work on the task, and (b) interpersonal techniques that are intended to improve the overall quality of inter-member relationships in the group, and thus indirectly enhance task effectiveness.

Structured Techniques. A large number of techniques have been proposed to help groups improve their creativity, their problem-solving or decision-making capability, their ability to make accurate judgments and predictions, etc. (e.g., Delbecq, Van de Ven, & Gustafson, 1975; Kepner & Tregoe, 1965; Maier, 1963; Osborn, 1957; Stein, 1975; Thelen, 1954; Varela, 1971). Some such techniques derive from research findings; others are based more on intuitive considerations. All are intended to provide strategies for proceeding with work in the group that will immediately aid group effectiveness. Many of these techniques have shown themselves to be very helpful to groups working on a specific type of task or problem. However, structured techniques that are useful for one kind of task tend not to be appropriate for other tasks, and little is known about precisely what task characteristics moderate their relative effectiveness. Moreover, structured approaches tend to ignore the interpersonal and emotional dynamics that take place in task-oriented groups, and for that reason they may not be helpful in achieving long-term and general improvements in group performance capability.

Interpersonal Techniques. This approach assumes that group effectiveness is strongly determined by the quality of the interpersonal relationships that develop among members, and that with training group members can increase their skills in working together competently (e.g., Argyris, 1962, 1965; Blake & Mouton, 1975; Kaplan, 1973). Change techniques, such as experiential laboratory training and team building with intact work groups, tend to focus directly on the relationships among group members, rather than on the interface between the group and its task. The goal is to help members gain the interpersonal skills required for competent interdependent work on the group task, and/or to help the group as a whole understand and change norms that may be constraining the behavior of group members (e.g., norms that minimize interpersonal openness about ideas, that inhibit individual and group risk-taking and experimentation, etc.). In general, research evidence suggests that interpersonal techniques can be quite powerful in changing the patterns of behavior that occur in groups during training, and in affecting member attitudes—but that *task effectiveness* is rarely enhanced (and often suffers) as a consequence (Deep, Bass, & Vaughan, 1967; Hall & Williams, 1970; Hellebrandt & Stinson, 1971; Kaplan, 1973; Wagner, 1964). Apparently the link between the interpersonal competence of group members and the task effectiveness of the group as a whole is not so direct or straightforward as one might wish.

Overall, research on the effects of interventions that focus on the group interaction process suggests the following conclusions:

1. Such interventions do alter the behavior that members exhibit in the group, and do affect member attitudes about each other and about the group

as a whole. This is true for both the structured and the interpersonal intervention strategies.

2. There is, however, no general intervention that increases group effectiveness for all groups and tasks. By design, the structured techniques focus on particular types of tasks or problems, and appear not to be useful for other task types. And there is no evidence that groups trained in a given structured technique attempt to generalize that technique to new situations, or to incorporate the technique into the group's standard repertoire of performance strategies.

3. Therefore, it appears that interventions that focus on group interaction processes should *not* be relied upon as the sole or primary means for creating (or redesigning) work groups in organizations. Instead, such interventions might be better used to *support and maintain* a group that is already well-designed (i.e., that has a meaningful group task, that is staffed with an appropriate configuration of competent members, and that has norms that support interdependent task work). Process interventions, whether of the structured or the interpersonal variety, would be employed to aid the group in overcoming interpersonal and procedural rough spots, or to help members invent new ways of working together that could enhance the overall effectiveness of the group. Such interventions would be focused on aspects of the group process of particular salience for the kind of work being done by the group, as in the "process consultation" model of Schein (1969), but they would not be expected to compensate for major flaws in the design of the work or of the group.

TOWARD AN INTEGRATED APPROACH TO THE DESIGN OF SELF-MANAGING WORK GROUPS

Each of the strands of research, theory, and practice reviewed in the previous section has something of importance to contribute to understanding about the design and maintenance of self-managing work groups in organizations. Yet it is also the case that none of the approaches reviewed can provide the full theory and technology required for such purposes—even if knowledge about them were substantially more advanced than it is at present. Therefore, a more encompassing view, integrating the materials reviewed in the previous sections, seems called for.

A first approximation toward the development of such a view is presented in Figure 2. The key concepts in the framework shown there are the three "interim criteria" of group effectiveness. These are: (a) the level of *effort* members bring to bear on the task, (b) the amount of *knowledge and skill* available for task work, and (c) the appropriateness of the *task performance strategies* used by the group in performing the task.

```
                          ┌─────────────────────────────┐
                          │      WORK TECHNOLOGY         │
                          └─────────────────────────────┘
┌───────────────────────┐ ┌───────────────────────────┐
│    DESIGN FACTORS     │ │      INTERIM CRITERIA     │
├───────────────────────┤ ├───────────────────────────┤
│1. Design of the group │ │1. Level of effort brought │
│   task                │ │   to bear on the task     │  ┌──────────────────┐
│                       │→│                           │→ │  WORK GROUP      │
│2. Composition of the  │ │2. Amount of knowledge     │  │  EFFECTIVENESS   │
│   group               │ │   and skill applied to task│ └──────────────────┘
│                       │ │   work                    │
│3. Group norms about   │ │3. Appropriateness of task │
│   performance process │ │   performance strategies  │
└───────────────────────┘ └───────────────────────────┘
                          ┌─────────────────────────────┐
                          │   INTERPERSONAL PROCESSES   │
                          └─────────────────────────────┘
```

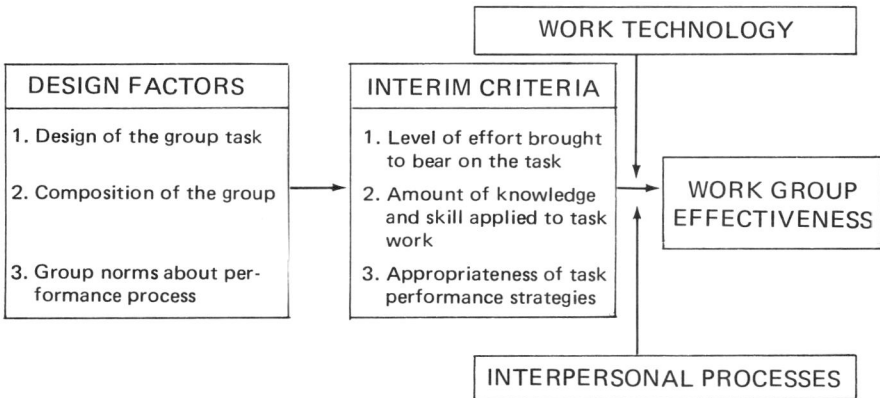

Fig. 2. A framework for understanding the determinants of work group effectiveness.

The organizing principle of the framework is the assumption that these three interim criteria, taken together, control a great deal of the variation in the overall effectiveness of any task-oriented group. That is, if one could simultaneously influence the effort, the knowledge and skill, and the performance strategies of a group, one would have substantial control over the task effectiveness of that group (Hackman & Morris, 1975).

If one views the three interim criteria as having a central role in determining work group effectiveness, then the following two questions emerge.

1. *How can a work group be designed so that its standing on the interim criteria will be as high as possible?* As is shown in Figure 2, three aspects of the design of a group seem particularly potent in affecting the interim criteria. These are: (a) the design of the group task, (b) the composition of the group, and (c) group norms about performance processes. As will be seen below, each of these design factors has an especially powerful impact on one of the three interim criteria, and each is potentially manipulable when a work group is created or redesigned.

2. *How is the standing of a group on the interim criteria translated into the overall level of effectiveness eventually achieved by that group?* Two factors are shown in Figure 2 as moderating the relationship between the interim criteria and overall group effectiveness: (a) the technology with which the group deals in doing its work, which serves to *weight* the contribution of each of the interim criteria in determining group effectiveness; and (b) the interpersonal processes that occur among group members, which can result

either in "slippage" (process losses) or in synergistic process gains as the group carries out its work.

With that general overview of the proposed framework, we turn now to a more detailed discussion of (a) the effects of work group design on the interim criteria, and (b) the factors that moderate the link between the interim criteria and overall group effectiveness.

Effects of the Design Factors

Task design: The design of the group task directly affects the level of effort group members apply to their work. When one reads discussions about the level of effort expended in work groups, comments invariably are made about the norms of the group—for example, norms that maintain production quotas, norms that encourage members to give their all for the group, and so on. The question, rarely answered, that emerges from such discussions is *where such norms come from.*

It is proposed here that in many cases group norms about effort derive from the nature of the group task. Consider, for example, a task that is structured so that it is very low in motivating potential. Members find work on the task to be boring, frustrating, and generally unpleasant. Over time, members may begin to share these reactions with one another, and eventually they may come to an implicit or explicit agreement that the best way to minimize the unpleasant feelings they get from working on the task is simply not to work so hard—and a group norm enforcing low effort emerges. On the other hand, if the task is high in motivating potential, and members find the work exciting, fulfilling, or otherwise rewarding, these experiences also are likely to be shared with one another—and a group norm encouraging high effort may develop.

The implication, then, is that alteration of the design of the group task (which directly affects the personal consequences of hard work) may more powerfully influence the effort members expend working on the task than would direct attacks on group norms about productivity.[5] To do the latter, in many cases, would be to address the outcropping of the problem rather than the problem itself.

---

[5] It also is true, of course, that the level of effort a group expends in carrying out its work is affected by the relationship among group members, and by aspects of the organizational environment (such as the reward system, performance objectives that the group may have accepted, supervisory expectations, etc.). But the focus here is on factors intrinsic to the *design* of the work group that influence the standing of a group on the interim criteria of effectiveness; the role of interpersonal and extrinsic factors, including managerial behavior and reward systems, will be addressed later in the chapter.

How should group tasks be designed to increase the chances that members will choose to expend high effort in their work? As a start, the five core dimensions specified by the job characteristics theory of individual work motivation would seem useful (i.e., skill variety, task identity, task significance, autonomy, feedback). Although originally intended to be applied to jobs done by individuals, there is no reason why these dimensions could not be used to assess the motivational properties of group tasks as well. If group tasks were designed so that they were high on the five job characteristics, then an increase in the task motivation of group members would be expected—and, over time, group norms about productivity should change to become consistent with the increased motivation of individual group members.

It would be necessary, of course, to ensure that the job characteristics were defined (and measured) at the *group* rather than the individual level of analysis. That is, autonomy should be high for the group as a whole, feedback should be provided to the group and based on group (not individual) performance, and so on. But such a translation of the job dimensions from the individual to the group level would seem to pose no major problems, either conceptually or operationally.

Even so, positive outcomes should come about only if individual group members identify with and feel personal commitment to the group as a whole (it is, after all, a *group* task). The five motivational job characteristics have little to offer toward the creation of such conditions. Instead, what seems required is that the task be designed so that members will be necessarily interdependent in their work, and so that they have ample opportunity to relate to one another about task- and group-related issues. Therefore, for tasks to be done by interacting groups, it would seem appropriate to supplement the motivationally-relevant job characteristics discussed above with the following two:

1. Task-required interdependence: the degree to which the *task itself* requires members to work with and rely upon one another for the task to be completed.

2. Opportunities for social interaction: the degree to which the task is structured so that members are in social proximity to one another, under conditions that facilitate inter-member communication about the work and how it is being done.

Both of these dimensions should enhance inter-member communication around matters having to do with task accomplishment and (if the group task also is high in inherent motivating potential) should facilitate the development of shared high motivation and commitment to the group and its performance goals.

It should be emphasized, however, that high motivation in response to a well-designed task will come about for groups, just as for individuals, *only* if the group is composed of people who collectively have sufficient knowledge and skill to complete the task successfully. If not, the same kind of frustration and withdrawal observed for individuals with insufficient task-relevant skill will be observed for a group. A basketball team is a good case in point: By all standards, the task of a basketball team is well designed (i.e., it is high on four of the five motivational job characteristics—skill variety, task identity, autonomy, and feedback; it also is high on the two interpersonal dimensions proposed above—task-required interdependence and opportunities for social interaction). And if a basketball team is skilled enough to be competitive with its opponents on the court and to play *together* competently, then motivation invariably is high. But if a team loses almost all of its games because of a lack of skill, then psychological (and sometimes behavioral) withdrawal of team members is a common outcome.

Group composition: The composition of a group directly affects the amount of knowledge and skill that can be applied to task work. Presumably, when a self-managing work group is formed in an organization, an attempt will be made to staff it with individuals who collectively have sufficient knowledge and skill to perform the group task well. And, given the relatively sophisticated technologies available for assessing the skill requirements of jobs and the capabilities of people, this strategy seems to represent a relatively straightforward way of affecting the level of knowledge and skill available to the group for work on the task.

There are, however, two complicating factors that may compromise the success of attempts to compose a group with a workable "mix" of task-relevant skills. The first factor has to do with the *heterogeneity* of skills in the group. On the one hand, if the skills of members are too homogeneous, some of the special advantages of designing work for teams are lost—e.g., the special expertise of different individuals for different parts of the task, and the opportunity for individuals in the group to learn new skills from their co-workers. Yet it also is true that too much skill heterogeneity can impair group effectiveness, because insufficient "common ground" among members makes communication difficult and/or provides less-than-needed interchange-ability among members. Even when the heterogeneity of member skills is at about the right level, problems can develop, particularly around the reluctance of members to share with one another their own specific and "special" skills. Often individuals in a work group have a vested interest in keeping to themselves special expertise they have developed, for in that expertise lies their own distinctiveness and status.

A second complicating factor derives from the fact that an effective self-managing work group requires members to have (and to use) interpersonal as well as task-relevant skills in carrying out the work of the group. As Argyris (1965, 1969) and others have shown, such skills are not well-practiced by most individuals in organizations, nor are they easily learned (Argyris & Schon, 1974). Yet if the group task is challenging and requires real interdependence among members, interpersonal skills are needed simply to bring the *task* skills of members effectively to bear on the work of the group. This issue may become especially salient on those occasions (not infrequent among managerial groups) when the work group is composed of representatives of other groups that may have a conflictful or competitive relationship with one another.

In sum, the technology is readily available for placing individuals in a group so that sufficient talent is present for the work of the group to be carried out; it is, however, far from a simple undertaking to compose a group so that the talents of individual members form a compatible *mix*. Nor, unfortunately, is the problem of creating a good mix of individuals in a group one for which behavioral science research currently provides much guidance.

Group norms: The norms of a group regarding performance processes directly affect the task appropriateness of the performance strategies used by the group. Performance strategy refers to the choices group members make about how they will go about performing the task (Hackman & Morris, 1975). For example, a group might decide to focus its energies on checking and rechecking for errors, in the interest of a high quality product (and at the expense of quantity of production); or members might choose to free-associate about ideas for proceeding with a new task, rather than starting to work immediately on it.

Strategy choices can be very important in determining how well a group performs (e.g., Davis, 1973; Hackman, Brousseau, & Weiss, 1976; Maier, 1963; Shiflett, 1972; Shure, Rogers, Larsen, & Tassone, 1962; Stone, 1971). What *specific* strategies will work best for a given task, however, depends very heavily on the particular requirements of that task.

And there lies the rub. Research evidence suggests that group members rarely engage in spontaneous tests of the task-appropriateness of their performance strategies—even when they are told that it is to their advantage to do so, or when the strategies presently in use are demonstrably dysfunctional for task effectiveness (Hackman & Morris, 1975; Janis, 1972; Shure et al., 1962; Weick, 1969). Instead, group task performance strategies tend to be well-codified as norms of the groups: Members typically share a set of expectations about the "proper" way to carry out the work, routinely behave in accord with those expectations, and enforce to some degree adherence to them.

Such norms have the advantage of short-cutting the need to explicitly manage and coordinate group member behavior on a continuous basis;

everyone knows how things should be done, and everyone does them that way with minimum fuss and bother. Because little time must be spent in moment-by-moment behavior management activities, more time becomes available for actual task work, and the effectiveness of the group should be enhanced. This advantage accrues to a group, however, *only* if the norms that guide the use of task performance strategies are fully task-appropriate. If existing norms about strategy are dysfunctional for effectiveness, then performance will suffer unless the norms are changed, despite their time-saving advantages.

Norms about strategy (in contrast to those that may emerge about the level of effort to be expended on the task) should be relatively amenable to change, since they are more likely to be present out of "habit" than as a reflection of some more basic structural feature of the group task or the organizational environment. Yet, because such norms are rarely examined or tested by the group, it probably is necessary for the impetus for change of norms about strategy initially to come from outside the group.

One option for the creation or re-formulation of group norms about performance processes is for an outside agent to independently diagnose the requirements of the group task, and then to generate a strategy for the group that is objectively more task-appropriate than the one currently in use (i.e., as in the approach to improving group effectiveness through the use of structured intervention techniques, discussed earlier). The problem is that such an intervention would not be likely to help group members increase their *own* capability to consider and re-formulate their performance processes when effectiveness is poor, or when task demands change.

Therefore, it appears more appropriate to involve group members themselves in interventions that are intended to improve the task-appropriateness of group performance strategies. Such an approach would be consistent with the aspiration that members of self-managing work groups become adept at handling their own task and social processes insofar as possible, and that opportunities be made available for members of such groups to enhance their skills at process management.

One type of intervention that is consistent with this approach involves an outside diagnosis of existing group norms, followed by feedback of the diagnostic results to group members in a way that encourages them to take responsibility for designing and implementing any changes in norms about strategy that seem to be called for. Useful in this regard is the Return Potential Model developed by Jackson (1965). This model allows for direct measurement of the distribution of potential approval (and disapproval) group members feel for various behaviors that might be exhibited in a given situation. The special value of this Return Potential Model as a diagnostic device derives in large part from the quantitative indices that can be generated to describe the properties of specific group norms [for examples, see Hackman (1976) and Jackson (1965)]. These measures can be of considerable help to members in understanding existing group norms, and can serve as a basis for subsequent decisions about whether (and how) members wish to change them.

Diagnostic data about group norms also can be generated using other devices, including direct observation of behavior in the group by a consultant. Whatever the data collection technique, the idea simply is to provide group members with systematic and verifiable information describing existing group norms about performance processes. Group members will then have a concrete basis for planning how those norms might be altered to make them more appropriate to the task of the group. And the result of such planning, in many cases, will be newly-formulated performance strategies, strategies that are more task-appropriate than those that were in use prior to the group's review of its norms about performance processes (see, for example, Hackman, Brousseau, & Weiss, 1976).

Summary. Three design factors have been proposed as useful points of intervention for facilitating the work effectiveness of self-managing work groups. The design factors were viewed as differentially potent in affecting three interim criteria of work effectiveness. Specifically, as shown in Figure 3:

1. The level of *effort* members bring to bear on the group task is affected primarily by the design of the group task itself.

2. The amount of *knowledge and skill* available for task work is affected primarily by the composition of the group.

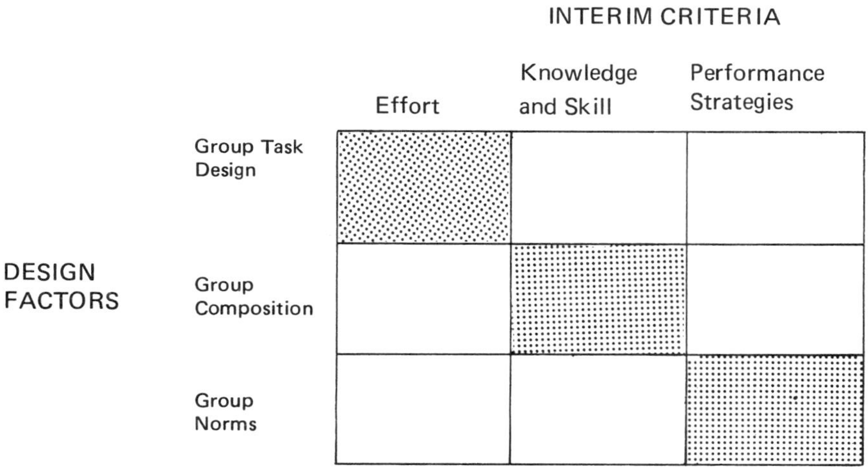

Fig. 3. Points of intervention for improving work group effectiveness: relationships between the design factors and the interim criteria.

3. The task-appropriateness of the *performance strategies* used by the group in carrying out its work is affected primarily by group norms about performance processes.

The off-diagonal cells in Figure 3 are not vacant. Performance strategies, for example, may also be affected by cues in the group task, or by the composition of the group (through the predispositions about strategy brought by different members); similar effects can be imagined for effort and for knowledge and skill. The point is simply that the most potent influences of the design factors on the interim criteria—and therefore the most useful points of intervention—are those indicated by the shaded diagonal cells in the figure.

Moderators of Group Effectiveness

As shown in Figure 2, the link between the interim and the final criteria of group effectiveness is moderated by two factors: the work technology with which the group deals, and the interpersonal processes that take place in the group.

Work Technology. By technology is meant "the complex of physical objects and technical operations (both manual and machine) regularly employed in turning out the goods and services" of an organization (Blauner, 1964). The technology with which a work group deals affects the *salience* of the three interim criteria in determining overall group effectiveness. That is, for some technologies, most of the variation in overall group effectiveness is determined by the level of effort the group applies to the task. A straightforward group assembly task in industry, where the pace of the work is controlled by the group itself, is an example of such a technology. In that case, effort is of high salience in determining group effectiveness, because overall group effectiveness covaries substantially with the amout of effort expended by the group.

For other technologies, of course, other interim criteria are more salient in affecting overall performance. The point can be stated more systematically as follows:

$$\text{Overall group effectiveness} = S_1\begin{bmatrix}\text{Level of}\\\text{effort}\end{bmatrix} + S_2\begin{bmatrix}\text{Amount of}\\\text{knowledge}\\\text{and skill}\end{bmatrix} + S_3\begin{bmatrix}\text{Appropriateness of}\\\text{task performance}\\\text{strategies}\end{bmatrix}$$

where S_1, S_2, and S_3 are the technologically-determined saliences of the three interim criteria.

How, then, does the technology enhance or depress the salience of the interim criteria? While systematic research and theory on the question have not yet been done, one possible answer is that salience is determined by the degree to which the technology *constrains* the variation of each of the interim criteria, as follows:

S_1 = 1—degree of technological constraint on effort
S_2 = 1—degree of technological constraint on performance strategy
S_3 = 1—degree of technological constraint on knowledge and skill

Thus, if one of the interim criteria is totally constrained by technological factors, it cannot be salient in determining group effectiveness for the work being done. The interim criterion, in such circumstances, is under the control of the technology rather than the group. So long as the technology remains relatively constant, variance in the interim criterion will be severely restricted, which means that it cannot have much causal impact on overall group effectiveness. On the other hand, if the technology places no constraint whatever on one of the interim criteria, it can have a substantial effect on how well the group performs its task. And when all three interim criteria are generally unconstrained by the technology, which is the case for many types of group work in organizations, all will have salience in affecting how well the group does.

A first cut at identifying the measurable features of technology that constrain each of the interim criteria follows:

1. The salience of *effort* is constrained by the degree to which work inputs are technologically controlled. When work is machine-paced, for example, the work group is in a reactive stance, and the relationship between effort and performance effectiveness is severely restricted—because the group is unable to exert control of its output by working especially hard. When, on the other hand, the technology is such that a group can work proactively at whatever pace it chooses (e.g., in group production where materials and equipment are available and sufficient), then effort will be a highly salient determinant of overall group effectiveness.

2. The salience of *strategy* is constrained by the degree to which performance processes are technologically determined. When, for example, work procedures are fully programmed, the relationship between performance strategy and group effectiveness will be restricted—because the group has little or no control about the strategies used in work on the task. On the other hand, when the work is unprogrammed there is a great deal of "room" for the group to alter its performance strategies, and strategy will be a salient determiner of group effectiveness.

3. The salience of *knowledge and skill* is constrained by the degree to which performance operations are simple and predictable, versus complex and unpredictable. When task performance requires routine use of skills that are well-learned in the general population, then knowledge and skill will be highly constrained as a determiner of group effectiveness. But when the technology

requires sophisticated or complex skills to be used on unpredictable occasions, then knowledge and skill will be unconstrained and of high salience in determining how well the group performs.

Some technologies are unconstrained for all three of the interim criteria. A group charged with development of a marketing plan for a new product is in such a position: The place of work is at the discretion of the group, task performance procedures are unprogrammed, and the work requires complex skills to deal with considerable uncertainty and unpredictability in the environment. For other technologies, all of the interim criteria may be constrained. For a group working on a mechanized assembly line, for example, task inputs are machine-paced, assembly procedures are completely programmed, and the performance operations are both simple and highly predictable. In such a situation, the fact that there is a work "group" is of little meaning or importance, because no matter how the group is designed it can do little to increase its own work effectiveness.

Most technologies will not have such clear-cut constraints as those described above, and instead will be relatively constrained on some interim criteria and relatively unconstrained on others. Consider, for example, the technology involved in the work done by a team of surgeons. There is little constraint regarding the use of knowledge and skill by work group members, and a moderate amount of constraint on strategy (some, but not all, procedures are specified) and on effort (some, but not all, task inputs derive from the nature of the surgical problem that is being dealt with and the responses of the patient as the operation progresses). In this case, all three interim criteria are salient—but one more than the other two. And, following the logic of Figure 2, one would wish to attend most carefully to the composition of the surgical team (because composition as a design factor strongly affects the most salient interim criterion—knowledge and skill).

In summary, it has been proposed that the nature of the work being done by a group—the work technology—affects which of the interim criteria are most salient or important in influencing the overall effectiveness of a work group. This suggests that there is no single approach to the design of a self-managing work group that will be generally appropriate for groups that deal with different work technologies. Instead, the design factors that serve as points of intervention for creating or redesigning a work group will be differentially useful, *depending on the nature of the technology with which the group must deal.*

Interpersonal Processes. The second moderator of work group effectiveness shown in Figure 2 has to do with the kinds of interpersonal processes that take place in a work group. It was argued that much of the variation in how well a work group performs is controlled by how well that group is designed, specifically in terms of its task, composition, and norms about performance strategy. Within a given design, however, the interpersonal processes that take place among group members can either impair or enhance group effectiveness.

Group effectiveness is *impaired* when the interaction among members creates process losses—i.e., group members relate to one another in ways that lead to inefficiencies or errors in their task behavior. Effectiveness is *enhanced* when the interaction leads to a process gain—i.e., a synergistic effect, in which the interaction among members leads to levels of efficiency or effectiveness that exceed what would be obtained by summing the inputs of individual group members.

The nature of the process losses likely to be encountered by a group, and the special opportunities of a group to generate process gains, depend largely on the kind of work being done. Listed below are some of the process losses and process gains that are likely to be of particular significance for each of the three interim criteria discussed in this chapter (cf. Hackman & Morris, 1975).

1. When *effort* is salient:
    Process loss: Members fail to coordinate their efforts in applying them to the task, resulting in a "coordination decrement" (Steiner, 1972).
    Process gain: Members develop strong commitment to each other and to the group that increases the amount of effort they are willing to expend in task work.
2. When *knowledge and skill* are salient:
    Process loss: The group imperfectly assesses and weights the inputs of members who have differential task-relevant talent.
    Process gain: Members share uniquely-held knowledge and skill, and cooperate to gain new learnings—thereby increasing the total pool of talent available to the group.
3. When *performance strategy* is salient:
    Process loss: Members imperfectly assess task requirements, and implement task-inappropriate strategies.
    Process gain: Members invent new or creative ways of proceeding with work on the task.

The implication, then, is that interventions intended to help self-managing work groups improve their internal processes might usefully be focused on the potential process losses and gains that are of special salience for the kind of work the group is performing. Indeed, an intervention focused on a nonsalient aspect of the group process might do more harm than good, in that it could direct the attention and energy of group members away from issues of particular importance for their task and toward phenomena that in fact could have little impact on the eventual effectiveness of the group. It would be inappropriate, for example, to intervene to help members become more competent at sharing their special skills with one another (a not uncommon type of process intervention) if effort (rather than knowledge and skill) were the sole salient interim criterion for the technology being dealt with by the group.

Conclusion

The conception of self-managing work groups presented in the preceding pages is both less complex and more complex than other treatments of work group behavior and effectiveness. It is less complex in that it focuses on a relatively small number of focal variables, each of which is assumed to control considerable variation in overall group effectiveness, and each of which is potentially open to planned change. It is more complex in that neither the design factors nor the variables proposed as moderators have direct effects on group performance outcomes that are constant for all circumstances.

The present conception is consistent with a diagnosis-based approach to the design and maintenance of self-managing work groups. This approach would begin with assessment of the imperatives of the work technology to identify the interim criteria that are most salient for the group being dealt with. Then would follow exploration of the usefulness of the three design factors in improving the standing of the group on the salient interim criteria. And finally, the interpersonal processes of the group would be assessed, with special attention given to identifying process losses likely to be experienced, and to opportunities that might be present for the group to achieve process gains as members work together on the group task.

The particular action steps called for on the basis of diagnostic exploration will, of course, vary from group to group and from technology to technology. The point is that there is no single best way to design a self-managing work group, nor a single type of process intervention that will be helpful to all such groups. Instead, the design factors and the process interventions that are likely to be of the greatest help to a given group depend upon the interim criteria that are most salient for the work being done by that group.

MANAGING WORK GROUPS IN ORGANIZATIONS

The material presented above has focused exclusively on the design of self-managing work groups and on the maintenance of effective internal group processes. Yet it must be emphasized that work groups do not operate in an organizational vacuum: How such groups are managed and the nature of the organizational context within which they function can have important implications for their long-term viability and task effectiveness—even if their internal design is excellent. In this section, we briefly review some of the major factors external to the group itself that can affect how self-managing work groups develop and function.

Reward and Control Systems

In almost every case in which self-managing work groups have been successfully created in organizations, pay systems have been arranged so that members are paid contingent upon the performance of the group as a whole, rather than in terms of the relative level of performance of individual employees. A group-based compensation arrangement increases the chances that internal cooperation and cohesiveness will improve as members work together to obtain the group-level rewards. Moreover, dysfunctional group interaction that grows from the fear (or the fact) of pay inequities among members can be reduced when compensation is tied directly to the output of the group as a whole (Lawler, 1977).[6]

The same line of reasoning applies to performance objectives that are set for self-managing work groups, and to organizational feedback and control systems that are used to monitor achievement of such objectives. In general, when a group accepts a moderately difficult performance objective, and has available to it feedback regarding its progress toward achieving that objective, group performance will be enhanced (Zander, 1971). Yet if such external motivational devices are instituted for a group that has a poor *internal* design, then there may be little improvement in overall group effectiveness—or even a performance backlash. The reason is that the external incentives to good performance may be neutralized by motivational disincentives or process difficulties that arise from a faulty design of the group itself. So once again the conclusion is that first priority must be given to the design of the work group—with external rewards, objectives, and control systems serving a supportive role. By themselves, such external devices probably cannot compensate for a group design that is inherently inappropriate for the kind of work being done.

Managerial Roles

It is clear that self-managing work groups must be provided with *substantial* autonomy in carrying out the group task and in managing internal group

---

[6] It should be recognized, however, that a group-based reward system does not necessarily solve all problems of pay equity among group members—especially for groups whose members were differentially skilled and differentially paid at the time the group was formed. In such cases, it may be necessary both to tie overall rewards to the performance of the group as a whole, and to help the group devise an equitable internal means for distributing those rewards among members.

processes if such groups are to be task-effective and internally healthy over the long term. Just as "pseudo-participation" in organizations may be worse than no participation at all, so it is that autonomous work groups should not be formed unless there is reasonable assurance that the result will not be a potentially frustrating state of "pseudo-autonomy." This, of course, requires careful attention to issues of management and supervision, to ensure that managers are both willing and able to provide the group with sufficient real autonomy to carry out the work assigned to it (cf. Gulowsen, 1972).

Moreover, what the manager *does* on the job after self-managing work groups have been formed may become problematic. No longer does the manager have ongoing responsibility for the work behavior and productivity of individual employees, and it is not unusual for a manager in such circumstances to feel that his or her own status has been compromised and that the meaningfulness of the managerial job has been stripped away.

One possibility for dealing with this problem is for the manager to move from managing what goes on within the boundaries of a group to helping the group manage those boundaries themselves. Thus, the manager would assist the group in liaison with other groups and serve as the advocate of the group with higher management—leaving to the group itself routine decision-making about the work and the management of work crises. Moreover, the manager might become something of a process consultant to the group, helping members meld themselves into an internally healthy and task-effective team.

The role is not an easy one, however, and such activities may require skills that are not familiar to, or well-practiced by, the manager. Moreover, there is inherent conflict in a managerial role that requires the occupant to exercise real authority in managing a group and simultaneously to serve as a process consultant to it. For these reasons, it would seen essential to give special attention to both the role and the person of the first-line manager when self-managing work groups are created, and especially to provide managers with the opportunity to learn *new* managerial skills that they will need in their new leadership roles.

The Structure and Climate of the Organizational Context

When designed according to the principles suggested in this chapter, a self-managing work group will be inherently "organic" (as opposed to "mechanistic") in character. If the organizational context surrounding such groups also is organic, then self-managing work groups should find nurturance and support in the environment: Flexibility among units would be valued, authority would be located relatively low in the organization and at the site where decisions are made and work is done, and rules and procedures would be viewed as less important than doing what needs to be done to complete organizational tasks successfully. In a mechanistic system, on the other hand, a self-managing work group might repeatedly run afoul of organization policies, procedures, and values. With decision-making and planning the clear prerogative of management, and consistency and regularity highly valued, predictions about the future of even a well-designed self-managing work group would not be optimistic. Instead, it would be expected that the group would have a relatively short and troubled life—or that the group would become congruent with the surrounding system, and survive by becoming as rigid and as mechanistic as that system.

One specific aspect of the organizational context that has special relevance for self-managing work groups is the nature of the relationships *among* work groups in the organization. There are two schools of thought on the matter. One is that healthy competition among groups should be encouraged, because competition increases the motivation of group members to perform well. The other is that the risk of dysfunctional consequences from competition is too great to tolerate—and that instead organizations should be structured so that work groups are *interdependent* with one another. While this strategy should lead to better communication between and coordination among groups, it runs the risk that the boundaries of individual groups (perhaps especially newer or weaker ones) will become excessively permeable, with a resultant loss in the internal integrity of the separate groups.

Clearly more research on inter-group relations and on boundary maintenance of self-managing work groups is needed. At present, perhaps all that can be said with confidence is that the strength of group boundaries—and the way relationships are managed across boundaries—will have important effects on what happens both within the separate groups and in the larger organization (cf. Alderfer, 1977).

INDIVIDUAL VS. GROUP WORK DESIGN: WHICH WHEN?

The choice between designing work for individuals or for groups is complex and, in many cases, depends on factors idiosyncratic to a given situation. In general, however, a group-based design seems indicated when one or more of the following conditions is present.

1. When the product, service, or technology is such that meaningful individual work is not realistically possible (e.g., when a large piece of heavy equipment is being produced). It often is possible, in this instance, for a group to take autonomous responsibility for an entire product or service—while the best possible job design for individuals would involve only small segments of the work. In such cases, the motivating potential of even the best possible individual job would be constrained to a relatively low level.

2. When the technology or physical work setting is such that high interdependence among workers is essential (cf. the concept of "technically required cooperation" proposed by Meissner, 1969). For example, Susman (1970) has suggested that one effect of increased automation (especially in continuous process production) is to increase interdependence among workers. The creation of autonomous work groups under such circumstances would seem to be a rather natural extension of the imperatives of the technology itself.

3. When individuals have high social need strength—and the enrichment of individual jobs would run significant risk of breaking up existing and satisfying groups of workers. In such cases (assuming technological and other considerations are appropriate), designing work for teams would capitalize on the needs of employees, whereas individual-oriented job enrichment might require that employees give up important social satisfactions to obtain a better job. Some people might be reluctant to make such an exchange (Reif & Luthans, 1972). There is, however, some risk present when members of self-managing work groups are all high in social needs, especially when these individuals also are relatively *low* in growth need strength. In such a case, there is a possibility that individuals will use the group primarily as a setting to obtain social satisfactions. Even if the task were very high in inherent motivating potential, such individuals might find the group itself so much more involving than the task that productivity would suffer.

4. When the overall motivating potential of employees' jobs would be expected to be *considerably* higher if arranged as a group task rather than as a set of individual tasks. Probably, in most cases, the motivating potential of a job would increase if the job were designed as a group task, simply because a larger piece of work is possible for a group than for an individual. This should not, however, automatically tilt the decision toward group work design, because of the difficult interpersonal factors that must be attended to in effectively designing work for interacting groups. When the expected benefits are commensurate with the costs and risks of implementation, then a group design would be called—but only then.

On the other hand, there are a number of circumstances that seem to call for work to be designed to be done by individuals, working more or less independently on motivationally well-constructed tasks. These include:

1. When individuals have high needs for personal growth and development, but relatively weak needs for meaningful social relationships at work—or, as is sometimes the case, a strong antipathy for working in groups. Such individuals would find it difficult to generate the considerable energy required to develop an effectively functioning group, because the personal benefits of group membership would not be sufficiently great.

2. When there are strong prospects that high and dysfunctional conflict will emerge either within or between work groups. As noted earlier, within-group conflict sometimes develops when there are marked differences in skills held by individual employees—especially when those skill differences are correlated with demographic factors such as age, race, or sex. Between-group conflict often develops when groups are at different levels of status in the organization, are in competition for resources or for rewards, and/or are organizationally positioned so that complete and undistorted communication from group to group is difficult. Because such conflict can be destructive both to task effectiveness and to the people involved—and because working through conflict can be very demanding of time and energy on the part of all parties involved—self-managing work groups should be created with considerable caution when the seeds of destructive intra- or inter-group conflict are evident beforehand.

3. When there is no natural interdependence among the people who would be members of the work group. If individuals are considered a "group" only because they perform the same function, or report to the same manager, then the prospects of developing a meaningful self-managing work group may be slim (e.g., a number of telephone installers who operate their own trucks, coordinating only with a central dispatcher, or a group of flight attendants who travel so much that they see each other and their supervisor infrequently). There would seem to be no *task-based* reason for forming work teams in such circumstances, and enrichment of individual jobs (or formation of inter-departmental teams of people who *do* work in close physical and temporal proximity) would be the better alternative.

4. When the behavioral science sophistication of those charged with carrying out the design (or redesign) of the work is not high, and/or when the managerial competence of those who supervise the work is low. As indicated above, designing work for groups is demanding—not only of energy and commitment, but also of behavioral science sophistication and managerial skill. If such talent is not readily available in the work setting, it might be advisable to opt for individual task design—which, although not a routine undertaking, is at least less likely to stretch the competence of managers and consultants quite as far. While some "stretching" is of course necessary for people to increase existing skills and learn new skills, such learning is unlikely to take place if the difference between present competence and project-required competence is too great.

Perhaps of special importance in this regard is the degree to which use of self-managing groups to carry out the work of an organization is consistent with the organizational values and philosophy of top management. The device of the self-managing work group moves *control* of the work being done downwards in the organization—a move that is sometimes at odds with the views of top management about how organizations should function. In such cases, it may not be advisable to proceed with the creation of work groups unless and until top management can understand the full implications of such groups for organizations functioning—and can accept that the creation of self-managing work groups may lead to significant changes in how control is exercised within the organization.

Conclusion

What has been attempted in this chapter is a relatively general treatment of factors that influence the effectiveness of self-managing work groups. The emphasis has been on a small number of variables and intervention strategies, each of which has been viewed as controlling considerable variance in work group effectiveness. The position taken does not deny that idiosyncratic design issues and interpersonal problems may arise in groups that have special or unique tasks—such as the development of a highly creative advertisement, the establishment of organization-wide policy by a group of top managers, or the conduct of research by an interdisciplinary scientific team. Because such groups may have unusual task and interpersonal problems, they may require design features or process interventions that are specifically focused on those problems—and that extend beyond the general kinds of design and process variables considered in this chapter. It is maintained, nonetheless, that even such special types of groups, if they are to perform well, must meet the basic criteria for effective group design and interpersonal process that have been proposed.

Overall, there is much to be said in favor of the creation of self-managing work groups in organizations. They can be motivationally advantageous, and it is a truism that more task-relevant resources are brought to the work by a group than by an individual performing the same task. Yet the material reviewed in this chapter suggests that the device of the self-managing work group is far from a panacea for the solution of organizational problems. In the first place, such teams are *not* always technologically or motivationally appropriate, and attempting to create them by force in an environment where they do not really fit is a sure route to organizational difficulties. Moreover, it is usually very difficult to create and maintain such groups—more difficult, for example, than individual job enrichment, which itself has been shown to be a more substantial undertaking than often is suspected (Hackman, 1975).

So the message of this research favors rather conservative use of self-managing work teams in organizations, despite their high overt attractiveness, at least until such time as more and better research on the determinants of what happens within such groups becomes available—and until better understanding is generated about how most effectively to install and maintain them.

REFERENCES

Alderfer, C. P. Group and intergroup relations. In J. R. Hackman & J. L. Suttle (Eds.), *Improving life at work: Behavioral science approaches to organizational change.* Santa Monica: Goodyear, 1977.

Argyris, C. *Interpersonal competence and organizational effectiveness.* Homewood, Ill.: Irwin-Dorsey, 1962.

Argyris, C. Explorations in interpersonal competence. *Journal of Applied Behavioral Science,* 1965, **1**, 58–83.

Argyris, C. The incompleteness of social psychological theory: Examples from small group, cognitive consistency, and attribution research. *American Psychologist,* 1969, **24**, 893–908.

Argyris, C., & Schon, D. *Theory in practice.* San Francisco: Jossey-Bass, 1974.

Blake, R. R., & Mouton, J. S. Group and organizational team building: A theoretical model for intervening. In C. L. Cooper (Ed.), *Theories of group processes.* London: Wiley, 1975.

Blauner, R. *Alienation and freedom.* Chicago: University of Chicago Press, 1964.

Bucklow, M. A new role for the work group. *Administrative Science Quarterly,* 1966, **11**, 59–78.

Cherns, A. The principles of sociotechnical design. *Human Relations,* 1976, **29**, 783–792.

Davis, J. H. Group decision and social interaction: A theory of social decision schemes. *Psychological Review,* 1973, **80**, 97–125.

Davis, L. E. The design of jobs. *Industrial Relations,* 1966, **6**, 21–45.

Davis, L. E., & Trist, E. L. Improving the quality of work life: Sociotechnical case studies. In J. O'Toole (Ed.), *Work and the quality of life.* Cambridge, Mass.: MIT Press, 1974.

Deep, S. D., Bass, B. M., & Vaughan, J. A. Some effects on business gaming of previous quasi-T group affiliations. *Journal of Applied Psychology,* 1967, **51**, 426–431.

Delbecq, A. L., Van de Ven, A. H., & Gustafson, D. H. *Group techniques for program planning.* Glenview, Ill.: Scott, Foresman, 1975.

Dunnette, M. D. *Personnel selection and placement.* Belmont, Calif.: Wadsworth, 1966.

Emery, F. E., & Trist, E. L. Socio-technical systems. In F. E. Emery (Ed.), *Systems thinking.* London: Penguin, 1969.

Evans, M. G., Kiggundu, M., & House, R. J. *A partial test and extension of the job characteristics model of motivation.* Working paper, Faculty of Management Studies, University of Toronto, 1976.

Gulowsen, J. A measure of work group autonomy. In L. E. Davis & J. C. Taylor (Eds.), *Design of jobs.* Middlesex, England: Penguin, 1972.

Hackman, J. R. On the coming demise of job enrichment. In E. L. Cass & F. G. Zimmer (Eds.), *Man and work in society*. New York: Van Nostrand Reinhold, 1975.

Hackman, J. R. Group influences on individuals in organizations. In M. D. Dunnette (Ed.), *Handbook of industrial and organizational psychology*. Chicago: Rand McNally, 1976.

Hackman, J. R. Work design. In J. R. Hackman & J. L. Suttle (Eds.), *Improving life at work: Behavioral science approaches to organizational change*. Santa Monica: Goodyear, 1977.

Hackman, J. R., Brousseau, K. R., & Weiss, J. A. The interaction of task design and group performance strategies in determining group effectiveness. *Organizational Behavior and Human Performance*, 1976, **16**, 350–365.

Hackman, J. R., & Lawler, E. E. Employee reactions to job characteristics. *Journal of Applied Psychology Monograph*, 1971, **55**, 259–286.

Hackman, J. R., & Morris, C. G. Group tasks, group interaction process, and group performance effectiveness: A review and proposed integration. In L. Berkowitz (Ed.), *Advances in experimental social psychology* (Vol. 8). New York: Academic Press, 1975.

Hackman, J. R., & Oldham, G. R. Development of the job diagnostic survey. *Journal of Applied Psychology*, 1975, **60**, 159–170.

Hackman, J. R., & Oldham, G. R. Motivation through the design of work: Test of a theory. *Organizational Behavior and Human Performance*, 1976, **16**, 250–279.

Hall, J., & Williams, M. S. Group dynamics training and improvised decision making. *Journal of Applied Behavioral Science*, 1970, **6**, 39–68.

Haythorn, W. W. The composition of groups: A review of the literature. *Acta Psychologica*, 1968, **28**, 97–128.

Hellebrandt, E. T., & Stinson, J. E. The effects of T-group training on business game results. *Journal of Psychology*, 1971, **77**, 271–272.

Herzberg, F. *Work and the nature of man*. Cleveland: World, 1966.

Herzberg, F., Mausner, B., & Snyderman, B. *The motivation to work*. New York: Wiley, 1959.

Hill, R. E. Interpersonal compatibility and workgroup performance. *Journal of Applied Behavioral Science*, 1975, **11**, 210–219.

Jackson, J. Structural characteristics of norms. In I. D. Steiner & M. Fishbein (Eds.), *Current studies in social psychology*. New York: Holt, Rinehart & Winston, 1965.

Janis, I. L. *Victims of groupthink: A psychological study of foreign-policy decisions and fiascos*. New York: Houghton-Mifflin, 1972.

Kaplan, R. E. *Managing interpersonal relations in task groups: A study of two contrasting strategies*. Technical Report No. 2, Dept. of Administrative Sciences, Yale University, 1973.

Kepner, C. H., & Tregoe, B. B. *The rational manager: A systematic approach to problem solving and decision making*. New York: McGraw-Hill, 1965.

Lawler, E. E. Reward systems. In J. R. Hackman & J. L. Suttle (Eds.), *Improving life at work: Behavioral science approaches to organizational change.* Santa Monica: Goodyear, 1977.

Leavitt, H. J. Suppose we took groups seriously . . . In E. L. Cass & F. G. Zimmer (Eds.), *Man and work in society.* New York: Van Nostrand Reinhold, 1975.

Maier, N. R. F. *Problem solving discussions and conferences: Leadership methods and skills.* New York: McGraw-Hill, 1963.

Meissner, M. *Technology and the worker: Technical demands and social processes in industry.* San Francisco: Chandler, 1969.

Oldham, G. R., Hackman, J. R., & Pearce, J. L. Conditions under which employees respond positively to enriched work. *Journal of Applied Psychology*, 1976, **61**, 395–403.

Osborn, A. F. *Applied imagination* (Rev. ed.). New York: Scribner, 1957.

Reif, W. E., & Luthans, F. Does job enrichment really pay off? *California Management Review*, 1972, **15**, 30–37.

Schein, E. H. *Process consultation.* Reading, Mass.: Addison-Wesley, 1969.

Schneider, B. *Staffing organizations.* Santa Monica: Goodyear, 1976.

Schutz, W. C. *FIRO: A three-dimensional theory of interpersonal behavior.* New York: Holt, Rinehart & Winston, 1958.

Shiflett, S. C. Group performance as a function of task difficulty and organizational interdependence. *Organizational Behavior and Human Performance*, 1972, **7**, 442–456.

Shure, G. H., Rogers, M. S., Larsen, I. M., & Tassone, J. Group planning and task effectiveness. *Sociometry*, 1962, **25**, 263–282.

Susman, G. I. The impact of automation on work group autonomy and task specialization. *Human Relations*, 1970, **23**, 567–577.

Stein, M. I. *Stimulating creativity* (Vol. 2). New York: Academic Press, 1975.

Steiner, I. D. *Group process and productivity.* New York: Academic Press, 1972.

Stone, T. H. Effects of mode of organization and feedback level on creative task groups. *Journal of Applied Psychology*, 1971, **55**, 324–330.

Thelen, H. A. *Dynamics of groups at work.* Chicago: University of Chicago Press, 1954.

Trist, E. L., Higgin, G. W., Murray, H., & Pollock, A. B. *Organizational choice.* London: Tavistock, 1963.

Turner, A. N., & Lawrence, P. R. *Industrial jobs and the worker.* Boston: Harvard Graduate School of Business Administration, 1965.

Varela, J. A. *Psychological solutions to social problems.* New York: Academic Press, 1971.

Wagner, A. B. The use of process analysis in business decision games. *Journal of Applied Behavioral Science*, 1964, **1**, 387–408.

Weick, K. E. *The social psychology of organizing.* Reading, Mass.: Addison-Wesley, 1969.

Whyte, W. F. *Money and motivation.* New York: Harper, 1955.

Zander, A. *Motives and goals in groups.* New York: Academic Press, 1971.

ORGANIZATIONAL CONTROL OF PERFORMANCE THROUGH SELF REWARDING

Milton R. Blood
Georgia Institute of Technology

Throughout the last two decades, considerable attention has been devoted to the distinction between intrinsic and extrinsic components of the work situation. This differentiation of job components and work outcomes originated with Herzberg, Mausner, Peterson, and Capwell (1957; see also Herzberg, Mausner, & Snyderman, 1959). Their treatment of this categorization and development of an associated theory of job satisfaction and dissatisfaction generated a heated controversy in the professional literature (e.g., Behling, Labovitz & Kozmo, 1968; Burke, 1966; Ewen, Smith, Hulin, & Locke, 1966; Grigaliunas & Herzberg, 1971; House & Wigdor, 1967; Whitsett & Winslow, 1967).

Though much of the dispute raged over the relative contributions of intrinsic and extrinsic job components to affective job responses, the intrinsic-extrinsic distinction proved itself as a viable and often useful dichotomy. Further, there were demonstrations that the intrinsic components were more influential than extrinsic components in the determination of job affect. Hulin and Smith (1967) found satisfaction with intrinsic job components to relate more strongly than satisfaction with extrinsic components to both overall job satisfaction and job dissatisfaction. In an experimental setting, Herold and Greller (1975) studied the relative effects of intrinsic and extrinsic feedback on performance and attitudes. They confirmed the greater impact of intrinsic feedback. King (1970) pointed out that data generated in support of Herzberg's notions also displayed this greater importance for the intrinsic job characteristics (contrary to some of Herzberg's own theoretical statements).

More recent work, dealing with problems of motivation, has focused on the roles of intrinsic and extrinsic rewards in the determination of behaviors. One of the concerns in this regard has been for the interaction between intrinsic and extrinsic rewards in their behavioral influence. Some investigators (Calder & Staw, 1975; Deci, 1971, 1972a, 1972b; Greene & Lepper, 1974; Kruglanski, Alon, & Lewis, 1972; Lepper & Greene, 1975; Lepper, Greene, & Nisbett, 1973) have suggested that the use of extrinsic rewards destroys the reward value of intrinsic outcomes as suggested by De Charms (1968). Others (Hamner & Foster, 1975; Salancik, 1975) have questioned this assertion. The contention remains unresolved (Scott, 1975), though Levine and Fasnacht (1974) and Notz (1975) have reviewed portions of the relevant empirical data.

While considerable effort has now been expended in investigations and discussions of intrinsic variables in the work situation (see Deci, 1975; Staw, 1975), important questions remain to be explored. This study pursues conceptually some of the issues concerning one of the important intrinsic work outcomes—self rewarding. This variable has been chosen as an important member of the intrinsic reward category. Self rewarding is defined as the private, cognitive, affective consequence of a job behavior. Colloquial language would describe extreme positive self rewarding as pride and extreme negative self rewarding as shame. It is intrinsic in that it derives from the person doing the behavior. Though it may be influenced by extrinsic events, this personal, thought response is not synonymous with extrinsic consequences singly or in combination. It is what the person says to him or herself as a result of the job behavior. Though other sources, e.g., supervisor, company records, or public acclaim, may tell an individual that she/he should be proud, the individual is not constrained to administer corresponding self rewards. Whether self rewards parallel externally administered rewards will be influenced by personal standards, evaluations of the veracity of the information on which external rewards are based, evaluations of the external sources that provide the rewards, etc. These possible influences provide research suggestions for adding to our understanding of self rewards.

Self-administered rewards have two characteristics that make them especially noteworthy as behavioral consequences (Nord, 1969). First, the self-administered reward is contingent on the behavior. When the behavior has occurred to the satisfaction of the worker s/he administers the self reward, i.e., s/he tells him-herself that s/he had done a good job. S/he does *not* self reward without the behavioral occurrence. Contingency on performance is indigenous for self rewards. Important problems related to the contingency of self rewarding are (1) the reliability with which the person recognizes the behavior (i.e., is the behavioral definition stable and clear or does it change from occasion to occasion), and (2) the correspondence between the behaviors desired by the organization and those desired by the person. Both of these problems will be addressed later in this study.

The second beneficial characteristic of self-administered rewards is their immediacy. The person doing the behavior can dispense the reward as soon as the behavior is performed. There is no delay required, as with rewards that must await a foreman's visit, the end of a pay period, an annual bonus, etc. Immediacy should increase the reinforcement value of self rewards.

The purpose here is to make a conceptual exploration of the concept of self rewarding and to develop an initial, working conceptual framework for the operation of self rewarding in organizations. If, as is suggested by previous literature, self rewarding is one of the important influences on work performance, then there is a need to understand the working of this variable and to clarify its relation to work behaviors. There is a need to discover what the organization can do to enhance the operation of self rewarding, and what the organization should avoid that might inadvertently inhibit self rewarding.

This report is *not* a statement, or an extension of the debate, about the relative importance of self-administered rewards and other-administered rewards. It begins with the assumption that self rewarding is one important behavioral influence that deserves study and elucidation, and presents a position for beginning that study.

THE CONCEPTUAL FRAMEWORK

The Focal Relationship

The focus of the conceptual model is the relationship between self rewarding and job performance. As indicated by the bidirectional arrow in Figure 1, the relationship is presumed to be interactive. Self rewarding has an influence on job performance and, likewise, job performance is a determinant of self rewarding. This is not meant to imply that this model is completely specified. Both self rewarding and job performance are affected by other variables outside the scope of this model. However, for both variables, it is this particular covariation that is the focus in the present analysis.

Self rewarding is defined as above. It is the evaluative, cognitive response an individual makes to his/her own job performance. To self reward, one tells oneself how well (or poorly) the job has been done. This is an affective reaction to one's own performance.

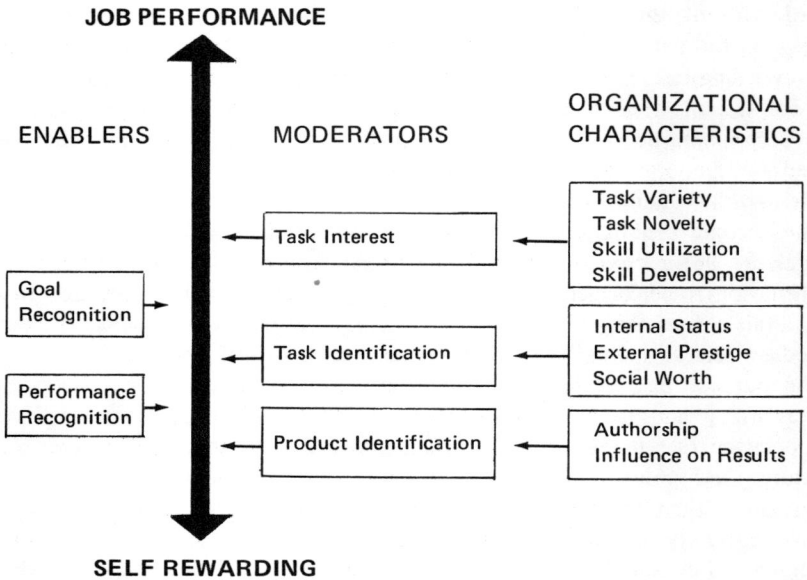

Fig. 1. Organizational influences on the relationship between job performance and self rewarding.

The job performance component of the model can be any job behavior. A worker can make an evaluative, cognitive response to any aspect of his/her task performance. The self reward may be in response to attendance, the decision to join or remain with the organization, social interactions on the job, or productivity tasks. Flexibility in defining the focal job behavior gives the model widespread usefulness.

The relationship specified by the bold arrow in the figure operates as the relationship between an operant behavior (job performance) and a reinforcing stimulus (self rewarding). The occurrence of the self rewarding is contingent on the behavior. The behavior is increased or decreased depending on whether the self rewarding is a reinforcement or a punishment.

The Enablers

Two variables are posited to behave as enablers of the focal relationship. That is to say, the relationship cannot occur without their existence. Some threshold amount of these cognitive characteristics is necessary (but not sufficient) for self rewarding and job performance to be related. Though the threshold notion might suggest that they would act in an all-or-none fashion, the enablers actually operate as moderators, i.e., they influence the strength of the relationship by degree. They can be totally present or totally absent, but they might also be partially present. Or, they might be present in a form that is an inaccurate, but correlated, version of reality. The enablers are perceptions of two aspects of the work situation.

The first of the enablers is goal recognition, the accuracy of the perception of the behavioral goal of the particular job performance being considered. As mentioned above, any aspect of the job behaviors can be chosen. If promptness is the job performance to which we are attending, the perception of the goal may be "at the plant by 7:30 a.m.," "at the work station in work clothes by 7:30 a.m.," "finished check-in procedures with previous shift by 7:30 a.m.," etc. If the job performance in question is the task outcome, a worker might perceive the goal to be "235 assemblies completed during the shift," "200 test-adequate assemblies completed during the shift," "less than 10 rejected assemblies during the shift," etc.

For the purpose of the model, goal recognition is the accuracy with which the worker perceives the performance goal of the organization. If inaccuracies or discrepancies exist between the worker's goal recognition and the organization's goal, the results can be dysfunctional for the organization. For example, if the worker's performance goal is less stringent than the organization's, s/he will self reward for substandard performance. To the extent that self rewarding influences performance in that situation, it will be detracting from performance. On the other hand, if the worker's performance goal is too stringent, s/he may sacrifice quantity for quality (or vice versa), or the influence of self rewarding will be diminished because the worker will pass up appropriate opportunities for self rewarding.

Should the worker self reward for qualitatively different performance goals, there will also be dysfunctional consequences. For instance, the performance goal of the worker might be to outwit the supervisor and take a nap in the stock room, to go for a joy ride in the delivery car, or to jam the production line so there will be an unscheduled mid-afternoon break. Self rewarding could follow any of these behaviors, but the self rewarding would only foster increases in these inappropriate performances, not organizationally approved performance. Recognition of the organization's goal is necessary to enable the focal relationship of the model to operate in a way that will be functional for the organization.

The second enabler is performance recognition, the perception of how one has performed relative to the behavioral goal. The worker must be able to assess his/her performance level before the self rewarding—job performance relationship will occur. If the job is analogous to playing golf in a thick fog, the relationship can't take place.

The stimulation for this perception of performance may come from any number of sources. It may be self-evident from the work itself. Peers or supervisors may provide feedback about performance. Organizational records or formalized feedback systems could tell the worker how s/he is doing. Whatever the source, the appropriateness of the self rewarding depends on the accuracy of the perception. Selective or distorted perceptions and misinformation will diminish the self rewarding-job performance relationship.

The Moderators

Three variables are proposed to act as moderators of the self rewarding-job performance relationship. As these variables increase, the relationship will be strengthened. Though the enablers discussed above were conceptualized as necessary conditions for the relationship, the moderators are not. Any of the moderators might be totally absent and still the relationship could exist. Their effects should be cumulative and, in fact, they are likely to be interrelated. These cognitive variables represent the personal reactions of the individual to his/her work situation.

The first moderator is the personal interest that the worker takes in the task. If the worker is interested in the work, good performance should lead to high self rewarding and poor performance should lead to low or negative self rewarding. On the other hand, if the worker is uninterested in the task, the performance level will be unlikely to lead to self rewarding, i.e., knowing that s/he has performed especially well (or poorly) on a task in which s/he is not interested should not cause personal pride (or shame).

The second moderator is the degree to which the worker identifies with the task. This is the extent to which the worker's self image is defined by the fact that s/he is a doer of that task. If that identification is strong, the performance level should influence self rewarding and vice versa. If the personal identification with the task is low, the relationship will be weakened.

The third moderator is similar to the second, but it involves identification with the product rather than with the task. For example, a worker may identify as a contributor to the construction of quality grand pianos (product), but not as an ivory gluer (task). The level of product identification, like the other two moderators, is assumed to be positively related to the strength of the relationship between self rewarding and job performance.

Organizational Intervention

If the organization wishes to enhance the relationship in order to increase job performance, it can act through changes in the enablers and moderators. The enablers can be affected directly by the organization. Goal recognition can be altered by the specification of performance goals. Workers should be told what behaviors and outcomes constitute good job performance. Performance recognition can be aided by structuring jobs and feedback systems so that the worker is able to discern how well s/he is performing relative to the performance goals. For both goal and performance recognition, the organizational influence comes *directly* from providing the necessary information to the worker.

The organization operates on the moderators in an indirect manner. The figure specifies characteristics that the organization can use to accomplish changes in the moderators. Some of these relationships are similar to those demonstrated by Hackman and Oldham (1975). For example, Hackman and Oldham show that Skill Variety, Task Significance, Autonomy, Feedback from the Job, and Experienced Responsibility are all strongly ($> .40$) related to Experienced Meaningfulness of the Work. Four job characteristics are specified that will influence task interest. They are task variety, task novelty, skill utilization, and skill development. Task variety is a measure of the diversity of activities or stimuli on the job. Task novelty indicates the expectations of unpredictable or novel events on the task. Skill utilization is an index of the amount that the task uses valued skills. Skill development depicts the personal growth derived from the task. Skill development may be especially important because of the general importance of Opportunity for Growth as a work reward (Blood, 1973).

Internal status, external prestige, and social worth are all characteristics that influence task identification. Internal status is the position of the job within the formal and informal hierarchies of the organization. The public value of the job in the community outside of the organization constitutes its external prestige. Social worth denotes the contribution of the task to society.

Product identification is influenced by the two characteristics of authorship and influence on results. Authorship is the ability to identify an individual worker as the creator of a particular product. Influence on results indicates the amount of control the worker exercises over the quantity and quality of the work product.

The organization structures tasks and work positions in ways that influence the work characteristics. These, in turn, influence the moderators of the relationship between self rewarding and job performance. The enablers of the relationship are influenced directly by the organization.

IMPLICATIONS OF THE MODEL

The conceptual model presented above has implications for several areas of interest to organizational psychologists. These implications will be sketched here, though a full appreciation of their scope and worth will await empirical investigation.

One of the most intriguing aspects of the model is the possibility of increasing our understanding of the relationship between job performance and job satisfaction. Since self rewarding is an affective response to the job, it can be considered one aspect of the multifaceted area of job satisfaction. It can be thought of as satisfaction with one's own performance. The model specifies that a positive relationship can exist when the enablers are present and the relationship will be strengthened by the moderators. When the moderators and/or the enablers are low, no relationship would be expected.

The model adds to our understanding of the relative success of job enrichment and organizational development programs. When the job or organizational changes increase the enablers and moderators, the changes can be expected to result in a strengthened relationship which will operate to raise both self rewarding and job performance. When the job or organizational changes leave the enablers insufficient and do not affect the moderators, they would be expected to leave performance and satisfaction unaltered. Of course, many job enrichment and organizational development procedures are specifically aimed at the types of variables specified by the model. For example, job enrichment often adds inspection and quality control duties to assembly tasks. Such an addition would increase goal recognition, performance recognition, task variety, task novelty, skill utilization, and influence on results.

The model emphasizes the use of cognitive behavioral self control as an influence on job performance. Though many behavioral approaches enlist extrinsic consequences to influence performance, this model makes explicit how the organization can utilize its resources to increase intrinsic consequences. The approach of using organizational influence on a private process is unique in the organizational psychology literature and opens new areas for investigation drawing on the behavioral self control and cognitive behavior control literature (e.g., Goldfried & Merbaum, 1973; Mahoney, 1974; Mahoney & Thoresen, 1974; Thoresen & Mahoney, 1974; Watson & Tharp, 1972).

The conceptual model suggests how the process of goal setting can influence job performance. This contributes explanatory power to current understanding of the efficacy of goal setting (see Latham & Yukl, 1975; Steers & Porter, 1974). Goal setting operates by establishing the standard that will act as a cue for self rewarding. The worker knows what performance will allow him/her to tell him-herself that s/he has done a good job.

A final implication of the model is its suggestion for the practice of management. Empirical verification of the relationships in the model will allow the description of work positions according to their suitability for motivation through self rewarding. When positions are found that prohibit the use of self reward as a consequence (enablers or moderators are unalterably lacking), then motivation attempts should be designed with extrinsic rewarding. Self rewarding would be ineffective in that situation. On the other hand, the model will suggest modifications for some jobs that will increase performance by strengthening the relationship between self rewarding and job performance. When possible, this emphasis on self rewarding should be an important management tool. Self rewarding is an efficient consequence with low cost to the organization. To the extent that self rewarding can be designed into jobs as an integral part of their operation, supervisory activities can turn from motivational efforts to matters of expertise and coordination (managers can be coaches, not cheerleaders).

Empirical research is ongoing to test the relationships assumed by the model. The research problems are particularly suited to a combination of field and laboratory research in a sequence of field research, laboratory experiment, and field experiment. The initial field research is to establish whether the predicted direct and moderated relationships occur and to determine their strengths. The second, laboratory phase of the research will manipulate the variables that are under organizational control. This will demonstrate the relative strength of potential organizational changes, and will allow the refinement of strategies for field implementations. The third phase of the research program will be a series of field interventions to enhance job performance through increasing self rewarding. This field research will be "hands-on" intervention projects rather than survey research, i.e., it will consist of field experiments with constant, rather than static, monitoring of the relationships.

REFERENCES

Behling, O., Labovitz, G., & Kozmo, R. The Herzberg controversy: A critical reappraisal. *Academy of Management Journal*, 1968, **11**, 99–108.

Blood, M. R. Intergroup comparisons of intraperson differences: Rewards from the job. *Personnel Psychology*, 1973, **26**, 1–9.

Burke, R. J. Are Herzberg's motivators and hygienes unidimensional? *Journal of Applied Psychology*, 1966, **50**, 317–321.

Galder, B. J., & Staw, B. M. The self-perception of intrinsic and extrinsic motivation. *Journal of Personality and Social Psychology*, 1975, **35**, 599–605.

De Charms, R. *Personal causation: The internal affective determinants of behavior.* New York: Academic Press, 1968.

Deci, E. L. Effects of externally mediated rewards on intrinsic motivation. *Journal of Personality and Social Psychology*, 1971, **18**, 105–115.

Deci, E. L. The effects of contingent and non-contingent rewards and controls on intrinsic motivation. *Organizational Behavior and Human Performance*, 1972, **8**, 217–229. (a)

Deci, E. L. Intrinsic motivation, extrinsic reinforcement, and inequity. *Journal of Personality and Social Psychology*, 1972, **22**, 113–120. (b)

Deci, E. L. *Intrinsic motivation.* New York: Plenum, 1975.

Ewen, R. B., Smith, P. C., Hulin, C. L., & Locke, E. A. An empirical test of the Herzberg two-factor theory. *Journal of Applied Psychology*, 1966, **50**, 544–550.

Goldfried, M. R., & Merbaum, M. (Eds.). *Behavior change through self-control.* New York: Holt, Rinehart & Winston, 1973.

Greene, D., & Lepper, M. R. Effects of extrinsic rewards on children's subsequent intrinsic interest. *Child Development*, 1974, **45**, 1141–1145.

Grigaliunas, B. S., & Herzberg, F. Relevancy in the test of motivator-hygiene theory. *Journal of Applied Psychology*, 1971, **55**, 73–79.

Hackman, J. R., & Oldham, G. R. Development of the job diagnostic survey. *Journal of Applied Psychology*, 1975, **60**, 159–170.

Hamner, W. C., & Foster, L. W. Are intrinsic and extrinsic rewards additive: A test of Deci's cognitive evaluation theory of task motivation. *Organizational Behavior and Human Performance*, 1975, **14**, 398–415.

Herold, D. M., & Greller, M. M. *Intrinsic and extrinsic performance feedback: Their relative effectiveness.* Paper presented at the meeting of the Eastern Psychological Association, New York, April 1975.

Herzberg, F., Mausner, B., Peterson, R. D., & Capwell, D. F. *Job attitudes: Review of research and opinion.* Pittsburgh: Psychological Service of Pittsburgh, 1957.

Herzberg, F., Mausner, B., & Snyderman, B. *The motivation to work.* New York: Wiley, 1959.

House, R. J., & Wigdor, L. A. Herzberg's dual-factor theory of job satisfaction and motivation: A review of the evidence and a criticism. *Personnel Psychology*, 1967, **20**, 371–373.

Hulin, C. L., & Smith, P. A. An empirical investigation of two implications of the two-factor theory of job satisfaction. *Journal of Applied Psychology*, 1967, **51**, 396–402.

King, N. A clarification and evaluation of the two-factor theory of job satisfaction. *Psychological Bulletin*, 1970, **74**, 18–31.

Kruglanski, A. W., Alon, S., & Lewis, T. Retrospective misattribution and task enjoyment. *Journal of Experimental Social Psychology*, 1972, **8**, 493–501.

Latham, G. P., & Yukl, G. A. A review of research on the application of goal setting in organizations. *Academy of Management Journal*, 1975, **18**, 824–845.

Lepper, M. R., & Greene, D. Turning play into work: Effects of adult surveillance and extrinsic rewards on children's intrinsic motivation. *Journal of Personality and Social Psychology*, 1975, **31**, 479–486.

Lepper, M. R., Greene, D., & Nisbett, R. E. Undermining children's intrinsic interest with extrinsic rewards: A test of the "overjustification" hypothesis. *Journal of Personality and Social Psychology*, 1973, **28**, 129–137.

Levine, F. M., & Fasnacht, G. Token rewards may lead to token learning. *American Psychologist*, 1974, **29**, 816–820.

Mahoney, M. J. *Cognition and behavior modification*. Cambridge, Mass.: Ballinger, 1974.

Mahoney, M. J., & Thoresen, C. E. *Self-control: Power to the person*. Monterey, Calif.: Brooks/Cole, 1974.

Nord, W. R. Beyond the teaching machine: The neglected area of operant conditioning in the theory and practice of management. *Organizational Behavior and Human Performance*, 1969, **4**, 375–401.

Notz, W. W. Work motivation and the negative effects of extrinsic rewards: A review with implications for theory and practice. *American Psychologist*, 1975, **30**, 884–891.

Salancik, G. R. Interaction effects of performance and money on self-perception of intrinsic motivation. *Organizational Behavior and Human Performance*, 1975, **13**, 339–351.

Scott, W. E., Jr. The effects of extrinsic rewards on "intrinsic motivation": A critique. *Organizational Behavior and Human Performance*, 1975, **15**, 117–129.

Staw, B. M. *Intrinsic and extrinsic motivation*. Morristown, N.J.: General Learning Press, 1975.

Steers, R. M., & Porter, L. W. The role of task-goal attributes in employee performance. *Psychological Bulletin*, 1974, **81**, 434–452.

Thoresen, C. E., & Mahoney, M. J. *Behavioral self-control*. New York: Holt, Rinehart & Winston, 1974.

Watson, D. L., & Tharp, R. G. *Self-directed behavior: Self-modification for personal adjustment*. Monterey, Calif.: Brooks/Cole, 1972.

Whitsett, D. A., & Winslow, E. K. An analysis of studies critical of the motivator-hygiene theory. *Personnel Psychology*, 1967, **20**, 391–415.

PART 2

THEORIES OF LEADERSHIP AND ORGANIZATIONAL CONTROL

SITUATIONAL CONTROL AND A DYNAMIC THEORY OF LEADERSHIP[1]

Fred E. Fiedler
University of Washington

Although empirical studies of leadership behavior and performance became a serious concern of social scientists some 50 years ago, we are just now beginning to understand the structure of the leader-situation interaction and the dynamics of the leadership process. By dynamics, we mean here how the leader and organization interact, and how group performance is affected by a change in the leader's personality or experience, or by the changes in the organization which occur almost continuously in the course of time. An insight into these interactions is essential if we are more fully to understand and improve organizational performance. This study presents an integration of some key concepts which may enable us to develop a dynamic theory of leadership that takes into account the ever changing leader-organization interaction.

Traditionally, the main business of leadership research has been the relationship between personality attributes of the leader and the performance

[1] Keynote address, NATO International Conference on Coordination and Control of Group and Organizational Performance, July 17, 1976.

of his or her group or organization. At first, this search focused on finding the magic personality trait which might predict leadership performance. This enterprise finally received the coup de grace from Stogdill's (1948) and Mann's (1959) now classical reviews of the literature.

The emphasis then shifted to the identification of specific types of leader behavior which would determine the effectiveness of a group. While this effort did not succeed, it did result in the monumental factor analytic research by the Ohio State group under Carroll Shartle and his associates (Stogdill & Coons, 1957) which identified the Consideration and Structuring dimensions as the two major types of leadership behavior which are seen by subordinates. Others, e.g., Cattell (1951), Likert (1961), and Bales (1951), identified similar types of behavior on which leaders differed in their interactions with groups. The hope that these or similar behaviors would be directly related to leadership performance has not been realized, although a number of investigators still deal with this problem.

In particular, a number of leadership training programs have been devoted to teaching managers how to be more considerate or more structuring. The well-known Fleishman, Harris, and Burt (1955) study showed that training of this type would not give lasting results unless the entire organization were to be changed. However, other types of training, working with the entire organization, have not been able to report much success in improving organizational performance. This applies to the orthodox approaches as well as such avant garde programs as T-group and sensitivity training. Stogdill (1974), in his authoritative and comprehensive *Handbook of Leadership*, summarizes this type of research by censuring its "failure to employ legitimate criteria of the effects of training" (p. 199). And he goes on to say,

> It is necessary to demonstrate that change in leader behavior is related to change in group productivity, cohesiveness, esprit, or satisfaction in order to claim that leadership is improved or worsened by training. Only a few of the studies examined for this report satisfy the above requirements. The results of this small body of research suggest that group cohesiveness and esprit increase after sensitivity training of the leader but productivity declines.

The acid test of leadership theory obviously must be its ability to improve organizational performance. For this reason, the ability to change and control and especially to train leaders is a very powerful test of our understanding of the process and theory. Our previous difficulties in this area may well derive from our inadequate understanding of the complex interaction which is inherent in leadership and even the way in which training itself affects the dynamics of the process. The simple notion that a particular type of behavior, or a particular behavior pattern, will result in effective leadership performance is no more viable than the earlier notion of a leadership trait. Leadership exists in the context of an organizational environment which determines, in large part, the specific kind of leadership behavior which the situation requires.

Since the publication of the Contingency Model (Fiedler, 1964, 1967), leadership theory has increasingly turned to formulations which consider not only the leader's personality or behavior, but also critical situational factors. Such situational effects or contingencies also have been explicitly recognized by theorists like House (1971), Vroom and Yetton (1973), and others. It seems fair to say that we are now beginning to predict the relationship between certain leader attributes and organizational performance at a given point in time with a reasonable degree of accuracy.

However, most of our predictions in this field tend to be cross-sectional. We cannot predict well for organizations which are undergoing change and we do not understand fully what factors are critical to leadership performance in this change process. Our major challenge in the area of leadership is to develop a theory which takes account of the changing organizational environment as well as the changes which occur in the leader.

The key concept, which is here proposed as a basis for developing a dynamic theory of leadership, is the leader's situational control. This is essentially the "situational favorableness" dimension of the Contingency Model. I hope to show that this concept gives us considerable understanding of the leadership process and also enables us to control the process, that is, to develop an effective leadership training program which meets Stogdill's requirement that it affect organizational performance.

The Contingency Model

Although the Contingency Model has been fully described in numerous publications, a brief summary provides the basis for the remainder of this study. This theory holds that the effectiveness of a group or an organization depends upon two interacting factors: (a) the personality of the leader (leadership style) and (b) the degree to which the situation gives the leader control and influence, or, in somewhat different terms, the degree to which the situation is free of uncertainty for the leader.

The leader's personality, and more specifically, his or her motivational structure, is identified by a measure which reflects the individual's primary goals in the leadership situation. One type of person, whom we call "relationship-motivated," obtains self-esteem from good interpersonal relationships with groups members and accomplishes the task through these good relations. These basic goals are most apparent in uncertain and anxiety-provoking situations in which we try to assure that our most important needs are secured. Under these conditions, relationship-motivated individuals will seek the support of those who are most closely associated with them. In a leadership situation, we hypothesize that these are, of course, their immediate subordinates and coworkers. Once the support of coworkers and subordinates is assured and this basic goal is no longer in doubt, relationship-motivated leaders will seek support and esteem from others who are important. In a leadership situation in which esteem and approbation are given for good task performance, these individuals will devote themselves to the task in, order to obtain the approval of their superiors, even if this means correspondingly less concern with the well being and approval of subordinates. Thus, when relationship-motivated leaders enjoy a high degree of situational control, they tend to show task-relevant behavior which is most likely to impress superiors.

The other major personality type is the "task-motivated" leader who obtains satisfaction and self-esteem from the more tangible evidence of his or her competence. In a leadership situation which is uncertain and anxiety-provoking, this individual will focus primarily on the completion of the task. However, when task-accomplishment is assured, as would be the case whenever the leader enjoys a high degree of situational control, the leader will relax and devote more time to cementing the relationship with his or her subordinates. Thus, "business before pleasure," but business with pleasure whenever this is possible.

These two motivational systems are measured by the Least Preferred Coworker (or LPC) score which is obtained by asking the individual to think of all those with whom he or she has ever worked, and then to describe the one person with whom he or she has been able to work least well. This description is made on a short bipolar scale of the Semantic Differential format, shown below. We have used 16 or 18 eight-point scale items, e.g.,

$$\text{friendly:}\underline{\ }:\underline{\ }:\underline{\ }:\underline{\ }:\underline{\ }:\underline{\ }:\underline{\ }:\underline{\ }:\text{ unfriendly}$$
$$8\ 7\ 6\ \ 5\ 4\ 3\ \ 2\ \ 1$$

$$\text{cooperative:}\underline{\ }:\underline{\ }:\underline{\ }:\underline{\ }:\underline{\ }:\underline{\ }:\underline{\ }:\underline{\ }:\text{ uncooperative}$$
$$8\ 7\ 6\ 5\ 4\ 3\ 2\ 1$$

The LPC score is simply the sum of the item scores. A task-motivated person describes the least preferred coworker in very negative and rejecting terms. This person says, in effect, that the task is so important it is impossible to differentiate between others as coworkers and as individuals apart from the work relationship. That is, an individual who does not perform well must also have a very objectionable personality, i.e., unfriendly, uncooperative, unpleasant, etc.

The relationship-motivated person is less dependent on esteem from task accomplishment and is, therefore, quite capable of seeing another as a poor coworker but as otherwise quite pleasant, friendly, or helpful. Since this leader's emotional involvement in the task is comparatively less intense, a person who is difficult to work with is seen in a more positive manner.

Although the LPC score is normally distributed, there is a relatively small segment in the middle of the distribution which cannot be clearly identified as task or relationship-motivated persons. For the purposes of this chapter, we shall be concerned primarily with the high and the low LPC leaders who are much better understood.

A recent review of the literature by Rice (1977) shows that the LPC score reflects a relatively stable personality attribute. Rice located 23 test-retest correlations which ranged "from .01 to .92 with a median of .67 and a mean (using Fisher's Z transformation) of .64 (standard deviation = .36, n = 23)." He goes on to say, "Somewhat surprisingly the test-retest reliability data . . . show only a moderate negative correlation between length of the test-retest interval and the magnitude of the stability coefficient (r = −.30, n = 23, ns). This analysis suggests that the variance in stability coefficients is primarily due to factors other than the simple passing of time." Exactly what other factors might affect the stability of the score is still not clear.

It is also of interest to note that the median retest reliability of LPC is well within the range of several other widely used personality measures. For example, Sax (1974) lists the stability of the MMPI for a period of only one week as .60, and the median stability coefficient of the Hartshorne and May honesty scales of a six month interval as .50. Mehrens and Lehmann (1968) report the stability of the California Psychological Inventory for 13,000 subjects over a one-year period as .65 for males and .68 for females. While the retest correlations for such measures of cognitive abilities as intelligence are generally higher, relatively few stability coefficients of personality test scores fall above .70 for intervals of several months.

The Leadership Situation. The other major variable of the Contingency Model is the leader's situational control or "situational favorableness." The method for operationally defining this concept is based on three subscales which indicate the degree to which (a) the leader is or feels accepted and supported by group members (leader-member relations); (b) the task is clear-cut, structured, and identifies the goals, procedures, and progress of the work (task structure); and (c) the leader has the ability to reward and punish, and thus to obtain compliance through organizational sanctions (position power).

Groups can be categorized as being high or low on each of these three dimensions by dividing them at the median or on the basis of normative scores. This leads to an eight-cell classification from high situational control (Octant I) to low control (Octant VIII) (shown in Fig. 1). Leaders will have high control if they enjoy the support of the group, have a clearly structured

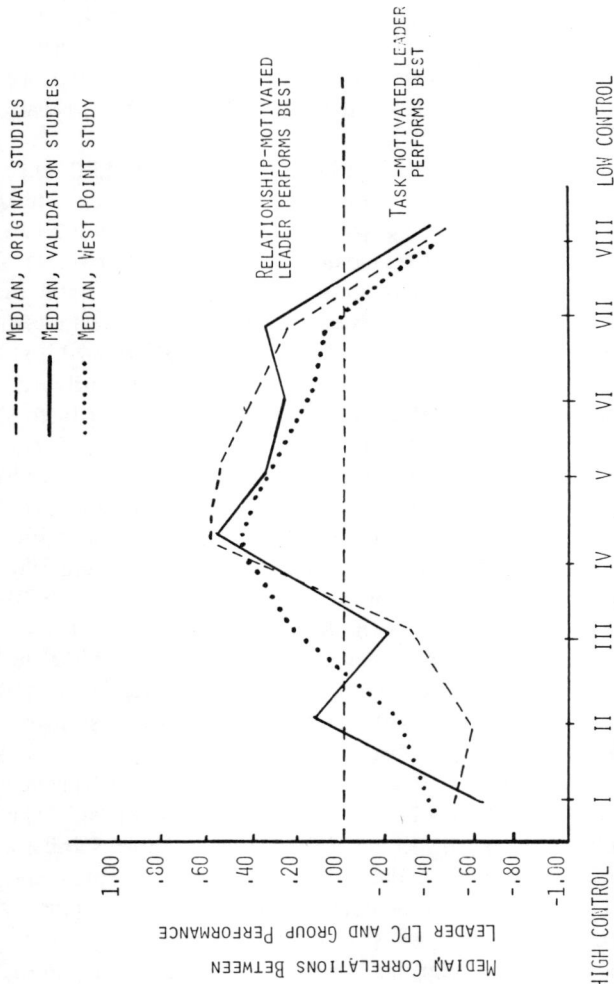

Fig. 1. Median correlations between leader LPC and group performance for studies conducted to test the Contingency Model.

task, and high position power. They will have low control if the group does not support them, the task is vague and unstructured, and position power is weak. When measuring situational control, leader-member relations are given a weight of 4, task structure a weight of 2, and position power a weight of 1. This weighting system has been supported by several empirical studies (Beach, Mitchell, & Beach, 1975; Nebeker, 1975).

Having high control implies that leaders will be assured that their particular goals and needs will be attained. Under these conditions, relationship-motivated leaders will worry less about interpersonal relations with the group and more about earning esteem from their boss or other important people in the organization. They accomplish this by showing concern for the job and exhibiting task directive behavior. Task-motivated leaders in a high control situation are assured that the job will be accomplished and will devote themselves to improving and cementing relations with group members.

Low situational control will result in uncertainty and greater anxiety that the leader's goals will not be attained. Under these conditions, task-motivated leaders will concentrate on their goal of task accomplishment, while the relationship-motivated leaders will focus on achieving their goal of good interpersonal relations with the group.

The Personality-Situation Interaction. The Contingency Model has shown that task-motivated leaders perform best when situational control is high as well as in situations where control is low. The relationship-motivated leaders tend to perform best in situations in which their control is moderate. These findings are summarized in Figure 1. The horizontal axis indicates the eight cells of the situational control dimension, with the high control situations on the left of the graph and the low control situations on the right. The vertical axis indicates the correlation coefficients between leader LPC scores and group performance. A high correlation in the positive direction (above the midline of the graph) indicates that the high LPC leaders performed better than did the low LPC leaders. A negative correlation indicates that the low LPC leaders performed better than the high LPC leaders.

The broken line in Figure 1 connects the median correlation coefficients of studies conducted prior to 1963; the solid line connects the median correlations obtained in validation studies since 1964. The dotted line shows the results of a major validation experiment conducted by Chemers and Skrzypek (1972) and provides the most convincing support of the Contingency Model.

In this study, LPC scores as well as sociometric ratings to determine leader-member relations were obtained six weeks prior to the study. Eight groups were then experimentally assembled for each of the octants so that half the groups had high LPC leaders, half had low LPC leaders. Half of the groups consisted of men who had chosen each other sociometrically as

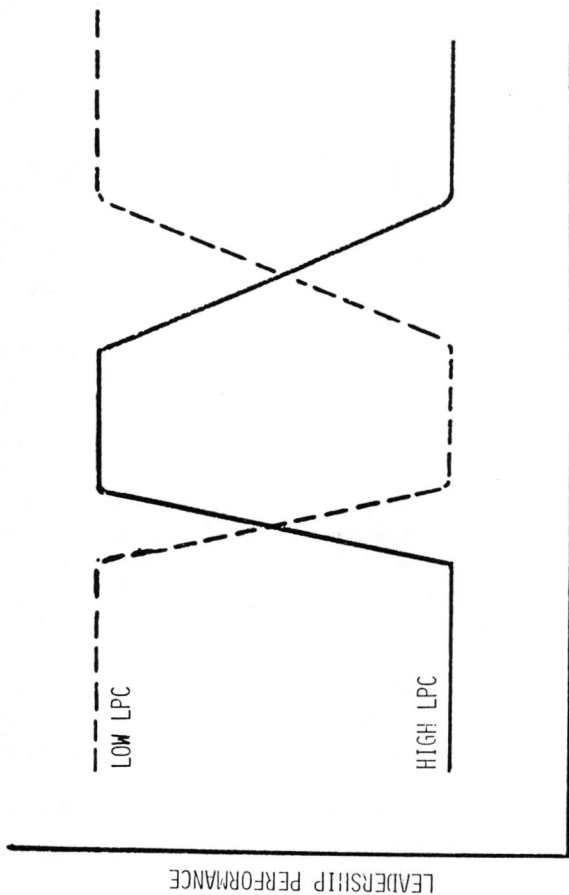

Fig. 2. Schematic representation of the Contingency Model.

	1	2	3	4	5	6	7	8
LEADER MEMBER RELATIONS	+	+	+	+	-	-	-	-
TASK STRUCTURE	+	+	-	-	+	+	-	-
POSITION POWER	+	-	+	-	+	-	+	-
	HIGH CONTROL			MODERATE		LOW CONTROL		

preferred work companions while the other half had indicated a dislike for working with others who were placed on the same team. Half the groups, further, were given leaders with high position power and half the groups had leaders with low position power.

As can be seen, the results of the Chemers and Skrzypek study almost exactly replicated the findings of the original studies. The correlation points of the original studies and the West Point study correlated .86 ($p < .01$) and a subsequent reanalysis by Shiflett (1973) showed that the West Point study accounted for 28% of the variance in group performance.

As Figure 1 clearly indicates, the effectiveness of the group or organization depends on leader personality (leadership style) as well as situational control. For this reason, we cannot really talk about a "good" leader or a "poor" leader. Rather, leaders may be good in situations which match their leadership style and poor in situations in which leadership style and situational control are mismatched.

Situational Control and the Dynamics of the Leadership Process

Let us now extend the Contingency Model to encompass the dynamic interactions in the leadership process. The integrating concept which allows us to do this is the leader's situational control and influence. Situational control will change partly in response to environmental and organizational events and in part as the leader's abilities to cope with the organizational environment change. Thus, leaders may be given different assignments, greater or lesser authority, more compliant or more "difficult" subordinates, or a more or a less supportive boss. Leaders may also learn through experience or training how to cope more effectively with the situation which confronts them, giving increased situational control or, in some cases, less control over their leadership situation.

As the Contingency Model has shown, leadership effectiveness depends on the proper match between situational control and leadership style as measured by the LPC score. A major change in the organization or in the leader will necessarily change this match and thus increase or decrease leadership performance. The nature of this relationship is schematically shown in Figure 2. The horizontal axis indicates the degree to which the situation gives the leader control. The vertical axis indicates leadership performance. The solid line shows the performance of relationship-motivated (high LPC) leaders and the broken line the performance of task-motivated (low LPC) leaders. Again, of course, task-motivated leaders are shown as performing best in high and low control situations; relationship-motivated leaders are shown as performing best in moderate control situations. Some of the major factors which would cause changes in the match to occur are presented below.

Experience. The most obvious and inevitable change which generally takes place in the leader's control is the result of time on the job and the concomitant increase in experience. The first days and months on a new job are almost invariably bewildering to the point where it is difficult to cope with the many problems which arise. This feeling of being out of control and in need of help gradually gives way, over time, to increasing confidence that we know what is going on. This process of feeling in control may take no longer than a few days for simple jobs, or several years for the complex and difficult assignments. Indeed, there are some jobs in which a leader may never really feel in control, no matter how long he or she has been in the position.

What does experience do for us? First of all, we learn the routines of the job. We know where things are, how we can get certain things done, and what the exact standards and requirements of the job are. In other words, the task, in our eyes, becomes more structured. Leaders also will become more familiar with subordinates. They learn what the group's idiosyncracies are and how to handle them, and relations with them tend to become easier, more cordial, and mutually more supportive. Moreover, leaders will get to know their boss, what the superior's standards and expectations are, how to manage a relationship with him or her. Finally, with greater support from the boss and a better grasp of the informal and formal rules of the organization, leaders will know exactly how much power their position has, and how to use it.

By and large, then, we expect that the typical experience which comes with time on the job will correspondingly increase the leader's control over the leadership situation. This means that inexperienced leaders who come into low control situations will perform well if they are task-motivated, but will gradually decrease in performance as the gain in experience makes the situation one of moderate control. Under the same conditions, relationship-motivated leaders will perform poorly, intially, and gradually become better as experience increases.

Similarly, if we take a situation in which the leader has moderate control upon beginning the job, we should find that the relationship-motivated person performs well at first, but decreases in effectiveness as he or she gains in experience and the situation becomes high in control. The opposite will be true of task-motivated leaders.

A study by Fielder, Bons, and Hastings (1975), using squad leaders of an infantry division, supports this hypothesis. These are first level supervisors who command a squad of between 8 and 12 soldiers. The squad leaders were evaluated by two superiors shortly after the squads were formed, that is, while the division was still in a rather unsettled state; the leaders did not yet know their subordinates well, nor did they know their superiors well. A second performance evaluation was obtained from the same raters about five months later, after the unit had gone through training and completed their combat readiness tests.

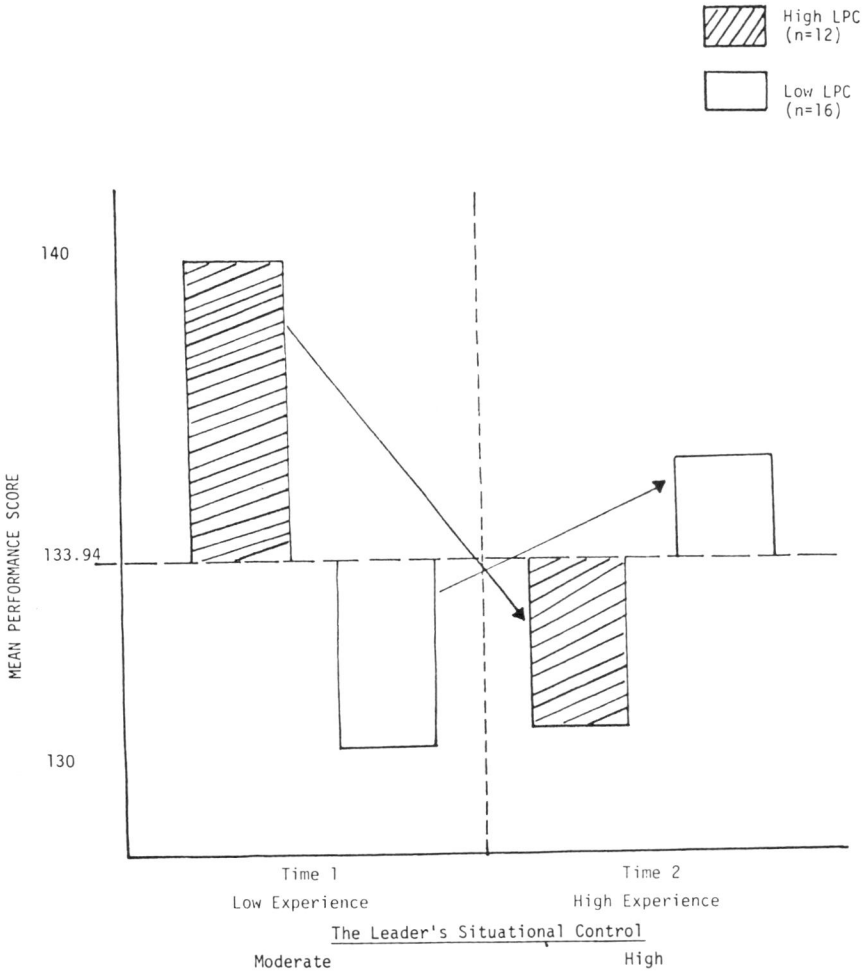

Fig. 3. Change in performance of high and low LPC leaders as a function of increased experience over five months (interaction significant).

An assessment of the leadership situation was obtained from outside judges and indicated that the situational control was moderate for the leaders at the time the division was established, but high after the leaders had gained experience and the division had shaken down. Figure 3 shows the results when we compare the performance ratings of the same leaders by the same raters at the first and second time of evaluation. Similar results have been reported elsewhere (Fiedler & Chemers, 1974).

Training. We would expect, of course, that the effect of training will be quite similar to that of experience, provided that the training is relevant and reflects the experience of others who have been successful in the position. However, a considerable amount of leadership training has been devoted to participative and nondirective approaches which would, by and large, reduce the leader's control since the leader must share information and decision making functions with group members. It is, therefore, not always clear what effects training will have on leadership control. On the other hand, task training almost certainly will increase the perceived structure of the assignment and the leader's situational control.

A well-designed leadership training experiment, conducted by Chemers, Rice, Sundstrom, and Butler (1975), demonstrates the effects of this intervention. A sample of 20 ROTC cadets with high and 20 with low LPC scores were selected as leaders, while those with intermediate LPC scores along with students from a psychology class served as group members in this experiment. The three-man groups were further divided at random into those who received task training and those who were given no training. The assignment consisted of deciphering a series of coded messages. The training consisted of teaching the leaders some simple rules of decoding, e.g., that the most frequent letter in the English alphabet is "e," that the most frequent three-letter word with "e" at the end is "the," that the only one-letter words are "I" and "a," etc.

The group climate scores were quite low, and the position power of the leaders was also low. Untrained leaders, who had an unstructured task, had low control while trained leaders had a moderate degree of situational control. This means that the untrained low LPC leaders should perform better than the untrained high LPC leaders, while the trained high LPC leaders should outperform the trained low LPC leaders. The interaction between LPC and training is statistically highly significant (Fig. 4). The finding is especially startling since the trained low LPC leaders not only performed less well than high LPC leaders, but they also performed less well than did the untrained low LPC leaders.

Organizational Turbulence. Changes in the organizational structure and function also affect the leader's situational control. These changes require the leader to adapt to new conditions and to learn how to cope with situations which are unfamiliar and which have less certain and less predictable outcomes. This is particularly true when the leader is given a new job which typically also means that the boss is new as are the leader's subordinates.

A study by Bons and Fiedler (1976) of squad leaders illustrates the effects of these changes on leader performance and behavior. One additional point needed to be considered in this study. Some of the squad leaders were newly appointed to this first-level command position while others had been squad

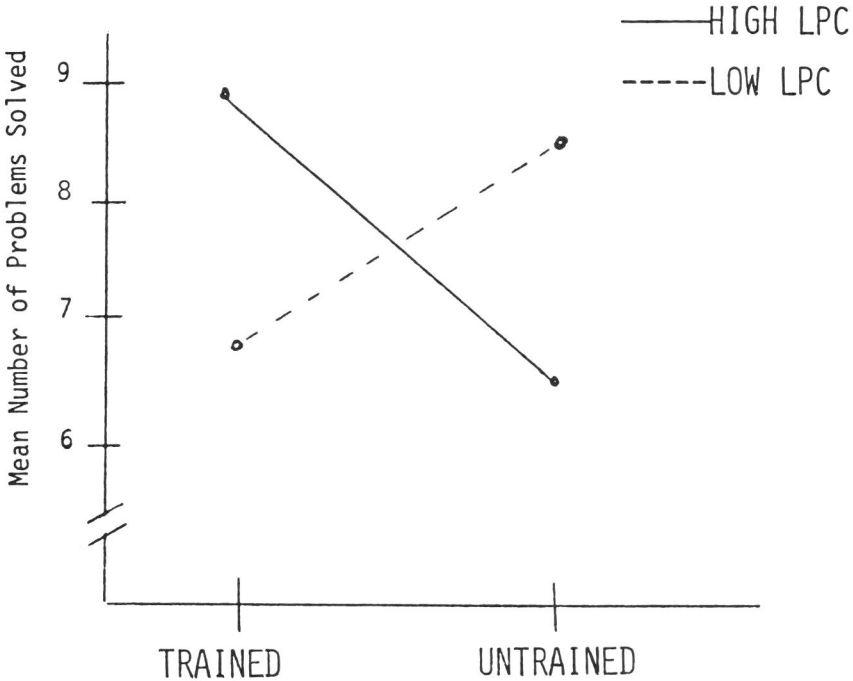

Fig. 4. The effect of training and LPC on group productivity.

leaders for several years—in fact, some for as much as ten years. For the latter, the situation obviously presented fewer new elements than it did for the newer, younger soldiers. For this reason, data for experienced and inexperienced squad leaders were analyzed separately with the expectation that the situation would provide more control for the experienced than for the inexperienced leaders. Performance was assessed on the basis of ratings by two superiors.

In the sample of experienced leaders there was no evidence that task performance had been affected substantially by organizational turbulence. In the group of inexperienced leaders, however, a change in job was associated with a markedly lower task performance on the part of high LPC leaders at time 2. Since we had made covariance adjustments for time 1 performance scores, these data imply that task performance of relationship-motivated leaders had decreased as a result of change in job, while that of task-motivated leaders had slightly increased. (See Figure 5; the broken line indicates the grand mean of task performance scores at time 1. The interaction of LPC $\times$ Experience $\times$ Change is significant at the .05 level.)

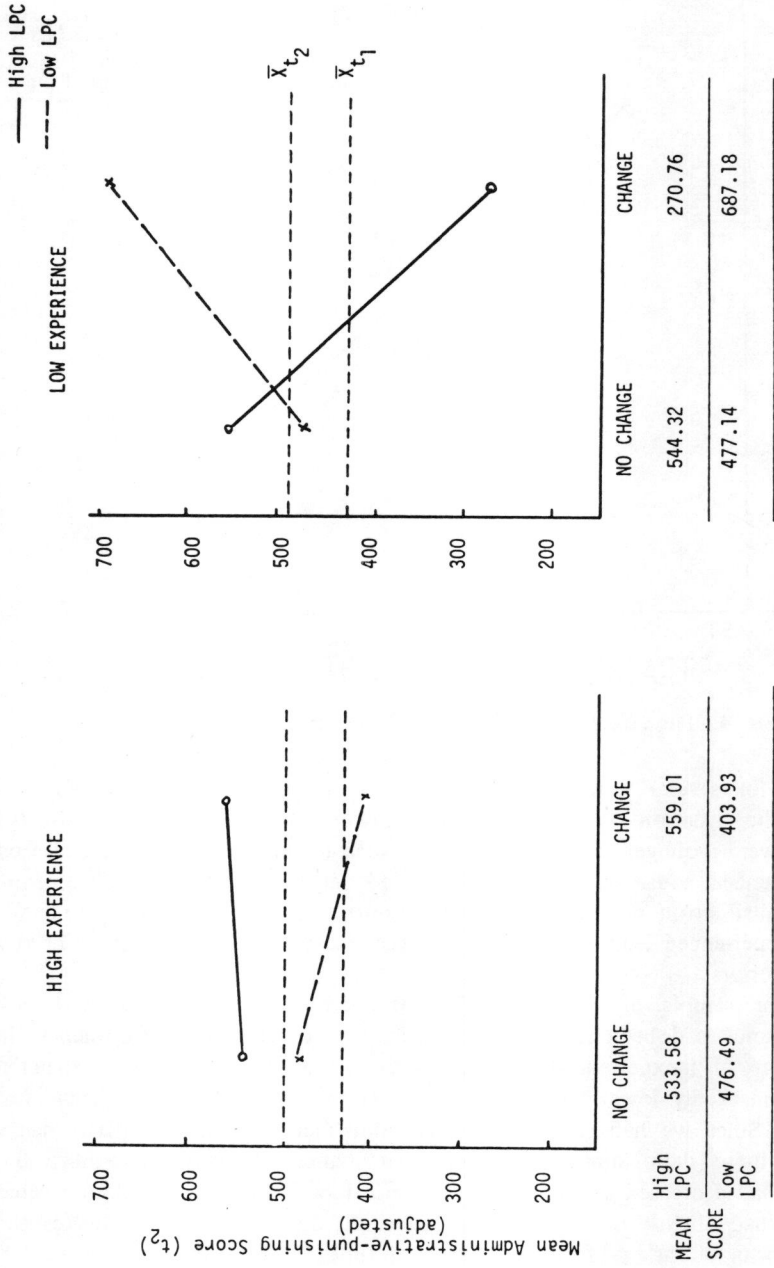

Fig. 5. Task-performance behavior as a function of LPC and change in job for given levels of leader experience.

Leadership Selection and Placement

Current theory and practice in leadership selection best typifies the nondynamic nature of present thinking in this area. We try to select managers and leaders with the well-worn notion that the round pegs belong in round holes and square pegs in square holes. This is fine as long as the pegs and holes do not change their shape. In fact, however, as we have seen, changes in leaders' ability and job knowledge affect their situational control, and thus the match between leadership style and situational control.

This match may be excellent as the leader enters on a new job and he or she tends to perform well at first. However, leadership performance is likely to change as the leader gains greater control over the situation through experience and training. Thus, if the situation provides low control for the new leader, we would expect that the task-motivated individual will perform well and the relationship-motivated person will perform poorly. As experience and training increase situational control to "moderate," the performance of the task-motivated leader will decrease and that of the relationship-motivated leader will increase. The opposite will be the case if the situational control is moderate in the beginning and high later on. Then, the relationship-motivated leader will perform well at first and poorly later on.

If selection and placement procedures are to be effective, they must take account of these dynamic changes. We must explicitly decide on the strategy which the organization should follow. As a rule, of course, selecting leaders to perform well when they are experienced will be best if the leadership job can be learned within a few weeks or months, even though the chosen leader may perform poorly at first.

A long-run strategy also will be more appropriate in very stable organizations in which the turnover of managerial personnel is very slow. However, in many organizations and especially in the military, it is rather unusual for a person to remain in the same job for more than one, two, or three years. This is also true in large organizations which have a policy of rotation as part of a managerial development program. Rapid change in the leadership structure may also be the result of various economic and environmental forces which impinge on the organization. Examples are found in large manufacturing and research and development organizations which utilize matrix or program management in order to accomplish special tasks or to develop specific product lines which are expected to discontinue after a given period of time.

Under these latter conditions, the requirements of the organization call for immediate top performance and a short-run strategy is clearly indicated. The organization must then be prepared to accept the possibility that a particular leader, who has been assigned to the same job for an extended period of time, is likely to become less effective and must again be moved to a more challenging job.

The amount of time which will elapse before a leadership situation will change from low control to moderate control, or from moderate to high control, will depend on the degree of structure and complexity of the task, and the intellectual abilities of the personnel who are available for these positions. For such tasks as infantry squad leader, the time at which this occurs may be 4 or 5 months; for school principals, it appears to be between 2 and 3 years; and for community college presidents, between 5 and 6 years. Some management jobs may require even longer before the leader gains maximum control.

The important point is, of course, that a rational selection and placement strategy cannot assume that the match between leader and job will remain a good fit forever. Rather, we must consider the effects which increased or decreased situational control will have on the selection process.

Situational Control and Leader Behavior

Having shown that a change in situational control results in a change of leadership performance, we must now ask why a situational change should have this effect. Since we must eventually look to leader behavior as the mainspring for leadership performance, we need to determine how situational control affects the behaviors of relationship- and task-motivated leaders.

As mentioned earlier, the behavior of task- and relationship-motivated leaders differs in relaxed, high control situations and in stressful, anxiety-arousing, low control situations (Fiedler, 1972). A study by Meuwese and Fiedler (cited in Fiedler, 1967) will serve as an illustration. In this laboratory experiment, we compared the behavior of task- and relationship-motivated leaders of Reserve Officer Training Corps teams which were engaged in creative tasks. In one condition, the cadets worked under low stress, assured that their performance would have no bearing on their future military career. In another condition, the cadets were asked to appear in uniform and were continuously evaluated by a high ranking officer who was seated directly across the table from the team. This latter condition was rated as quite stressful.

The comments made by leaders were categorized as relevant to developing good interpersonal relationships in the team, specifically, involving group participation and democratic leadership behavior, and as task-relevant (proposing new ideas and integrating ideas of others.). The results are shown in Figure 6 and support the interpretation that high and low LPC scores reflect different goal or motivational structures. That is, the behavior of the leader in the stressful condition appears directed toward achieving the more

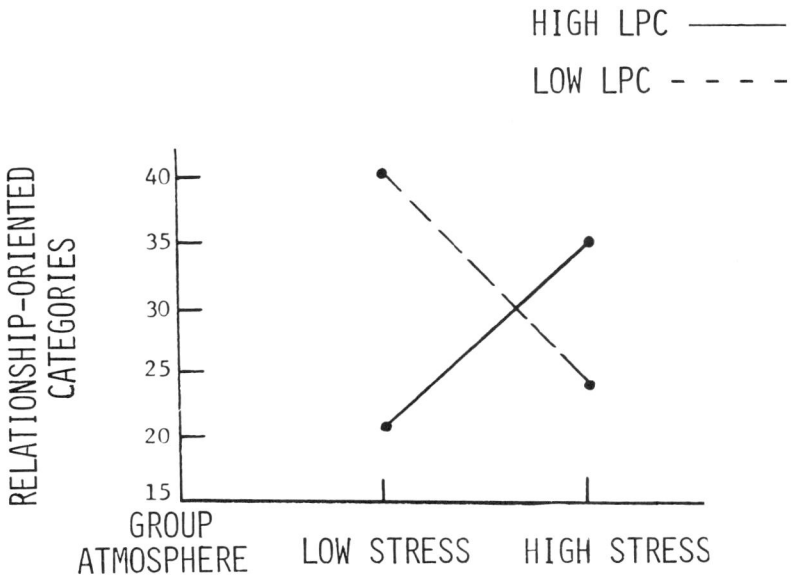

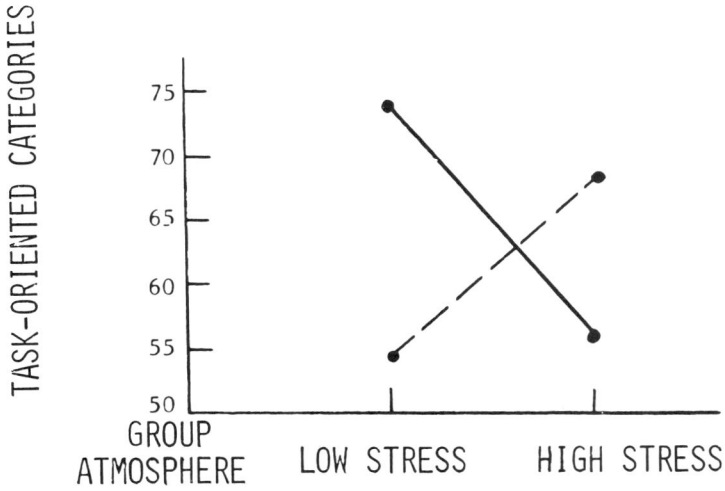

Fig. 6. Effect of stress on behavior of relationship-motivated (high LPC) and task-motivated (low LPC) leaders.

basic goals, namely task achievement for the low LPC, and good interpersonal relations for the high LPC leader. In the nonstressful condition in which the leader's control is high, and he can feel sure of achieving his basic goals, the leader's behavior appears directed toward the attainment of secondary goals. These are a pleasant relationship for the low LPC leader, and gaining approval of others by task relevant behavior on the part of the high LPC leader.

It is also possible to ask whether the leader's behavior will change as a result of a deliberate change in the leadership situation or one caused by organizational turbulence. According to the Contingency Model, an increase in the leader's control should make task-motivated individuals behave in a more considerate, social-emotional manner while it should lessen the relationship-motivated leader's concern for group members. Lowering the leader's situational control should increase the relationship-motivated leader's concern for the group but decrease that of the task-motivated leader. Chemers (1969) tested this hypothesis using a culture training program which was designed to improve the American leader's ability to deal with Iranian coworkers in a more effective and more secure manner.

Chemer's experiment used three-person groups which were to make recommendations on two controversial issues in Iran at the time: (a) employment of women and (b) appropriate training for low-status supervisors. At the end of the task sessions, the two Iranian group members described the leader's consideration behavior, the group climate, and their evaluation of the leader.

Half the leaders in the experiment were high and the other half low LPC persons. These were randomly assigned either to the culture training condition or to a condition involving control training, that is, training in the physical geography of Iran. The culture training was, of course, expected to increase the leader's control enabling more effective interaction with group members.

As can be seen from Figure 7, the task-motivated leaders with culture training were seen as more considerate. They also were more esteemed and developed better group climate. The relationship-motivated leaders, on the other hand, were seen as less considerate, and as having developed a poorer group climate. (The interaction between LPC and training is significant.)

Let us now consider the effects which a stable leadership situation and an unstable, turbulent leadership environment will have on leader behavior. A stable environment should increase the leader's control and thus cause the relationship-motivated leader to become less concerned with group member relations while the task-motivated leader should become more concerned with interpersonal relations in the group. However, a leadership environment characterized by change and turbulence should cause anxiety and insecurity. Under these conditions, the relationship-motivated leader will seek the support of group members while the task-motivated leader will become more

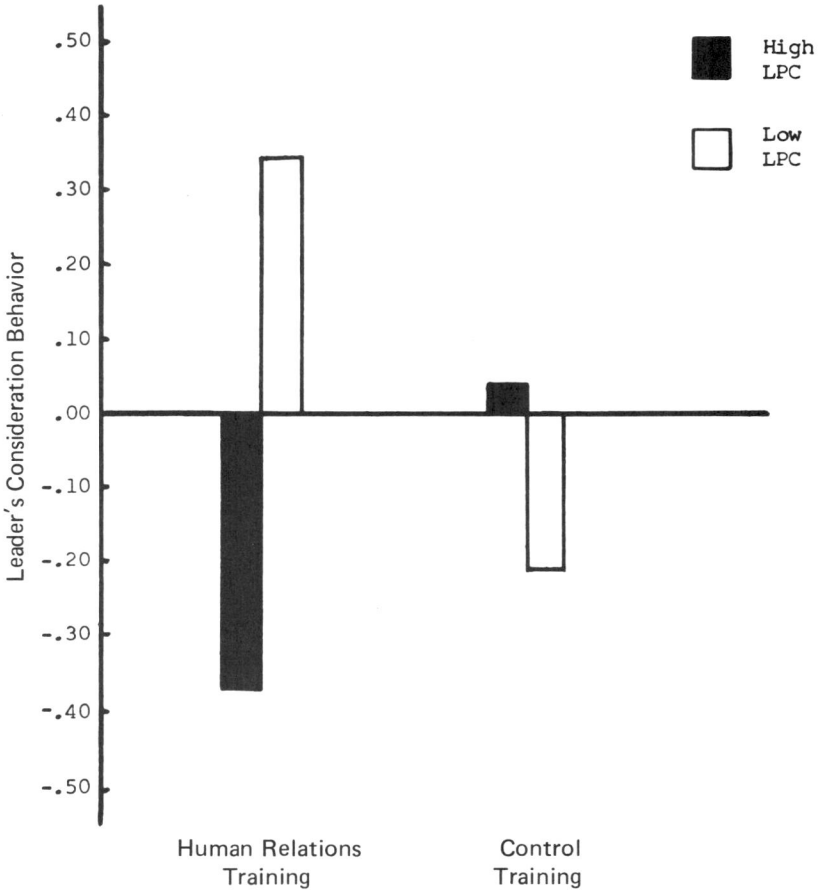

Fig. 7. Effects of human relations training on considerate behavior of high and low LPC leaders.

controlling in order to assure that the job gets done. We assume, then, that a tendency to reward will improve interpersonal relations while a tendency to be punitive implies the desire for stronger control and concern for task accomplishment.

The study of infantry squad leaders, discussed earlier, provides data which support this hypothesis. Figure 8 shows the time 2 mean scores on rewarding behavior as rated by subordinates and adjusted for time 1 scores. The broken line indicates the grand mean for time 1. As can be seen, there is little

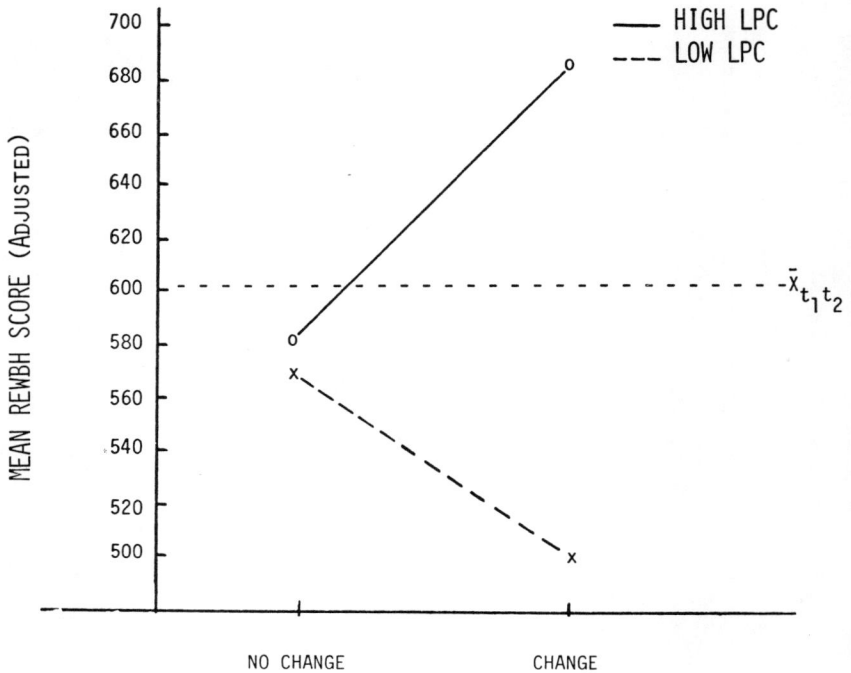

Fig. 8. Rewarding behavior (REWBH) as a function of LPC and change in job.

difference in rewarding behavior for the group leaders who experienced no job change in the six to eight months which intervened between the first and second testing sessions. However, in the group which experienced a turbulent environment, the differences in time 2 rewarding behavior are substantial and the LPC × Change interaction is significant. We may thus infer that the high LPC leaders became more rewarding while the low LPC leaders became less rewarding as a consequence of the lower situational control which resulted from being assigned to a new job.

The opposite trend emerged from the analysis of administrative punishment behaviors (e.g., threatened or actual reduction or demotion or placement in the stockade). Figure 9 indicates the effects on administrative punishment behavior when both of the leader's superiors (platoon sergeant and platoon leader) are replaced in the time period $t_1 - t_2$. The LPC × Experience × Change interaction is significant. For the inexperienced leaders, the turbulent condition (new superiors) is associated with more punitive behavior on the part of low LPC leaders but less punitive behavior on the part of high LPC

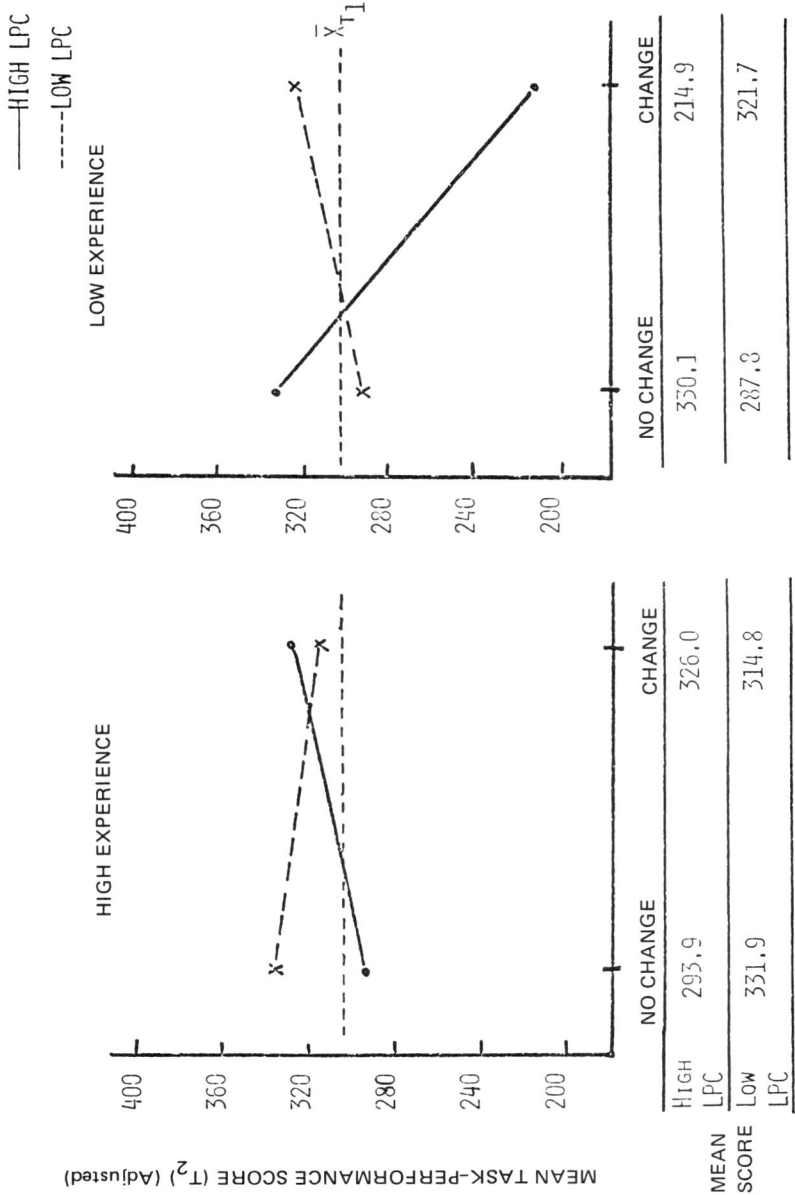

Fig. 9. Administrative-punishing behavior as a function of LPC and change in boss for leaders with high and with low experience.

leaders. Among leaders with high experience who have considerable control over their situation, the high LPC leaders are generally more punitive at time 2 than are low LPC leaders.

The data described in this study make an important point. Situational control substantially influences leader behavior, and, presumably, leader behavior determines group performance. Behavior and performance change, therefore, as the situational control of the leader changes.

The Leader Match Program

One type of evidence that we understand a process is the ability to change the process in the desired manner. A demonstration that we know how to improve leadership performance, therefore, gives some hope that we are beginning to understand the dynamics of organizational leadership.

We recently developed a self-paced programmed instruction manual, entitled *Leader Match* (Fiedler, Chemers, & Mahar, 1976), which incorporates the principles of the Contingency Model. Specifically, leaders are instructed to take the LPC scale and to interpret their score. They are given detailed instructions on how to measure leader-member relations, task structure, and position power, using various scales and appropriate exercises and feedback. Finally, the manual provides guidance on how to modify the leadership situation so that it will provide the appropriate degree of situational control.

As of this date, eight successive validation studies have yielded significant results which indicate that leaders who are trained with this program tend to perform significantly more effectively than do those not so trained. Four of these studies were conducted in various civilian organizations and involved second level leaders of a volunteer public health organization, middle managers of a county government, supervisors and managers of a public works department, and police sergeants. In each of these studies, a list of eligible leaders was obtained from which a trained and control group was randomly selected. While all studies yielded significant findings, attrition clouded the results.

Better control over the subject population was possible in a study of junior officers and petty officers of a navy air station and a study of junior officers and petty officers of a destroyer. Again trained and control subjects were selected at random, and performance ratings were obtained at the time of training and six months later from the same supervisors. There was no voluntary attrition in either study. As can be seen from Table 1, the trained group significantly improved in performance when compared to the control group.

Two other studies were conducted by Csoka and Bons (personal communication). The first used officer trainees who were scheduled to

Table 1. Comparison of Mean Change Scores for Trained and Control Group Leaders

Change score for	Group	N	$\overline{X}$	S.D.	t	p^{a}	ω^2
Overall performance	Trained	27	.5741	.786	3.58	<.001	.174
	Control	29	−.4595	1.257			
Task performance	Trained	27	.5872	.696	3.89	<.001	.202
	Control	29	−.5158	1.283			
Personnel performance	Trained	27	.5213	.921	2.93	<.002	.120
	Control	29	−.3659	1.246			

[a]Probability is one-tailed.

become acting platoon leaders in operational units. One third of 154 men were randomly selected for training while the others were used as controls. At the end of the test period, the unit officers' evaluations showed the *Leader Match*-trained leaders as performing better than untrained men within the same unit.

A second study involved training 1 randomly selected platoon leader of 3 in each of 27 training companies. At the end of a 4-month period, evaluation of all platoon leaders showed that the trained leaders were significantly more often chosen as the best of the three in their company.

Although the investigations are not yet complete, preliminary data show that the training with the *Leader Match* program did enable leaders to modify their leadership so as to maintain the appropriate balance between their leadership style and situational control. Thus, using situational control as the key concept in a dynamic interpretation of the leadership process appears to be a highly promising and cost effective approach.

Conclusion

This study presents a dynamic interpretation of the Contingency Model in which the leader's situational control emerges as the critical variable for interpreting the complex processes of leadership performance in changing organizational environments. This interpretation accounts for the disappointing results which previous leadership training programs have yielded, and the low correlations between years of leadership experience and leadership performance. Training and experience typically provide the leader with greater control while organizational turbulence, shake-ups in management, and similar events, cause uncertainty and lessen the leader's control over the situation.

Recent research shows that we can improve organizational performance by teaching the leader how to diagnose and modify situational control in order to maintain an optimal match between leadership style and situation in a continuously changing organizational environment. These findings provide further important evidence that we are beginning to understand the dynamics of the leadership process.

REFERENCES

Bales, R. F. *Interaction process analysis.* Cambridge, Mass.: Addison-Wesley, 1951.

Beach, B. H., Mitchell, T. R., & Beach, L. R. *Components of situational favorableness and probability of success.* Organizational Research Technical Report 75-66, University of Washington, Seattle, 1975.

Bons, P. M., & Fiedler, F. E. The effect of changes in command on the behavior of subordinate leaders in military units. *Administrative Science Quarterly*, 1976, 21, 433–472.

Cattell, R. B. New concepts for measuring leadership in terms of group syntality. *Human Relations*, 1951, 4, 161–184.

Chemers, M. M. Cross-cultural training as a means for improving situational favorableness. *Human Relations*, 1969, 22, 531–546.

Chemers, M. M., Rice, R. W., Sundstrom, E., & Butler, W. Leader esteem for the least preferred coworker score, training, and effectiveness: An experimental examination. *Journal of Personality and Social Psychology*, 1975, 31, 401–409.

Chemers, M. M., & Skrzypek, G. J. An experimental test of the Contingency Model of leadership effectiveness. *Journal of Personality and Social Psychology*, 1972, 24, 172–177.

Fiedler, F. E. A contingency model of leadership effectiveness. In L. Berkowitz (Ed.), *Advances in experimental social psychology* (Vol. I). New York: Academic Press, 1964.

Fiedler, F. E. *A theory of leadership effectiveness.* New York: McGraw-Hill, 1967.

Fiedler, F. E. Personality, motivational systems, and behavior of high and low LPC persons. *Human Relations*, 1972, 25, 391–412.

Fiedler, F. E., Bons, P. M., & Hastings, L. L. The utilization of leadership resources. In W. T. Singleton & P. Spurgeon (Eds.), *Measurement of human resources.* London: Taylor and Francis, 1975.

Fiedler, F. E., & Chemers, M. M. *Leadership and effective management.* Glenview, Ill.: Scott Foresman, 1974.

Fiedler, F. E., Chemers, M. M., & Mahar, L. *Improving leadership effectiveness: The leader match concept.* New York: John Wiley & Sons, 1976.

Fleishman, E. A., Harris, E. F., & Burt, H. E. *Leadership and supervision in industry.* Columbus, Ohio: Ohio State University, 1955.

House, R. J. A path goal theory of leader effectiveness. *Administrative Science Quarterly*, 1971, **16**, 321–338.

Likert, R. *New patterns of management*. New York: McGraw-Hill, 1961.

Mann, R. D. A review of the relationships between personality and performance in small groups. *Psychological Bulletin*, 1959, **56**, 241–270.

Mehrens, W. A., & Lehmann, I. J. *Standardized tests in education*. New York: MacMillan, 1973.

Nebeker, D. M. Situational favorability and environmental uncertainty: An integrative study. *Administrative Science Quarterly*, 1975, **20**, 281–294.

Rice, R. W. Psychometric properties of the esteem for least preferred coworker (LPC) scale. *Academy of Management Review*, 1977, in press.

Sax, G. *Principles of education measurement and evaluation*. Belmont, Calif.: Wadsworth, 1974.

Shiflett, S. C. The contingency model of leadership effectiveness: Some implications of its statistical and methodological properties. *Behavioral Science*, 1973, **18**, 429–440.

Stogdill, R. Personal factors associated with leadership: A survey of the literature. *Journal of Psychology*, 1948, **25**, 35–71.

Stogdill, R. *Handbook of leadership*. New York: The Free Press, 1974.

Stogdill, R. M., & Coons, A. E. *Leader behavior: Its description and measurement*. Columbus, Ohio: Ohio State University Monograph No. 88, 1957.

Vroom, V. H., & Yetton, P. W. *Leadership and decision making*. Pittsburgh: University of Pittsburgh Press, 1973.

THE VROOM-YETTON MODEL OF LEADERSHIP: AN OVERVIEW[1]

Philip W. Yetton
Manchester University, England

Victor H. Vroom
Yale University

INTRODUCTION

It would not be unusual for a manager to make an individual autocratic decision on Monday morning and then to call a meeting on a different matter, for the afternoon, at which he and his subordinates make a highly participative or group decision. Furthermore, such a pattern of behavior would not surprise his subordinates. They would see no inherent contradiction in his behaving both autocratically and participatively on the same day. However, his behavior might pose a problem for the student of managerial psychology who was nurtured on a diet of Theory X and Theory Y, and other individual difference models of leadership.

In such theories, a manager is implicitly or explicitly assumed to have a dominant or modal style. Furthermore, the writings of many behavioral

[1] Preparation of this paper was partially supported by the Psychological Sciences Division, Office of Naval Research, Control No. N00014-67-A-0097-0027 (Control Authority Identification No. NR-171-935).

Table 1. Taxonomy of Decision Processes

AI	—You solve the problem or make the decision yourself, using the information available to you at the present time.
AII	—You obtain any necessary information from subordinates, then decide on a solution to the problem yourself. You may or may not tell subordinates the purpose of your questions or give information about the problem or decision you are working on. The input provided by them is clearly in response to your request for specific information. They do not play a role in the definition of the problem or in generating or evaluating alternative solutions.
CI	—You share the problem with the relevant subordinates individually, getting their ideas and suggestions without bringing them together as a group. Then *you* make the decision. This decision may or may not reflect your subordinates' influence.
CII	—You share the problem with your subordinates in a group meeting. In this meeting you obtain their ideas and suggestions. Then, *you* make the decision which may or may not reflect your subordinates' influence.
CII	—You share the problem with your subordinates as a group. Together you generate and evaluate alternatives and attempt to reach agreement (consensus) on a solution. Your role is much like that of chairman, coordinating the discussion, keeping it focused on the problem and making sure that the critical issues are discussed. You can provide the group with information or ideas that you have but you do not try to "press" them to adopt "your" solution and are willing to accept and implement any solution which has the support of the entire group.

scientists appear to suggest that if his modal style is participative, he is a good manager, whereas if it is not, he is a bad manager. Within such individual difference models, the variance in the manager's behavior on Monday would be treated simply as error, implicitly normally distributed with mean zero.

In this study we review the Vroom-Yetton theory of leadership in which it is this variability in a manager's behavior rather than his modal style which is the subject of the analysis (Vroom & Yetton, 1973). Their shift from a trait theory to a contingency theory is analogous to a switch from the question of which single style a manager does or should use, to the questions of which combination of styles does or should a manager use, and how does he or should he map them onto the needs of different problem situations.

To develop a normative model for the purpose of relating a manager's behavior to the demands of different situations, Vroom and Yetton distinguish five management styles and seven situational variables. The styles range from autocratic, through consultative, to group democratic decision-making (see

Table 2. Situational Variables

A. *Quality:*	Does the problem possess a quality requirement?
B. *Information:*	Do I have sufficient information to make a high quality decision?
C. *Structure:*	Is the problem structured?
D. *Acceptance:*	Is acceptance of decision by subordinates important for effective implementation?
E. *Prior proba-* *bility:*	If I were to make the decision by myself, is it reasonably certain that it would be accepted by my subordinates?
F. *Goal con-* *gruence:*	Do subordinates share the organizational goals to be attained in solving this problem?
G. *Conflict:*	Is conflict among subordinates likely in preferred solutions?

Table 1). The seven situational variables include characteristics such as the degree of problem structure and the level of conflict among subordinates (see Table 2). Vroom and Yetton argue that a profile of a particular organizational problem or occasion for decision-making on the seven situational characteristics should determine the appropriate leadership style.

Descriptively, they present evidence to show that managers do, in fact, vary their style as a function of the same seven characteristics. Thus, their normative and descriptive theories employ the same theoretical concepts but have different structures to account for different phenomena. Unlike a number of studies, Vroom and Yetton carefully distinguish between the behaviorally linked, but analytically quite separate, normative and descriptive questions of which style a manager should and would use in a particular situation.

To examine their two models of leadership behavior, this study is divided into three sections. In Section I, we examine the Vroom-Yetton normative model; in Section II, the descriptive model; and in Section III, the relationship between these two models. Each section begins with a statement of Vroom and Yetton's initial research on that topic. This study concludes with a brief discussion of plans for future research within the Vroom-Yetton paradigm.

I. THE VROOM-YETTON NORMATIVE MODEL

The traditional answer to the normative question of how a manager should act has been to prescribe participative behavior (Blake & Mouton, 1964; Likert, 1961; McGregor, 1960). However, comprehensive reviews of the

Table 3. Rules Underlying the Model

Rules to protect the quality of the decision

1. The Leader Information Rule:

   If the quality of the decision is important and the leader does not possess enough information or expertise to solve the problem by himself, then AI is eliminated from the feasible set.

2. The Goal Congruence Rule:

   If the quality of the decision is important and subordinates are not likely to pursue the organization goals in their efforts to solve this problem, then CII is eliminated from the feasible set.

3. The Unstructured Problem Rule:

   In decisions in which the quality of the decision is important, if the leader lacks the necessary information or expertise to solve the problem by himself, and if the problem is unstructured, the method of solving the problem should provide for interaction among subordinates likely to possess relevant information. Accordingly, AI, AII, and CI are eliminated from the feasible set.

Rules to protect the acceptance of the decision

4. The Acceptance Rule:

   If the acceptance of the rule by subordinates is critical to effective implementation and if it is not certain that an autocratic decision will be accepted, AI and AII are eliminated from the feasible set.

5. The Conflict Rule:

   If the acceptance of the decision is critical, an autocratic decision is not certain to be accepted and disagreement among subordinates in methods of attaining the organizational goal is likely, the methods used in solving the problem should enable those in disagreement to resolve their differences with full knowledge of the problem. Accordingly, under these conditions, AI, AII, and CI, which permit no interaction among subordinates and therefore provide no opportunity for those in conflict to resolve their differences, are eliminated from the feasible set. Their use runs the risk of leaving some of the subordinates with less than the needed commitment to the final decision.

6. The Fairness Rule:

   If the quality of the decision is unimportant, but acceptance of the decision is critical, and not certain to result from an autocratic decision, it is important that the decision process used generate the needed acceptance. The decision process used should permit the subordinates to interact with one another and negotiate over the fair method of resolving any differences with full responsibility on them for determining what is fair and equitable. Accordingly, under these circumstances, AI, AII, CI, and CII are eliminated from the feasible set.

Table 3 (cont'd)

---

7.   The Acceptance Priority Rule:

If acceptance is critical, not certain to result from an autocratic decision and if subordinates are motivated to pursue the organizational goals represented in the problem, then methods which provide equal partnership in the decision-making process can provide greater acceptance without risking decision quality. Accordingly, AI, AII, CI, and CII are eliminated from the feasible set.

---

evidence concerning the effectiveness of participation (Lowin, 1968; Vroom, 1970; Wood, 1973) reveal inconsistencies and strongly suggest the need to treat the situation as a moderator variable. Developing a contingent normative model in which the prescribed style (Table 1) is a function of seven situational variables (Table 2), Vroom and Yetton are able to explain some of these apparently inconsistent findings.

Building on the work of Maier (1963), Vroom and Yetton (1973) distinguish three components of the effectiveness of a decision. These are the *quality* of the decision, the degree of subordinates' commitment to or *acceptance* of the decision, and the *resource* cost (man hours) expended in making the decision. Their approach is essentially a cost/benefit analysis in which the cost would be the opportunity cost of holding a meeting, and the benefits would be an improved decision in a technical sense, or a more effectively implemented solution as a result of the subordinates' participation in that meeting.

To map a manager's decision-making style onto the acceptance and quality needs of the problem, Vroom and Yetton propose a model consisting of seven rules. Each rule eliminates the use of styles in particular kinds of situations on the basis of research evidence concerning their deleterious effects on either decision quality or solution acceptance. The rules in combination identify the *feasible set* of styles (which may range from one to all five of the styles in Table 1) that would satisfy the acceptance and quality needs in the situation. Four rules protect the acceptance of the final solution and three rules protect the quality of that solution (Table 3).

Now any increase in participation implies a cost in terms of the additional manpower resources it consumes. Assuming that the managerial manpower consumed by decision-making increases monotonically with an increase in participation, Vroom and Yetton define the optimal short-term managerial style as the minimum level of participation (minimum cost) which would generate a decision that would satisfy the quality and acceptance needs in the situation. This is called the minimum cost strategy.

A. Does the problem possess a quality requirement?
B. Do I have sufficient information to make a high-quality decision?
C. Is the problem structured?
D. Is acceptance of the decision by subordinates important for effective implementation?
E. If I were to make the decision by myself, am I reasonably certain that it would be accepted by my subordinates?
F. Do subordinates share the organizational goals to be attained in solving this problem?
G. Is conflict among subordinates likely in preferred solutions?

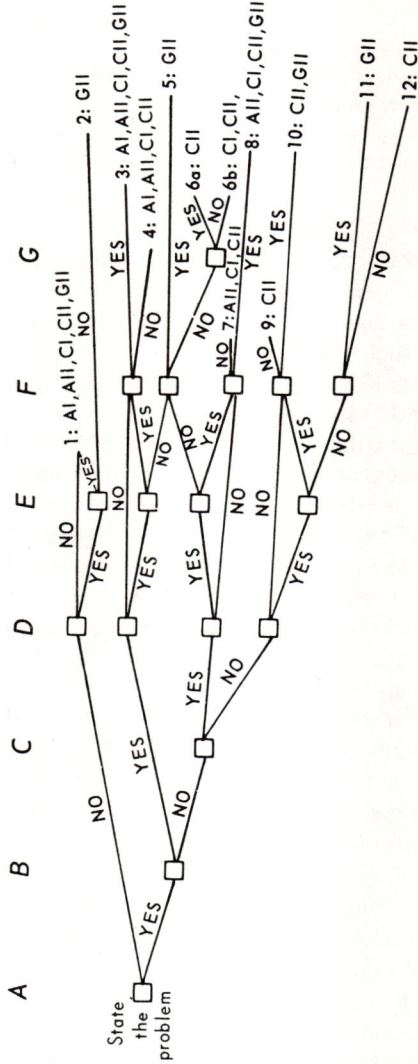

Fig. 1. Vroom-Yetton normative model.

1: AI,AII,CI,CII,GII
2: GII
3: AI,AII,CI,CII,GII
4: AI,AII,CI,CII
5: GII
6a: CII
6b: CI,CII,
7: AII,CI,CII
8: AII,CI,CII,GII
9: CII
10: CII,GII
11: GII
12: CII

State the problem

A B C D E F G

The model is presented in Figure 1 in a decision tree format. To use the tree, the manager begins at the left hand side and asks the questions along the top whenever he encounters a box. The rules are incorporated into the structure of the tree and the feasible set is identified for each terminal node on the right. This format makes visible how an error in a manager's judgment about the characteristics of the problem could have major implications for the problem's feasible set. This problem will be considered in some detail in Section III.

At the time of its initial presentation (Vroom & Yetton, 1973), the model's validity rested largely on its face validity and the fact that the rules in Table 3 are consistent with a large body of empirical evidence.

Vroom and Yetton (1973) did describe one limited investigation of the model's validity. They asked a set of managers to write a description of a problem with which they had been confronted, to code it on each problem attribute, to specify which of the five styles they had used, and to evaluate the acceptance and the quality of their solutions on a 7-point scale. These data were then used to test three hypotheses: (a) managers whose behavior fell into the feasible set for their problem would report higher decision quality and solution acceptance than those whose behavior deviated from the model; (b) managers whose behavior violated a quality rule (rules #1, 2, and 3) would report lower decision quality than those whose behavior was consistent with these rules; and (c) managers whose behavior violated an acceptance rule (rules #4, 5, 6, and 7) would report lower solution acceptance than those whose behavior was consistent with those rules.

The results were consistent with the above hypotheses but did not reach statistical significance. This failure to find significant results was attributed by Vroom and Yetton to the research design employed. Each manager reported only one problem and tended to describe a success experience reflected in limited variance on the dependent variables of solution quality and acceptance. Consequently, adequate tests of the hypotheses were not possible.

Two recent studies by Vroom and Jago (1976) and Yetton (1976b) correct the above deficiencies. Vroom and Jago asked 96 managers to describe two problems, one dealing with a decision which proved to be successful, and the other pertaining to an unsuccessful decision. Both problems were within his sphere of responsibility and had effects on at least two of his subordinates. For each problem, the manager concerned wrote it up as a case, coded it on the situational variables, reported which of the five leadership styles was closest to the one he had used, and rated the overall solution effectiveness, the decision quality and solution acceptance on a 7-point scale. A similar strategy was followed by Yetton who asked 105 managers to describe three decisions, a success, a failure, and an average solution. Instead of using a 7-point scale, Yetton used an 11-point scale. Otherwise, the two studies are similar.

The 96 managers in the Vroom and Jago study reported 181 cases covering a wide variety of situations. Of these, 94 were success experiences and 87 were failures. The 105 managers studied by Yetton reported 311 cases of which 105 were success experiences, 103 were average, and 103 were failures. Table 4 shows that behavior which is consistent with that prescribed by the model was more likely to be successful than was behavior that deviated from the model. For example, Vroom and Jago report that 68% of the 117 situations in which the manager's behavior was consistent with the model were characterized as successful by the manager responsible, whereas only 22% of the instances in which the managers' behavior deviated from the model were rated successes.

Although the data in Table 4 are supportive of the Vroom-Yetton model, it is possible that an alternative hypothesis could account for the data. One possibility is that participative methods were employed more often in successful than in unsuccessful decisions. If so, the data would be more parsimoniously explained by the traditional model, advocating the use of a participative strategy in all situations, which Vroom and Yetton (1973) rejected.

To investigate the above possibility, Vroom and Jago performed a two-way analysis of variance using a hierarchical (step down) procedure. Yetton reports a similar investigation using a step wise regression model. In step one, only the level of participation was used as a predictor of overall effectiveness. Agreement with the feasible set (behavior which is consistent with the Vroom-Yetton model) was then included in the model to account for the residual variance from the first stage.

The two studies report similar findings. Level of participation is significantly ($p < 0.01$) positively correlated with overall effectiveness, decision quality and solution acceptance (step 1). Agreement with the feasible set is significantly ($p < 0.01$) positively correlated with all three measures of performance (step 2). As such, agreement with the feasible set accounts for a significant proportion of the unexplained variance from the simple participation model. In contrast, if the order in which the variables are introduced is reversed and the level of participation is introduced second, it does not account for any of the residual variance in overall effectiveness or decision quality and only accounts for a small although significant part of the variance in solution acceptance. It should also be noted that the variance in solution acceptance independently accounted for by level of participation is not related to overall decision effectiveness and as such would, at least in the short run, result in an unnecessary expenditure of resources.

A more specific test of the Vroom-Yetton normative model would involve examining the validity of each of the rules in Table 3. It is possible that while the rules collectively contribute to performance, any specific rule may make no contribution or even be counter-productive and reduce performance. Vroom and Jago report significant differences in the predicted direction for

Table 4. Relationship between Agreement with the Feasible Set and Decision Outcomes

Agreement with feasible set	Decision outcome					
	Successful	Unsuccessful	Successful	Average	Unsuccessful	
	(Vroom & Jago, 1976)		(Yetton, 1976b)			
Yes	68%	32%	44%	36%	20%	
No	22%	78%	7%	14%	79%	

five rules (rules #1, 3, 4, 6, and 7). On rule 5, the difference is large and in the predicted direction but the small sample size was inadequate to test the hypothesis. With a larger sample, Yetton reports significant differences on rule 5, as well as on the other five rules. Neither Vroom and Jago, nor Yetton, found evidence to support rule 2—a rule that prohibits the use of the group decision process in decisions possessing a quality requirement and low goal congruence between the manager and his subordinates.

In an effort to understand why this rule was not contributing to the validity of the model, the investigators examined the relationships between decision quality and solution acceptance and rule violation. The results indicate that decisions in which rule 2 was violated were of lower quality but higher acceptance than decisions in which the rule was applicable but not violated. These two factors are tending, in these instances, to cancel each other out. This possibility was not considered by Vroom and Yetton (1973) in their initial work where they made the implicit assumption that the risk to the decision quality inherent in using a group decision style in situations of low goal congruence is greater than any gain in solution effectiveness generated by a group process. The evidence suggests that the trade off implicit in rule 2 may be less clear cut than they imply.

In all of the validation studies that have been described so far, the coding of decisions in each of the problem attributes has been carried out by the manager involved. Since the manager also reports his behavior and evaluates the effectiveness of the decision, all data pertaining to a given problem come from a single source. Yetton (1976b) has reported another investigation in which judgments of decision effectiveness were made by the managers' subordinates and this group (three reporting to each manager) also furnished judgments of problem attributes.

The use of subordinates' rather than the managers' perceptions of the state of affairs provides slightly greater support for the validity of rule 2 but does not alter materially any other results reported above. It is true that subordinates tend to rate all three measures of performance lower than do managers. However, the bias is constant and not a function of the managers' agreement with the feasible set or propensity to violate rules. The differences in performance as a function of the agreement with the feasible set or rule violations (other than rule 2) remain significant and of the same order of magnitude regardless of whose perceptions are analyzed.

The results described above bear on the concurrent rather than the predictive validity of the model in the sense that judgments about style and problem characteristics were obtained after the decision had been made and its outcome observed. Yetton also presents evidence of a predictive nature. Thirty-seven managers were asked to each describe five problems before solutions were attempted and for which the gestation period was three to six months. As such, no judgments about success or failure could be made in less than three months. The managers were also asked to make judgments as to the problems' status on each of the situational variables and to indicate which style they intended to use. Six months later, the managers were asked to rate their decisions on quality, acceptance, and overall effectiveness. In addition, they were asked to recode the problems on the seven situational attributes and to recall which style they did, in fact, employ.

When the managers' ex post perceptions are used to identify the feasible set, the results are more strongly supportive of the Vroom-Yetton model than if their ex ante perceptions of the situation are used. The explanation appears to be that managers sometimes misread the situations prior to making the decision. Either at the time of the decision or when implementing the solution, the managers realize that they misjudged the situation and correct their coding of the problem. Thus, the weaker but still significant validity evidence using their ex ante perceptions of the situations rather than their ex post perceptions could be a function of initial coding errors. For example, the manager initially believes that he has all the relevant information and consistent with the Vroom-Yetton model makes an autocratic decision. Later he realizes that the decision was based on inaccurate or incomplete data which accounts for the low effectiveness of the decision and which also reveals that he did, in fact, violate rule 1 of the Vroom-Yetton model.

The results discussed in this section are generally supportive of the validity of the Vroom-Yetton model. The relationships between overall decision effectiveness and style are consistent with those specified by the model in general and by six of the seven rules in particular. However, there are a number of instances in which inappropriate behavior as defined by the model is successful and others in which the appropriate behavior is ineffective. Vroom and Yetton (1973), Vroom and Jago (1976), and Yetton (1976b) discuss a number of factors which could account for the successful deviant behavior and unsuccessful consistent behavior. These include methodological and measurement problems such as the treatment of both the feasible set and problem attributes as dichotomous variables. However, the major factor is probably that the choice of the right style does not guarantee that it would be effectively carried through. For example, in a number of instances Yetton (1976b) found that while subordinates may have agreed with their manager that he had used a group consultative approach, they commented on their questionnaire that this meeting had been poorly run. Equally, failure to act in line with the model does not preclude a manager from acting in other ways to save a poor decision from failing. Such behaviors could lead to results which would appear to contradict the Vroom-Yetton model but which are, in fact, independent of its validity. Instead, such findings would suggest that the model was an incomplete explanation of effective managerial performance.

II. THE VROOM-YETTON DESCRIPTIVE MODEL

Just as the traditional normative models advocated a single universally appropriate style, so the traditional descriptive models describe a manager's style in terms of his modal behavior. Any variance in an individual's behavior is implicitly assumed to be small and random. A manager may occasionally employ other decision methods adjacent to his modal behavior but his repertoire is assumed to be limited.

In contrast, the Vroom-Yetton normative model presented in Section I ⸱⸱⸱plicitly assumes that a manager's repertoire is not limited but ranges from autocratic to participative. In fact, it is the pattern of this variance in a manager's behavior and not his modal style which is the focus of their normative model. Similarly, the nexus of their descriptive model is the set of rules by which a manager fits his behavior to the situation, rather than the difference between his and another manager's average behavior.

Thus, Vroom and Yetton (1973) attempt to answer questions such as whether managers do, in fact, use all five styles prescribed by their normative model and which factors in the situation influence their choice of a decision process. Two different research methods were used to investigate these questions. In one, managers were asked to recall a problem they had recently solved, to describe its characteristics in terms of the seven situational variables in Table 2, and to indicate which of the five styles from Table 1 was closest to the one they had used. The other approach involved the use of a set of standard problems. Managers were asked to indicate which decision process they would use if faced with each problem.

Vroom and Yetton began their series of investigations by asking 268 managers to recall a problem, to describe it, and to say how they had acted. Table 5 reports the correlations between the managers' behavior and the problem characteristics. Decision Quality, Solution Acceptance, Goal Congruence, are positively correlated with participation; Leader Information,

Table 5. Relationships Among Situational Characteristics and Level of Subordinates' Participation

	A	B	C	D	E	F	G
A. Quality	1.00						
B. Information	−.12	1.00					
C. Structure	−.10	.08	1.00				
D. Acceptance	.17	−.04	−.07	1.00			
E. Prior Probability	−.20	.11	.11	−.13	1.00		
F. Goal Congruence	.02	.01	.08	.07	.12	1.00	
G. Conflict	.12	.03	.09	.06	−.16	−.12	1.00
Participation	.12	−.36	−.15	.24	−.23	.21	.08

Vroom & Yetton, 1973, pp. 82.

Problem Structure, and Prior Probability of Acceptance are negatively correlated with participation; and Conflict has no main effect on behavior. A simple linear multiple regression model of their main effects has an $r = 0.58$ and accounts for 33.4% of the variance.

Interpretation of these results is confounded by the intercorrelations among the situational variables shown in Table 5. The analysis is further complicated by the self-selected nature of the problems. Both of these are controlled for in the second research method where a set of 30 standardized problems was developed. Problems reported by the managers in studies similar to the one described above were selected and where necessary rewritten to conform to a multifactorial experimental design in which the seven situational characteristics are varied in a manner which permits nonconfounded estimates of their effects. Using this experimental design, it is possible to compare the relative importance of individual and situational factors as determinants of decision behavior, as well as to investigate the effect of each situational variable.

Five hundred and fifty-one managers were asked to read the 30 cases in the problem set and indicate which decision process they would use. A two-way analysis of variance showed that both individual and situational differences have main effects on a manager's choice of a decision process. Individual differences accounted for 8.5% of the variance and situational factors for 29.2%. Thus, problem characteristics accounted for three times as much as of the variance as did individual differences. These findings confirm the importance of the intra-individual variance in decision-making behavior and the inadequacy of any model of decision-making based purely on individual differences.

As well as permitting a comparative analysis of the influence of individual and situational factors, this research design distinguishes between the causal and spurious main effects reported in Table 5. Vroom and Yetton report significant main effects of Decision Quality and Problem Structure and interaction effects of Information × Goal Congruence, Solution Acceptance × Prior Probability of Acceptance, and Acceptance × Goal Gongruence × Conflict. A model incorporating these terms accounts for over 60% of the situationally determined variance in a variety of different populations. With participation measured on a 10-unit scale, the beta weights in the regression model range from −1.5 for Problem Structure to 2.3 for the interaction between Acceptance, Goal Congruence, and Conflict. Thus, changes in a problem's characteristic have a major influence on the decision process the typical manager would choose.

This model was cross-validated against the data on self-selected problems from the other study. Some shrinkage was obtained but the results confirm the general pattern of relationships specified by this model. Certainly, the evidence overwhelmingly supports the thesis of problem characteristics as determinants of leadership style.

In the above analysis, a linear model of seven situational variables accounts for a substantial proportion of the situational variance. In a similar way, part of the variance accounted for by individual as a nominal variable may be explained by differences such as functional responsibilities or level in the organizational authority structure. For example, Yetton (1976a) reports that prison governors use group decision-making processes less often on the cases in the problem set than do managers in the U.K. private sector or administrators in the Health Service. Such differences could be the result of selection procedures used to fill this position and/or the socialization of individuals in their jobs.

Whatever inter-organizational differences exist, it has always been accepted that within organizations more participative behavior is found near the top than at lower levels in the management structure. In contrast, Vroom and Yetton (1973) and Jago and Vroom (1975) report that managers perceive others above them to be more autocratic than themselves. Jago and Vroom (1977) show that the relationship between participation and organizational level is dependent on the type of analysis performed. They report that a between-level comparison of managers' behavior on the standard cases shows a positive correlation between level and participation. In contrast, a within-level comparison of a manager's behavior on the standard cases and his predictions of his superior's behavior on the same cases reveals a negative correlation between level and participation. Jago and Vroom discuss a number of factors which might account for these contradictory findings and conclude that participation typically increases with hierarchical level.

So far in this section we have only attempted to account for either problem or person main effects on decision behavior, the former in terms of specific problem characteristics such as the degree of problem structure, and the latter in terms of organizational identity. It will be recalled that problem differences accounted for 29.2% of the variance in behavior on the problem set and individual differences for 8.5%. What about the 63.3% of the variance which hitherto remains unaccounted for?

Obviously, part of this residual variance is a function of the experimental/analytic procedures. In the studies reviewed, participation is measured as a discrete variable while the variance and regression models used in the analysis assume it to be a continuous variable. Thus, some part of the 63.3% is likely to be measurement error on the dependent variable. Measurement errors on the situational variables which are also probably continuous rather than dichotomous, specification errors in the models, and the fact that managers' heuristics are not likely to be linear, are all additional factors which could account for more of the residual variance.

Although the above considerations are technically important, they contribute little to our understanding of decision behavior. More important, therefore, is the possibility that interactions between individual and situational factors may explain a significant part of this 63.3% variance in managers' behavior. Bowers (1973), in his critique of the situational and personality models of behavior, argues for interactional models. He presents data which suggests the interaction term typically accounts for more variance than does either of the two main effects. Yetton (1972), in passing, reports an interaction between individual differences and the level of conflict as a determinant of the decision method used. Unfortunately, with this minor exception, there are no studies of individual and situational interactions within the Vroom-Yetton paradigm.

The picture that begins to emerge from the studies discussed in this section is of an increasingly complex descriptive model of decision making. Whereas once there were only participative or autocratic managers, we now find that it makes as much sense to talk about participative and autocratic problems. Furthermore, there is likely to be interaction between individual and situational factors. Certainly, the studies have established the importance of situational factors as determinants of the level of subordinates' participation in decision making.

III. NORMATIVE VERSUS DESCRIPTIVE BEHAVIOR

The normative model presented in Section I says how a manager should act. The descriptive model in Section II attempts to explain how he does act. Of course, if managers acted in the way prescribed by the normative model, it would also be a descriptive model of their behavior. This would suggest asking how good the normative model would be as a descriptive model of managers' decision-making. At a minimum, such an analysis would reveal the behavioral changes which would follow if the normative model were adopted.

This comparative investigation was carried out using the data from the descriptive studies of recalled and standard problems. Vroom and Yetton (1973) report that the typical manager agrees with the most autocratic style in the feasible set as defined by the normative model approximately 40% of the time, and with the feasible set itself in over 60% of the situations. So, about one-third of the time, a manager's behavior violates at least one of the seven rules of the model.

The different rules are not violated with similar frequencies. The four rules designed to protect the solution acceptance are subject to higher rates of violation than are the three rules protecting the solution quality. The information rule (Rule 1) has the lowest violation rate of 3% and the fairness rule (Rule 6) the highest of almost 75%. If the two sets of rules have approximately equal validity, these findings would suggest that greater costs are likely to be incurred by the typical manager through ineffective implementation of decision rather than through adopting technically inadequate solutions.

To make any of the above comparisons between the model's and managers' behavior, it is necessary to identify each problem's status on the seven situational dimensions. Therefore, some differences between the model's and managers' behavior could be a function not of the rules governing their selection of a decision method but of the problem definitions they use. Against this, Vroom and Yetton (1973) and Yetton (1975) report that errors in judgments about the situational characteristics are fairly low. Yetton reports that these error rates vary from 0% for Quality to 13% for Problem Structure.

However, although these errors are small, they are importantly related to deviations in managers' behavior from the model. Vroom and Yetton (1973) and Yetton (1976b) report that if a manager's behavior agrees with the model, the probability is over 0.9 that he codes the problem accurately. In contrast, if his behavior violates the model, the probability is about 0.5 that he also misjudges the situation. Yetton (1975) notes that particularly on problems involving only questions of fairness and not technical issues, managers have a strong tendency to misread the situation, believe they can come up with a solution acceptable to their subordinates, and use an inappropriate autocratic style.

If anything, the above studies underestimate the importance of perceptual errors about the situation and the use of an inappropriate style. The results discussed refer to judgments made about the situation after the decision has been made or about written cases in which ambiguity had been minimized. Yetton (1976b) shows that if judgments about the situation are obtained before a decision is attempted, errors are higher and very frequently associated with the use of an inappropriate style. While lack of knowledge or misjudgments about the problem situation are infrequent, they could be a major cause of deviations from the model in managers' behavior.

FUTURE RESEARCH

To summarize an already highly concentrated overview would seem inappropriate. Instead, the intent here is the look to the future. Indeed, one of the questions to be asked of any new theory is the extent to which it generates new hypotheses about the world. Not only does the Vroom-Yetton theory reviewed here account for some of the existing inconsistencies between individual difference models and research findings, it also suggests a whole new range of questions to ask.

A simple extension of the existing model would involve the search for additional situational variables. A more substantial issue is the structure of the descriptive model. The normative model is non-linear, whereas the descriptive model is a simple linear function of situational main effects and interaction terms. As such, it is an "as if" model. A major revision is under way, in which a non-linear descriptive model is being investigated. Another logical step, as noted in Section II, would be the study of individual/situation interactions and their effect on the decision method employed.

Research is also being planned relevant to "dynamic" models of decision-making. The existing normative and descriptive models consider a problem as a discrete independent event in the sequence of such decisions. The basic questions to be asked in future research are whether behavior on decision K does and/or should effect the decision method chosen for problem K + 1. In particular, in what way does and/or should a manager's behavior influence the situational characteristics of subsequent problems?

In addition to these two major studies, a sequence of investigations is planned to further establish the predictive validity of the existing models. These studies involve the collection of data on behavior and performance in the work situation as opposed to hypothetical problem situations. Such studies are needed to throw light on the questions Argyris (1976) raises about "espoused" and "in use" models of managers' behavior.

It would appear that the Vroom-Yetton paradigm not only accounts for some existing inconsistencies between theory and data but is also fruitful in identifying a number of phenomena to investigate. If the studies mentioned above prove successful, their outcome will undoubtedly be a very much more complex theory about the social structure of decision-making, each part of which would only account for a small proportion of the variance in a manager's decision behavior.

REFERENCES

Argyris, C. Theories of action that inhibit individual learning. *American Psychologist*, 1976, **31**, 638–654.

Blake, R., & Mouton, J. *The managerial grid*. Houston: Gulf, 1964.

Bowers, K. S. Situationalism in psychology: An analysis and a critique. *Psychological Review*, 1973, **80**, 307–316.

Jago, A. G., & Vroom, V. H. Perception of leadership style: Superior and subordinates descriptions of decision making behavior. In J. G. Hunt & L. Larson (Eds.), *Leadership frontiers*. Kent, Ohio: Kent State University Press, 1975.

Jago, A. G., & Vroom, V. H. Hierarchial level and leadership style. *Organizational Behavior and Human Performance*, 1977, **17**, in press.

Likert, R. *New patterns of management*. New York: McGraw-Hill, 1961.

Lowin, A. Participative decision making: A model, literature critique and prescriptions for research. *Organizational Behavior and Human Performance*, 1968, 3 440–458.

Maier, N. R. F. *Problem-solving discussions and conferences: Leadership methods and skills*. New York: McGraw-Hill, 1963.

McGregor, D. *The human side of enterprise*. New York: McGraw-Hill, 1960.

Vroom, V. H. Industrial social psychology. In G. Lindzey & E. Aronson (Eds.), *Handbook of social psychology*. Reading, Mass.: Rand McNally, 1970.

Vroom, V. H., & Jago, A. G. *On the validity of the Vroom-Yetton leadership model*. ONR Technical Report #9, School of Organization and Management, Yale University, 1976.

Vroom, V. H., & Yetton, P. W. *Leadership and decision-making*. Pittsburgh: University of Pittsburgh Press, 1973.

Wood, M. J. Power relationships and group decision making in organizations. *Psychological Bulletin*, 1973, **79**, 280–293.

Yetton, P. W. *Participation and leadership style: A descriptive model of a manager's choice of a decision process*. Unpublished dissertation, Carnegie-Mellon University, 1972.

Yetton, P. W. *A manager's perception of the situation and the Vroom-Yetton model*. Technical Report No. 3, Manchester Business School, 1975.

Yetton, P. W. *Comparative study of prison governors', health service officers' and private sector managers' leadership style*. Working paper, 1976. (a)

Yetton, P. W. *Studies on the validity of the Vroom-Yetton leadership model*. Working paper, 1976. (b)

TOWARDS AN ORGANIZATIONAL CONTROL AND POWER THEORY OF LEADERSHIP

Richard J. Butler
University of Bradford
Yorkshire, U.K.

What makes a great leader? Organizational leadership theories have generally been characterized by two features. First is the search for the "one best way," defined as the style that produces the most productive, efficient, or happiest group regardless of other variables that might impinge in a given situation. The best style recommended frequently has an ideological stance extolling the virtue of democracy variously described as participative management, Theory Y, System 4 or employee centered management (for example, McGregor 1960, Likert 1961). Little or only implicit mention is made of situational features such as task structure, personal relationships in the group, or of the technology.

The second feature of organizational leadership theories has been the neglect of the power of the leader and the organizational context within which he has to operate. Yet organizations have authority structures in which formally appointed supervisors and managers have differing degrees of control over rewards and punishments.

This study sets out to develop a model of organizational leadership that takes account of task and situational variables and how these relate to the organizational structure within which the leader operates. Leadership is seen as a process in which the leader has certain choices to make concerning his style and manipulation of situational variables, but these choices are, in fact, partly constrained by structure. In particular, the model draws upon ideas from the contingency theory of leadership (Fiedler, 1967) and from a study of organizational inter-role power carried out by the author (Butler, 1976).

THE CONTINGENCY APPROACH TO LEADERSHIP THEORY

The trend in organization theory towards contingency theory illustrates the move away from the search for the one best way of organizing, whether in the search for the ideal span of control, the best leadership style, or the most efficient organization structure. The starting point for the contingency theorists is usually the lack of consistent relationships between variables associated with a cherished theory, for instance, that span of control varied with the kind of organizational technology (Woodward, 1965) or that the changing technological environment of electronics firms affected organizational structure (Burns & Stalker, 1962).

Similarly, the contingency approach in leadership theory follows from lack of consistent evidence as to the best leadership style where style refers to behavior exhibited by the leader towards the subordinates. The most comprehensive and tested contingency approach is that of Fiedler (1967) who noted the lack of a consistent correlation between employee centered leadership style and group performance across different studies.

This theory of leadership is an attempt to define the situations under which employee and task centered leadership is effective. The situation is summed up by the notion of a leader favorability scale which must be understood in terms of three constituent situational variables. The variable having the greatest effect upon situation favorability is leader/member relations, which means the liking of group members for the leader and is considered to have the greatest effect upon favorability; the next strongest is task structure and finally power position.

Replication across many situations usually shows that the correlation between employee centered leadership and group performance is positive and high when the leader member relations are good, the task unstructured, and position power weak. However, the correlation is also positive and nearly as high when the leader member relations are poor but the task structured and the leader position power strong. In other words, if the leader is employee centered the best situation is for him to be liked by the group, and then he does not have to worry about power or structuring the task. But a lack of liking can be made up for by a structured task and high position power and the leader can still maintain an employee centered leadership style.

The above two situations are of intermediate favorability. The most favorable situation for the leader is to have good leader member relations (high liking), a structured task, and high position power. Then the leader should use a task centered style (non-employee centered) for high group performance. The other extreme is the least favorable situation of poor relations, unstructured task, and low power. Here the correlation is also negative between employee centered leadership and group performance.

It is possible to see two strategies for improving group performance. First, leadership style may be changed to fit a particular combination of situational variables or style may be seen as constant and the situation adapted to a person's style. The innovation of this theory was to introduce the notion that leaders actually exist within a situation that imposed constraints.

Some limitations are evident in this approach to a contingency theory of leadership. First, the dependent variable is a correlation coefficient between employee centered leadership style and group performance; there is nothing to say what the level of group performance is. It is, for example, possible to have a high positive *correlation* between employee centered leadership and group performance with low performance. Second, the concept of power has not been elaborated sufficiently well. Is power unidimensional and might leader/member relationships be seen as a dimension of power? Another limitation concerns the ability to manipulate the situational variables. The "strongest" variable, leader-member relations, would seem to be the most difficult to control; how do you get the led to like the leader? If we move to the "weaker" task structure and power variables, these would seem easier to change. For example, tasks in organizations can be structured by techniques of bureaucratization or of work study and industrial engineering. Finally, there is no relationship between the situational variables and the wider organizational structure. Is not organizational structure likely to set constraints upon the degree to which task structure or position power can be manipulated?

These four limitations do not apply simply to Fiedler's theory; rather, this theory has been selected for discussion as representing a most promising current approach to leadership. The model developed below suggests ways in which these limitations may be overcome and associated suggestions for further research. In particular, the emphasis is upon producing a model that can take into account the leader's situation and the degree of control over that situation in order to produce effective groups.

PRODUCTIVITY AND THE LEADER SITUATION

Group productivity and effectiveness are notoriously difficult to measure. To relate leadership style and situation to group output must involve some notion of what is expected from a group. Furthermore, it is not only formally appointed leaders who have expectations of group output. Others in an organization can rely upon a group for a particular activity or service. Butler (1976) investigated the functional satisfaction of research engineers as users of complex equipment, such as computers or wind tunnels, with the service provided by support people who had to operate and maintain the equipment, and certain situational variables.

Functional satisfaction may be seen as an effectiveness or productivity measure, although only in this case measured through the eyes of one observer, the user of the equipment. It was operationalized through questionnaire items comparing, for example, the standard of service to previously used similar services. Of relevance to this discussion, the situational variables used were formal power, informal power, and specificity of evaluation of output of the technology.

Power was operationalized using the French and Raven (1959) five bases of power, i.e., reward, expert, coercive, referent, and legitimate power. An overall power score was obtained and was found to give a correlation of .21 ($p < .05$) with functional satisfaction obtained from a sample of 89 research engineers doing a variety of work.

Although treating power as a unidimensional concept has the merit of simplicity, the French and Raven conceptual schema provides a multi-dimensional schema for the operationalization of power. Butler found that power could reasonably be treated as a two dimensional concept corresponding to the notion of formal and informal power. Formal power is represented by items having to do with formal rewards and punishments that the organization provides as a power base to leaders and may be compared with Fiedler's situational variable of position power. Informal power is based upon the use of information, expertise and friendship patterns, and was found to be slightly more important for influencing support people in this sample than formal power, as shown by a slightly higher correlation with functional satisfaction. This dimension of power could be compared with Fiedler's leader liking variable which emphasizes affective relationships.

Although Butler found that the two kinds of power were found to be positively related to functional satisfaction, it was specificity of evaluation of the technology that was found to have the greatest influence over functional satisfaction as shown by a .39 correlation coefficient. Thus, if the equipment's output could be easily measured against precise standards of performance it seems to be easier for the user to obtain satisfactory performance from the support person. Specificity of evaluation of output, it is suggested, can be compared to Fiedler's situation variable of task structure.

Exactly why this is so cannot be explained using any existing theory. All we can go on is interview data collected at the time of the study. For example, engineers who relied upon computer programmers were more able to exert pressure upon the programmer when they could assess whether the job had been done correctly. This was easier on those programs when it was more immediately apparent when a mistake had been made.

More generally, high specificity of evaluation is likely to be related to routinization of procedures, that is, when jobs can be broken down into specific tasks each of which has an easily evaluated conclusion. Crozier (1964), in his study of maintenance engineers in the French tobacco industry, found that these engineers managed to keep their power position through prevention of routinization of their activities. Similarly, Goldner (1970) has shown how an industrial relations department managed to gain and keep a power position through their ability to manage difficult and complex industrial relations situations. Hickson, Hinings, Lee, Schneck, and Pennings (1971) and Hinnings, Hickson, Pennings, and Schneck (1974) have shown how organizational sub-units that can cope with organizational uncertaintities came to increase their power. It seems that the situational variable of specificity of evaluation could be considered as another dimension of leader power. If the leader succeeds in specifying and routinizing tasks, he will increase his power over his subordinates. The question addressed below is how much room to maneuver does a leader have to increase his power.

THE LEADER SITUATION AND ORGANIZATION STRUCTURE

The study of the functional satisfaction of the research engineers reported above concentrates upon the situational variables of leaders and not on the problem of style. We can see that a leader has certain situational variables which are, in a sense, at "his disposal"—they are resources that can be used to help group productivity. Similarities have been suggested between Fiedler's variables of leader liking, task structure, and position power to the variables of informal power, specificity of evaluation, and formal power.

The question that now arises is how does a leader get these resources and how can be increase what he already has? This question has an obvious connection to the two possible strategies that might be used to improve group performance. If there are ready possibilities for a leader to increase his scores on situational variables, then he can do this and not bother with changing style.

An indication of the kind of relationships that might be sought comes from the study on the functional satisfaction of equipment users with the service of support people described above (Butler, 1976). The workflow rigidity between the technology user and the equipment was measured. When there was high workflow rigidity, the users' work would stop quickly if the equipment stopped. Workflow rigidity was found to be negatively correlated with informal power ($r = -.22$). This suggests that in situations of low workflow rigidity the user has time to foster the kinds of relationships necessary to develop informal power. The way in which the process appeared to work, from interview data, was that research engineers working on projects that allowed flexibility of time scheduling would be more able to indulge in conversations, to have breaks or lunch with the service person. This data is impressionistic and unsystematic but does suggest that it should be possible to more thoroughly explicate the conditions under which informal power could be developed. For instance, the layout of buildings could be important; buildings that allow informal contacts would encourage informal power relationships to develop if it is necessary.

The concept of workflow rigidity was used by Hickson, Pugh, and Pheysey (1969) in their study of the impact of technology upon organization structure. At an organizational level of analysis, high workflow rigidity exists when there is a lack of "buffering" between individual workflow segments so that a stoppage in one place means a rapid stopping of all production. Workflow rigidity at an individual level of analysis has been suggested by Butler (1976) as an antecedent of informal power, but we could also expect that there might be a relationship between workflow rigidity at an individual and an organizational level of analysis.

More generally, we could expect that the leader situational variables are related to the organization structure within which the group operates. Structure will provide both opportunities and constraints for the leader, these opportunities and constraints coming from the impact of organization structure upon the leader situation.

Pugh, Hickson, Hinings, and Turner (1968) found three dimensions of organization structure: structuring of activities, concentration of authority, and line control of workflow. Structuring of activities means to lay down written procedures and standards about how to do the job when the emphasis is upon specifying and evaluating activities. High concentration of authority means that decisions are made at the top of the organization and passed down in the form of commands for implementation. The structural dimension of line control of workflow would be one in which the people doing the work control their own methods and pace of work. Typically, this situation would be found in organizations with a high proportion of professional or craft work.

These structural dimensions may be seen as methods of controlling an organization with each dimension suggesting a dominant control system. An organizational control system expressed in these structural terms will involve people influencing others to do things. Therefore, a particular kind of control system will manifest itself at an inter-role level in terms of the kinds of power processes that can be used by individuals. As already elaborated above, the bases of a person's power to get another to do things are resources that are available to him; these resources will be related to resources provided by the organizational control system.

Here, it is only possible to suggest the kinds of relationships shown in Figure 1 that might exist between dimensions of organizational structure and bases of power at the inter-role level. An organization in which structuring of activities is the predominant control method will lay down procedures and instructions for tasks. Part of the structuring would be technology with outputs that can be easily evaluated. Structuring of activities would work through specificity of evaluation of output and affect the technology user's ability to control the support person. This is the implication of the .34 correlation found by Pugh et al. (1968) in their sample between structuring of activities and workflow integration, their overall technology scale, an important constituent of which is specificity of evaluation of output. The structural dimension of line control of workflow would be related to the use of expert power. An organization in which the work is controlled by the line workers will tend to develop the bases of power at an inter-role level inherent in the expert power dimension. The most problematic of the suggested relationships between structural dimensions and inter-role power dimensions is that between concentration of authority and formal power. The assumption here is that an organizational control system based on formal authority would tend to emphasize the use of impersonal rewards and punishments at an inter-role level of analysis.

The data from the study of the research engineers and support people (Butler, 1976) and discussion suggest a complex inter-relationship, as shown in Figure 1, between variables of inter-role control and power, technology, and organizational control systems. Not all these relationships have been directly supported by data from Butler's study. But an important line of further research is indicated that would try to relate organizational control systems to the method of power activation and technology of an organization.

From the point of view of developing leadership theory, such a perspective should help us to determine which situational variable a leader should attempt to change. It should also help us to know whether, in fact, he should be changing his leadership style. As Child (1972) has pointed out, a correlation of less than one between two variables means that there is a degree of choice; a score on one does not automatically mean a score on another.

Survey data in correlational form does not tell us what level a variable needs to be for optimum performance but simply alerts us to relationships and choices. A contingency theory to be useful has to be a decision model; from it we can decide what the situational variables or the leadership style should be for high performance. We need also to understand how leaders in organizations can learn to develop their skills in changing variables, perhaps through better use of information as suggested by Randell (1976).

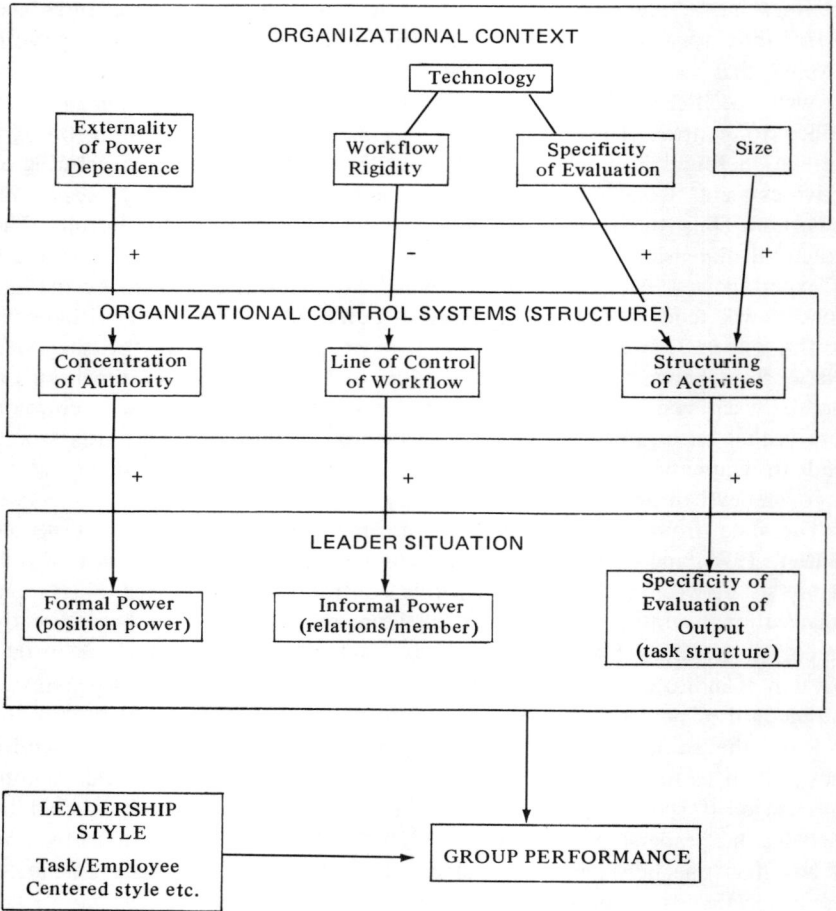

Fig. 1. Organizational control and leadership or group performance.

The model in Figure 1 could be used to tell us where the choices can be made. The procedure would work like this. If the leader's group is seen to be operating inefficiently, the situational variables he operates under should be measured. It might be found, for instance, that he is low on formal and informal power but high on structuring of activities. Examination of the organization structure might show a highly bureaucratic situation in which structuring of activities is high but concentration of authority and line control of workflow low. Under these circumstances it might be inappropriate to attempt to change the leader's situational variables. He is already high on task structure but the structure does not enable him to develop formal or informal power. The only possibility, then, is to change his style of leadership.

It is possible to think of other variable combinations but the essential point is to sensitize group leaders and trainers to the constraints imposed by the wider organization upon the possibilities of changing. This shows the necessity in leadership theory, as indeed in all theories, to proceed using both laboratory and field studies. The greater internal validity of laboratory studies is frequently at the expense of a wider perspective obtainable from field studies.

THE IMPACT OF ORGANIZATIONAL CONTEXT

It has frequently been observed that organization structure is a reflection also of the environment or context within which the organization operates. In particular, the Aston studies (Pugh et al., 1968) have shown that an organization may be seen as operating within certain contextual variables, the main ones identified being dependence upon other organizations, technology, and size. There was found to be a positive correlation between size and structuring of activities, dependence and concentration of authority, as shown in Figure 1. The relationship between the two technology variables of workflow rigidity and specificity of output evaluation and structural characteristics is less clear cut. There is suggested a positive correlation between specificity of evaluation and structuring of activities. Also indicated is a negative relationship between workflow rigidity and line control of workflow; an organization whose basic technology is highly integrated (i.e., line flow production) would allow little scope for professional control of the work flow. This argument simple transfers the relationship between informal power and workflow rigidity from an individual and group level to an organizational level of analysis.

More recently, Butler, Hickson, Wilson, and Axelsson (1976) and Hickson, Butler, Axelsson, and Wilson (1976) have indicated how the internal power processes of an organization would be affected by the internal/external power balance; power is external when it resides in one or more outside organizations. Drawing upon two cases, one an electricity board with high externality of power, and the other a university with comparatively high internality of power, it is shown how externality of power leads to small and routine decisions made centrally within the organization. The similarity between high externality of power and dependence can be seen; as a contextual variable it would give rise to concentration of authority and at the group level formal power processes. The electricity board (the paralytic organization) is contrasted to the university (the politicking organization) where the power processes are much more diffused. The leadership processes in the university would be quite different, if indeed one can talk about leadership in this setting. The main power base would be informal and concentration of authority low. Department heads have to develop close working relationships with junior staff who, for academic decisions, are treated more as colleagues than subordinates. In the electricity board we find much greater emphasis upon formal power processes and structuring of activities.

CONCLUSION

To revert to the initial question, what, then, does make a leader great? The answer suggested by this study is that leaders are overwhelmingly made by the organization within which they have to operate. The organization, in turn, is greatly influenced by the context within which it operates.

But the leader does have some choice. In order to increase his power he must assess his situation in relation to the organization structure within which he operates. An overwhelmingly strong organizational control system of one kind should tell him that he has to use that as his base of power. Thus, if his organization is a professional one with high line control of workflow, his power base should be an informal one using expertise and collegial relationships to achieve good group performance.

It has been suggested that power and its different dimensions can be a useful concept for examination of leader processes and has been much neglected up to now in leadership theories. Power has not been suggested in any Machiavellian sense of the word but simply as the kinds of resources that a leader has available to him. We have also seen that specificity of evaluation of output can be regarded as a dimension of the power process.

It has been argued that in order to understand leadership processes in organizations we must take into account the organizational structure and context. The model presented in Figure 1 presents what should be regarded as a number of tentative hypotheses, but the important point is that leadership research must take into account these wider aspects. In order to improve leadership practices, there needs to be an appreciation of where choices can be made and within what degree of freedom.

Finally, although it has been emphasized here that leaders are victims of their situation, we must always remember that our theories are never so good as not to allow room for individual characteristics to play their part.

REFERENCES

Burns, T., & Stalker, G. M. *The management of innovation.* London: Tavistock, 1961.

Butler, R. J. *Inter-role power, technology and control in organizations.* Working paper, University of Bradford Management Centre, Bradford, U.K., 1976.

Butler, R. J., Hickson, D. J., Wilson, D. C., & Axelsson, R. *The external/internal balance of power and organizational paralysis.* Paper presented at European Group for Organizational Studies Conference on the Organization and its Environment, Paris, February, 1976.

Child, J. Organizational structure, environment and performance: The role of strategic choice. *Sociology*, 1972, **6**, 1–22.

Crozier, M. *The bureaucratic phenomenon.* London: Tavistock, 1964.

Fiedler, F. E. *A theory of leadership effectiveness.* New York: McGraw-Hill, 1967.

French, J. R. P., & Raven, B. The bases of social power. In D. Cartwright (Ed.), *Studies in social power.* Ann Arbor: Research Center for Group Dynamics Institute for Social Research, University of Michigan, 1959.

Goldner, F. H. The division of labor: Process and power. In M. N. Zald (Ed.), *Power in organizations.* Nashville: Vanderbilt University Press, 1970.

Hickson, D. J., Butler, R. J., Axelsson, R., & Wilson, D. C. *Decisive coalitions.* Paper presented at NATO Conference on Co-ordination and Control of Groups and Organizational Performance, Munich, July, 1976.

Hickson, D. J., Hinings, C. R., Lee, C. A., Schneck, R. E., & Pennings, J. M. A strategic contingencies theory of intra-organizational power. *Administrative Science Quarterly*, 1971, **6**, 216–229.

Hickson, D. J., Pugh, D. S., & Pheysey, D. C. Operations technology and organization structure: An empirical reappraisal. *Administrative Science Quarterly*, 1969, **14**, 378–397.

Hinings, C. R., Hickson, D. J., Pennings, J. M., & Schneck, R. E. Structural conditions of intraorganizational power. *Administrative Science Quarterly*, 1974, **19**, 22–43.

Likert, R. *New patterns of management.* N.Y.: McGraw-Hill, 1961.

McGregor, D. *The human side of enterprise.* N.Y.: McGraw-Hill, 1960.

Pugh, D. S., Hickson, D. J., Hinings, C. R., & Turner, C. Dimensions of organization structure. *Administrative Science Quarterly*, 1968, **13**, 65–105.

Randell, G. A. *A management skills approach to developing people and organizations at work.* Paper presented at NATO Conference on

Co-ordination and Control of Groups and Organizational Performance, Munich, July, 1976.

Woodward, J. *Industrial organization: Theory and practice.* N.Y.: Oxford University Press, 1965.

TOWARDS A THEORY OF THE LEADERSHIP PROCESS

Ralph Katz
Sloan School of Management,
M.I.T.

The current contingency approaches to the study of leadership stress the need to relate various leadership activities and/or characteristics with various kinds of groups, tasks, and environmental conditions (Stogdill, 1974; Vroom, 1976). The efficacy of any specific leadership activity or quality, therefore, is dependent upon the particular context. Those individuals who possess the most suitable combination of skills necessary for meeting the needs and demands that have surfaced in a given setting will be the most effective leaders. They become effective not because they are intelligent, strong, considerate, or structuring, for example, but because intelligence, strength, consideration, and structuring are essential for satisfying the requirements and expectations occurring within the overall situation.

Furthermore, it seems reasonable that as conditions change, the actions or characteristics required of the leadership role might also shift. Those leaders who can recognize changing conditions and are able to meet any new leadership requirements will most likely maintain their effectiveness. Otherwise, pressures will develop for them either to be replaced by someone who can or for someone else to perform the necessary functions informally.

The effectiveness of leadership over time, therefore, is dependent upon the stability of the situation as well as the adaptability of the other group members.

Task Influence

In trying to increase our understanding of the linkages between situational variables and the effectiveness of different leadership dimensions, much of the recent work has focused on the nature of the assigned tasks, although other moderating variables have included job level, external pressures, group size, high-order needs, etc. (see Kerr, Schriesheim, Murphy, & Stogdill, 1974). House (1971), in his path-goal theory of leadership, hypothesizes that task complexity significantly influences the relationships between leadership style and performance and satisfaction. More specifically, House contends that with considerable task complexity or challenge, individuals are more likely to derive their satisfaction and motivation from the task itself. As a result, considerate leadership will be unrelated to effectiveness principally because it is perceived as redundant and unnecessary. On the other hand, initiating-structure will be seen as more facilitative of the path-goals and will be directly related to satisfaction and performance. Conversely, when the task is fairly routine and structured, considerate leadership will help moderate task frustration and will be significantly related to the dependent variables. Viewed as excessive control under these circumstances, initiating-structure will be uncorrelated with performance and negatively correlated with satisfaction.

In general, House (1971), Dessler (1973), and House and Dessler (1974) have presented evidence that supports the major tenets of the path-goal theory. Other researchers, however, have reported contradictory results. Stinson and Johnson (1975), for example, discovered that initiating-structure and satisfaction were more positively correlated under conditions of high task structure and repetitiveness rather than the reverse. Moreover, Downey, Sheridan, and Slocum (1975) found that considerate leadership was most related to job satisfaction while initiating-structure was most related to perceptions of performance, regardless of task structure.

Despite the contradictory findings among these studies, there seems to be general agreement with the notion that the function of leadership is to supplement the detracting deficiencies that are part of most job settings. As a result, a leader will be effective to the degree to which he can provide the support, feedback, definitions, constraints, pressures, and risks that are missing, yet are essential for enhancing task performance.

The multiple-linkage model presented by Yukl (1971) also supports this idea with its formulation that leadership affects overall performance primarily by influencing (1) subordinate task motivation, (2) subordinate task skills, and (3) the task-role organization. The influence of leadership, therefore, depends on how successfully the overall task situation has provided for other sources of motivation and skills or has established complete and well-defined task roles. Yukl (1971) hypothesizes that considerate leadership can only help determine subordinate motivation while initiating-structure can help determine all three intermediate variables. House (1971) has shown, for example, that when task-roles become highly ambiguous, initiating structure is more positively correlated with satisfaction than under parallel conditions of less ambiguity.

The Leader and His Group

Given this framework, the next step is to specify those pressures and demands that confront subordinates in various social and task environments and which moderate the influence of different leadership behaviors during the execution process. In carrying out their assigned tasks, most employees belong to a fixed, organized group. And ever since the Hawthorne experiments, it has been generally acknowledged that the conditions and interactions within a group can exert powerful pressures and stresses upon the individual members, such that their behaviors, motivations, and attitudes are significantly affected. Furthermore, because of the imperfect nature of people as well as organizations and their designs, tensions and conflicts invariably emerge from the interactions required of the group members. The extent to which such frictions occur should affect not only the effectiveness of the group process but also the relevance of different leadership behaviors.

Unfortunately, none of the studies pertaining to leadership style to date has focused on the complex set of interrelationships transpiring among all of the group members. Although the dependency of leadership style on the nature of the group has been recognized, investigations of this connection have not been pursued. Close to 30 years ago, Gibb (1947) suggested that whether a particular individual fits the leadership role is more contingent on the group and its members than upon the personality of the individual. In addition, Hemphill (1955) concluded that in order for leadership to be effective, it must respond to the specific demands and requirements imposed by the nature of the group that is being led.

During its existence, each group contends with its own task-related as well as socio-emotional problems. Interpersonal conflicts that occur between particular group members create social and psychological tensions that must be reduced. In addition, individuals may experience stress and pressure from problems and conflicts that are more task-related. For a whole host of reasons, certain individuals may not be working well together as part of the same group. For example, their individual work objectives, goals, or levels of commitment may be different, their relative degrees of status or power may be inhibiting, or the kinds of task roles that each tries to assume may not be compatible. Whatever the reasons, there is some degree of task conflict in any group. It should not be surprising that this conflict typology parallels the two dimensions of leadership style. As pointed out by Evan (1965), interpersonal conflicts are primarily handled by a considerate leader while the structuring leader devotes his energies towards solving the task problems. The leadership functions demanded by a particular group at a particular time, therefore, could depend on the comparative strengths of its task and socio-emotional problem areas.

Conflicts that arise from a group's interrelationships create tensions, stresses, and socio-emotional needs for certain group members. These individuals are in a continual struggle to relieve these tensions. It seems reasonable that leadership effectiveness, as well as the pressures for changes, will depend on the extent to which the leader can help reduce these tensions and meet these needs. Studies such as Crockett's (1955) have clearly shown that if a designated leader fails to meet his group's demands, pressures will develop for either informal or new formal leaders to fill these gaps. Furthermore, as the interpersonal and task conflicts vary in strength and in importance, the actions required of the leadership role could also change. Thus, an adequate theory of effective leadership must be dynamic—at least dynamic enough to capture the transitions in leadership style that occur in response to significant changes in the group members' interindividual relationships.

Leadership Process Model

Based on the ideas discussed above, the model presented in Figure 1 describes several relationships between changes in leadership behavior and changes in intragroup tensions and stress. If we assume that affective conflict adequately measures the interpersonal tensions that exist within the group, then the model postulates that increasing affective conflict will tend to precipitate a more considerate and a less structuring style of leadership in order to satisfy the needs of the group members. Similarly, increasing task conflicts between group individuals will tend to evoke a more structuring and a less considerate form of leadership. The inverse of these respective leadership changes are predicted when the reverse situations of decreasing affective conflict and task conflict are taking place.

The transitions proposed by the model could take a considerably long time to evolve, during which time many other changes could occur. The overall task, the individual assignments, the specific personnel, the pressures from the external environment, or the affective and task conflicts themselves could all change, thereby interfering with the long-term predictions of the model. The

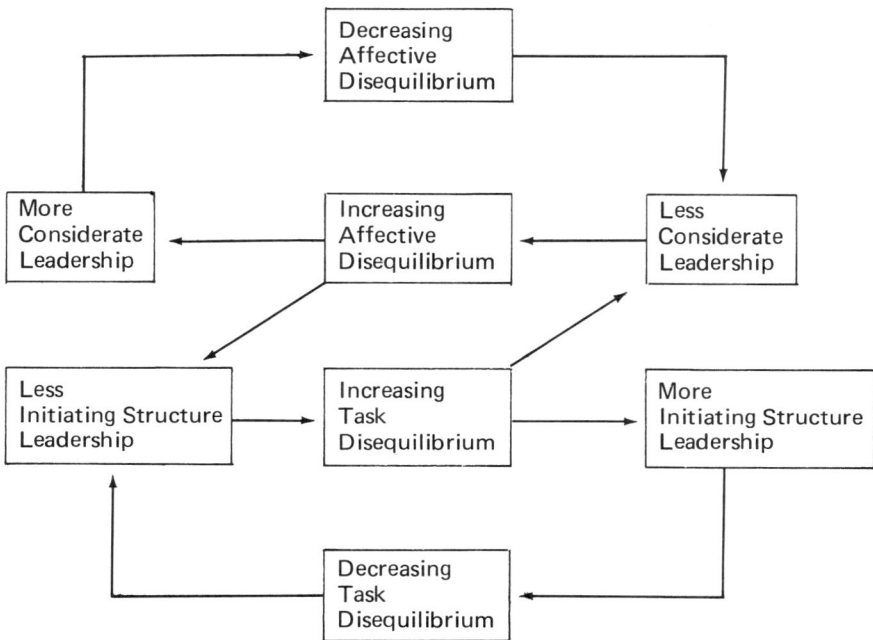

Fig. 1. The Leadership Process Model.

assumption underlying the leadership process model, however, is that the group members desire certain changes in leadership behavior depending upon their conditions of disequilibrium, i.e., their conditions of affective and task conflict. In other words, the discrepancy between the actual and desired leadership styles is a function of the perceived disequilibrium state, and such discrepancy measures are important by themselves as indicators of employee satisfaction, e.g., Porter (1962) and Locke (1969).

Yukl (1971) strongly recommends the use of a discrepancy model for studying the relationships between leadership style and subordinate satisfaction. He further speculates that subordinate preferences for initiating structure will be more situationally-contingent than preferences for consideration since subordinates will invariably prefer more of the latter. Based on the relationships described by the leadership process model, however, the following hypotheses are proposed:

1. The desired change in structuring leadership varies directly with task conflict.

2. The desired change in considerate leadership varies directly with affective conflict.
3. The desired change in structuring leadership varies inversely with affective conflict.
4. The desired change in considerate leadership varies inversely with task conflict.

With respect to performance, it is hypothesized that both affective and task conflict interfere with the path-goal relationships of group members and, consequently, are negatively associated with overall effectiveness. The notion that task conflict can also be positively linked with performance has been surfacing more and more. As pointed out by Assael (1969), however, constructive conflict implies that the individual disputants are able to frequently and effectively communicate with each other, readily express their grievances, and often have a standardized mode for resolving conflict. In short, they are able to work well together despite their differences.[1] As previously mentioned, the concept of task conflict as used in the leadership process model is one where the disputants do not work well together, thereby resulting in some degree of friction and tension between the individuals.

A number of researchers, e.g., Bass (1960), Torrance (1954), and Fiedler (1967), have asserted that groups experiencing tension and stress appear to perform better under task-oriented leaders who structure the situation. Since both affective and task-related conflict supposedly generate tension and stress, as well as hinder the path-goal relationships, structuring leadership is hypothesized to be more related to overall effectiveness than considerate leadership as long as conditions of either high affective or task conflict are present. Consequently, effectiveness is hypothesized to be directly related to both the interaction effect between affective conflict and perceived initiating structure and the interaction effect between task conflict and perceived initiating-structure. These relationships are hypothesized even though group members may prefer less structuring and more considerate leadership to help reduce the tension from high affective conflict.

To test the hypotheses derived from the leadership process model, a field study was conducted across a number of different academic groups. In addition, a laboratory experiment was designed to test a common subset of

---

[1]Studies by Evan (1965) and Pelz (1967) are often referenced to show that conflict and performance are positively related. In Evan's study, task conflict was a measure of technical heterogeneity rather than task conflict. Similarly, Pelz found that scientists were more effective if they differed from colleagues in technical style and strategy as long as they were also able to share similar sources of stimulation with these same colleagues, i.e., they could work well with their colleagues.

hypotheses. The use of both methodologies will hopefully add generaliz-ability and credibility to the findings.

FIELD STUDY

Methodology

The sample consisted of 84 randomly selected faculty members belonging to 20 different departments across two universities from the same metropolitan area. The departments varied in size, ranging from 7 to 13 members. Of the 120 potential subjects approached, 70% agreed to complete the individually administered questionnaires.[2]

Leadership Instrument. Each respondent was asked to rank order all of the professors in his department according to the degree to which they were described by a particular statement or short scenario. Actually, the subjects produced four separate rank orders—one for each of four different projective statements. Two of the statements represented functions from the consideration dimension (He finds time to listen to other department members; He is friendly and understanding with other department members). The other two statements typified the structuring dimension (He maintains definite standards of performance in teaching and research; He is helpful in the organizing and planning of many of the department's activities). Each respondent also rank ordered his departmental colleagues according to the degree to which he perceived they exhibited overall departmental leadership. Subsequently, he completed a final rank order according to how he would *like* to see them assume a leadership position. As will be discussed below, separate measures of the current and desired leadership styles were derived for each subject using these rank order vectors and some recent methodology from multidimensional scaling.

Conflict. As part of the questionnaire, each respondent rated the task relationship between every pair of individuals in his department. A 5-point rating scale, ranging from "would work very well with" (coded as +2) to "would work poorly with" (coded as −2), was used by each subject to rate the full sociometric-type matrix of task-related interrelationships. To collect the full matrix of interpersonal relationships, each faculty respondent also indicated on a 5-point scale the degree of friendliness between every pair of individuals. The scale ranged from "very friendly" (coded as +2) to "very unfriendly" (coded as −2).

Using Heider's (1958) theory of balanced triads as a model that describes and measures disequilibrium and tension, the degree of task conflict

---

[2] For more information regarding the sample and sampling procedures, see Katz (1974).

experienced by each subject was calculated by adding the task interrelationships from those triads in which he was a member. A simple transformation was used to normalize for the number of triads and to reverse the scoring so that high numerical values would signify high task conflict. The degree of affective conflict was similarly calculated using the data from the matrix of interpersonal relationships.[3]

To measure directly the overall feelings of tension and strain, each respondent was asked, using 7-point Likert-type items, how comfortable he was being in his department, how much tension he felt, and how much change he would like to see among the group members' interrelationships (interitem reliability of .89). Finally, two additional 7-point Likert-type items were averaged to measure perceived effectiveness by having each respondent rate the overall academic quality of his department plus the overall quality of education being provided to the students by his department (interitem reliability of .88).

Prelude to Results (Leadership Calculations)

Leadership is often defined in terms of intragroup influence (Cattell, 1951). Any justification for comparing only the formal leadership styles across different groups, therefore, requires that the influence of the remaining group members be somehow controlled for or "averaged out" (Campbell, 1956). In groups where the influence of some of the members can be as great, if not greater, than that of the formal leader, as in academic groups, this justification for comparability seems difficult to accept. Consequently, the measures of perceived leadership style should ideally reflect all of the leadership functions being carried out by the various group members.

To accomplish this, the multidimensional scaling model called INDSCAL (see Green & Rao, 1972) was used to obtain a spatial configuration of the faculty members of each department, derived from the four rank orders completed by the respondents in connection with the projective statements. The rank orders were regarded as a set of profile data from which a symmetric dissimilarity matrix was derived by calculating Euclidean distances between the ranks of every pair of professors. For example, if the respondent ranked professor "i" 3rd, 8th, 4th, and 7th and ranked professor "j" 5th, 1st, 5th, and 2nd on the same four scenarios, then the dissimilarity measure

---

[3]Heider's concept of balance involved the multiplication of the "signs" of the relationships among a single triad. For larger groups, however, the notion of additive balance, in which the "signs" are added rather than multiplied, has been formulated in opposition to multiplicative balance. In this field study, measures for both definitions were calculated, but only the results for additive balance are presented because it was significantly more related to tension and stress than multiplicative balance.

High Consideration

•B

•A   •C

                                      •E

•F   •D

Low Structuring ———————————————— High Structuring

   •G

      •H   •I

                  •J

Low Consideration

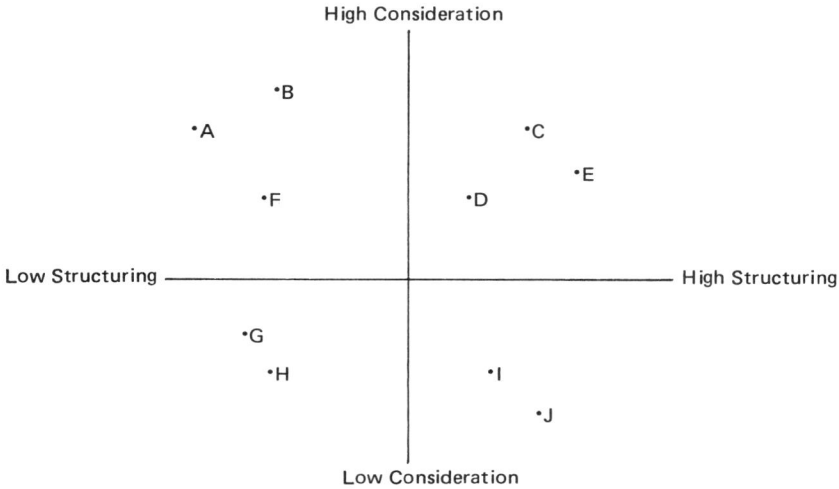

Fig. 2. A two-dimensional configuration of departmental members.

between professors "i" and "j" is the square root of $[(3\text{-}5)^2 + (8\text{-}1)^2 + (4\text{-}5)^2 + (7\text{-}2)^2]$. In this manner, a pairwise professor-by-professor dissimilarity matrix was computed for each subject.

By maximally using the information from the matrices of the subjects from the same department, two-dimensional solution spaces of faculty members were computed for each department by the INDSCAL model. The advantage of starting with profile measures from scenario rank orders is that the dimensions uncovered by INDSCAL's solution spaces must correspond with the characteristics embedded in the statements, i.e., the solutions' dimensions are easily identifiable as either consideration or initiating-structure. Figure 2 illustrates a typical 2-dimensional configuration of a department of size 10, whose faculty members are represented by points "A" through "J." Note, for example, that professors "A", "B", "C" are very similar with respect to considerate leadership but very dissimilar with respect to the structuring dimension.

Given the 2-dimensional spatial representations of the faculty members, there is some particular combination of values in the department's space that represents the perceptions of the overall leadership being displayed "better" than any other combination—commonly called the "ideal-point." The underlying notion is that those faculty members closest to this point exhibit more leadership than those members further away.

The location of a leadership ideal-point for each subject was derived so that the Euclidean distances between it and all of the professors from his department's solution space are as monotonically related as possible with the rank order that he completed for describing the present leadership. These ideal-points, representing each subject's consolidated viewpoint of current departmental leadership, were calculated with the PREFMAP model (Green & Rao, 1972). The degree of leadership along the consideration dimension was measured by the ratio of the differences between the coordinate value of the ideal-point and the maximum and minimum coordinates of the department's space. The degree of structuring leadership was similarly computed using the coordinate values along the structuring dimension.

Each subject's rank order of how he would like to see the leadership was also submitted to PREFMAP to obtain an ideal-point that represented his preferences for overall departmental leadership. By subtracting the coordinates of the "current" from "preferred" leadership ideal-points along each dimension, normalized by the appropriate dimensional range, measures for the desired change in considerate and structuring leadership, i.e., the discrepancy measures, were calculated for each subject.

With these methodological procedures, all of the leadership measures are based on the subject's perceptions of the combined influences of all departmental members. Furthermore, the derivation of the discrepancy scores circumvents the psychological constraints associated with asking respondents if the want more or less of a particular leadership behavior.

Finally, none of the variable measures calculated for the 84 subjects was significantly correlated with group size except for the tension index ($r = .24$). This is quite appropriate since many other studies, e.g., Corwin (1969) and Hackman and Vidmar (1970), have shown that dissatisfaction and tension generally increase as group size increases.

Results

A critical assumption is that individuals in a disequilibrium state of either affective or task conflict will feel tense and stressful until such conflict is resolved. As shown by Table 1, both affective and task conflict are significantly correlated with overall tension. Furthermore, even though task and affective conflict are significantly intercorrelated ($r = .37; p < .01$), the regression equation of Table 1 reveals that they are also jointly and significantly related to the subjects' feelings of stress. And as shown by their respective beta weights, both conflict types are about equally important in accounting for the individual differences in stress.

Not unexpectedly, neither leadership dimension is particularly associated with overall tension. The process model suggests, however, that subjects

Table 1. Multiple Regression Equation for Tension

Independent variables		Simple correlations	Regression coefficients	Beta weights	F-values
R-value = .58*	Affective conflict	.49*	.26	.36	13.1*
	Task conflict	.47*	.16	.33	10.7*
$F(4,79) = 10.2$	Considerate leadership	−.06	.48	.12	1.8
	Structuring leadership	−.07	.18	.03	0.1

*$p < .01$.
$n = 84$.

experiencing affective conflict will desire more considerate and less structuring leadership and vice versa for task conflict. If the model has validity, then the stress being suffered by respondents in a state of affective conflict should be magnified with high structuring leadership while task conflict will be aggravated by high consideration. In other words, the current leadership style moderates the relationships between tension and conflict. In support of the model, the correlations between affective conflict and tension significantly shift ($p < .05$) from .33 to .62 under conditions of low and high (median split) initiating-structure, respectively. Similarly, the correlations between task conflict and tension change ($p < .10$) from .36 to .58 under leadership conditions of low and high consideration, respectively.

Having established that the conflict measures are appropriately related to tension, one can next examine the connection between conflict and the desired changes in leadership style, i.e., the discrepancy measures presumably associated with satisfaction. Since the two conflict measures are positively correlated, one must control for affective conflict when testing for the effects of task conflict and vice versa. The partial correlations presented via Table 2 support the hypothesized leadership changes associated with the initiating-structure dimension. The respondents' preferences for more structuring leadership vary positively with task conflict while varying negatively with affective conflict. Despite these confirmations, the propositions regarding desired changes along the consideration dimension were not upheld.

Since the current leadership style significantly influenced the relationships between tension and conflict, it is also possible that leadership style moderates the relationships between the discrepancy and conflict variables. To investigate

Table 2. Partial Correlations Between Conflict and Desired Leadership Changes

Disequilibrium measure (control variable)	Structuring discrepancy	Consideration discrepancy
Affective conflict (task conflict)	−.29*	.03
Task conflict (affective conflict)	.31*	−.04

*p < .01.
n = 84.

this contingency, partial correlations were run between each of the conflict variables (controlling for its conflict counterpart) and the structuring discrepancy scores under conditions of low and high considerate leadership (median split).

The results revealed that the partial correlations between task conflict and structuring discrepancy increased significantly (p < .05) from .17 to .51 under conditions of low and high consideration, respectively. Similarly, the partials between affective conflict and structuring discrepancy shifted, albeit not quite significantly, from −.22 to −.44. Thus, the relationships between the desired changes for structuring leadership and the interaction effects between conflict and considerate leadership are completely consistent with the leadership process model; and furthermore, they are the same interaction effects that significantly influenced the overall tension scores.

Although current leadership style did not completely moderate the relationships between either type of conflict and the consideration discrepancy scores, it was found that affective conflict did significantly correlate with the desire for more considerate leadership, but only when structuring leadership was high (r = .31, n = 42, p < .05). This relationship provides the first supporting evidence for the leadership process model with respect to the consideration dimension. There were no conditions, however, under which task conflict was significantly correlated with the desire for less considerate leadership.

In summary, the preceding evidence tends to support the notion that the need for either more or less structuring leadership is contingent upon the comparative degrees of task and affective conflict being experienced, in conjunction with perceptions of the existing leadership style. Only some slight evidence was uncovered in favor of a similar conclusion for the consideration

Table 3. Correlations Between Effectiveness and Leadership Style

Leadership style	Task conflict		Affective conflict	
	Low	High	Low	High
Initiating structure	.38**	.51**	.29*	.63**
Consideration	.20	.11	.13	.13

Note. – Underlined correlations are significantly different ($p<.01$).
*$p < .05$.
**$p < .01$.
$n = 42$.

dimension. Consequently, it may seem that Yukl's (1971) previously mentioned speculation regarding preferences for leadership behavior is to some extent valid. Nevertheless, those wanting more considerate leadership were only slightly greater in number than those wanting less. Perhaps a more appropriate explanation lies in the path-goal theory in that consideration is simply not as relevant or as meaningful a dimension as initiating-structure for professors who have jobs with considerable intrinsic satisfaction and represent a rather task-oriented group. The degree to which individuals in various stages of stress will want either more or less leadership along a given dimension may itself be contingent on the nature of the task.

With respect to perceived effectiveness, both task and affective conflict have significantly ($p < .05$) negative correlations as previously suggested ($r = -.28$ and $-.29$, respectively). In contrast, initiating-structure is strongly correlated with effectiveness ($r = .45$; $p < .01$) while considerate leadership is not ($r = .16$). Such findings for the two leadership dimensions are completely compatible with the path-goal theory. But as revealed by Table 3, the strength of the relationship between initiating-structure and effectiveness is moderated by affective conflict, jumping from .29 for unstressed respondents to .63 for respondents who are experiencing considerable interpersonal stress.

Thus, initiating-structure is associated with effectiveness, especially when high affective conflict is present. This supports the tendered hypothesis that effectiveness is directly correlated with the interaction effect between structuring leadership and affective conflict even though respondents may desire less initiating-structure and possibly more considerate leadership with high interpersonal stress. Task conflict, however, did not significantly moderate the relationships between structuring leadership and effectiveness while considerate leadership remained consistently uncorrelated with effectiveness throughout the different conditions of conflict.

Table 4. Stepwise Regression for Perceived Effectiveness

Independent variables		Regression coefficient	Beta weight	F-value
	1) Initiating-structure	.56	.25	3.09*
R-value = .58**	2) Task conflict	−1.28	−.28	8.55**
$F(4,79)$ = 10.1	3) Interaction between structure and affective conflict	.79	.25	3.52*
	4) Consideration	.36	.17	3.29*

*$p < .05$.
**$p < .01$.
$n = 84$.

Finally, the stepwise regression reported in Table 4 was run to help clarify the joint influence of leadership style, conflict, and their assorted interactions on perceived effectiveness. The most important result is that both initiating-structure and the interaction effect between structure and affective conflict are included as significantly positive terms. In addition, only task conflict was selected by the stepwise procedures as being negatively related to effectiveness. Apparently, affective conflict by itself could not significantly explain any additional variance. Thus, it is possible that interpersonal conflict per se does not necessarily result in poorer performance, especially since its interaction effect with structuring leadership is positively related with effectiveness. Having taken into account the various effects of tension and stress, considerate leadership finally becomes significantly related with perceived effectiveness, although initiating-structure is certainly more important in this setting.

EXPERIMENT

Methodology

As a result of the field study, a two-factor experiment was designed to compare the relative effects of consideration and initiating-structure leadership on individual performance under treatments of low and high affective conflict. For the sake of brevity, only a brief overview of the experimental procedures will be included. A more complete description can be found in Katz (1974).

Forty-four male student subjects were separately hired for a few hours of coding work through a school newspaper advertisement. Subjects were randomly assigned to the various treatments. Upon reporting for work, the subject was to assist two other staff employees, one of whom was a formal leader and both of whom were confederates in the experiment. The subject was told that he would be working on the National Crime Survey Project, and that his help was needed to transfer survey questionnaire responses to code sheets to facilitate key punching. Before working with the questionnaires, however, the subject proofread several pages of a purported project report followed by some work on a "cluster-matching" task, lasting a total of about 35 minutes. During this period, the subject's perceptions of the assigned leadership style were shaped.

For the high consideration treatment, the leader continuously behaved in a friendly, encouraging, and appreciative manner. He thanked the subject for coming and stated that his help would be greatly appreciated. Similar kinds of concerned and appreciative behavior were used when the subject finished a task or when the leader interacted with the other staff member. In contrast, the high structuring leader greeted the subject by emphasizing that there was considerable work to do in a short amount of time and periodically repeated this concern throughout the experiment as well as a concern about the quality of work and the meeting of deadlines. Finally, when the subject completed his tasks, the structuring leader refrained from expressing appreciation but simply assigned the next task, emphasizing that there was much work to do.

Having completed the first two tasks, the subject was given a set of 10 survey questionnaires and the necessary instructions for the transfer of codes to key punch sheets. Essentially, the questionnaires consisted of a number of 5-point Likert-type attitudinal items about the problems of crime (e.g., most judges are too lenient on criminals, and harsher jail sentences would deter crime). This brief coding task, lasting about 10 minutes, not only helped to solidify the leadership perceptions but also acquainted the subjects with the questionnaires and the task of coding, in order to suppress the effects of learning on future coding tasks.

Prior to completing this first coding task, the subject was told that the leader had to leave for a few minutes and if he should finish the task before the leader returned, he should complete a blank questionnaire. Once the leader departed, the second set of treatments was introduced. For low affective conflict, the other staff member started a friendly conversation with the subject about the various issues covered by the questionnaire and basically agreed with and supported the opinions of the subject. For high affective conflict, however, the confederate reacted with considerable hostility towards the subject. Looking over the subject's completed questionnaire, the confederate antagonistically disagreed with his opinions and started to attack his personally, e.g., "I should have known by your clothes (or long hair) that you would think like this." The confederate also looked for particular inconsistencies in the answers of the subject to use in his personal attacks.

By the time the leader returned, the experimental treatments had been implemented. The rest of the experiment consisted of two coding-type tasks from which objective performance measures were obtained. In the first task (lasting about 25 minutes), the confederate read previously key punched codes from a computer listing while the subject scanned the actual questionnaires to make sure the codes were correct. The listing contained 30 built-in errors; consequently, the number of errors detected by the subject in this cross-checking task served as one of the performance measures. The next task (lasting about 35 minutes) required the subject to code a total of 60 questionnaires. The number of coding errors made by the subject in this task served as a second performance measure.

To permit the verification of the treatments, a departmental secretary administered a post-experimental questionnaire in the context of the experiment. Shortly before the subject completed the last task, the secretary entered the room and told the subject that the project's employees would be reassigned into small working groups. To do this more effectively, the administrator of the project would like the subject's honest impressions of the people with whom he had been working. The subject rated the interpersonal relations among all three group individuals using a 6-point Likert-type scale ranging from "very friendly" (1) to "very unfriendly" (6). He also completed six Likert-type items concerning his perceptions of the leadership style: three questions for each leadership dimension. Neither the leader nor the confederate was present when the questionnaire was administered, having left on the pretense of examining some equipment. When the subject finished coding the 60 questionnaires, the experiment was completed, and the subject was paid and debriefed.[4]

Treatment Verification

The data from the post-experimental questionnaires were analyzed to insure that the treatments were correctly introduced and perceived. The answers to the three consideration and initiating-structure items were submitted to a 2-group discriminant program. Except for one subject, all of the cases were correctly classified by the discriminant analysis into either the high

---

[4]During debriefing, most subjects were astonished that they had participated in an experiment and that all of the questionnaires, conversations, and project activities were fictitious. Some subjects confessed that they had been "on guard" for an experiment but that after all of the activity in the first 15 minutes, they dropped the idea.

consideration treatment or the high structuring treatment [D^2 = 10.4; $F(1.42)$ = 114.8; $p < .001$]. The misclassified subject was excluded from the rest of the analysis.

An examination of the subjects' responses about their interpersonal relationships with the confederate revealed that, except for two cases, all of the ratings for subjects assigned to a low affective conflict treatment were lower, i.e., friendlier, than all of the ratings for subjects assigned to high affective conflict. These two exceptions were also excluded from further analysis. Thus, the treatments appear to have been correctly introduced for the remaining forty-one subjects.

Results

Because the performance measures from the coding and cross-checking tasks are not significantly correlated, they are separately investigated. Table 5 presents the ANOVA results for the coding task where the performance measures are the number of coding errors committed by the subjects. The most striking result is that there is a highly significant interaction effect between the kind of leadership style and affective conflict—the same type of interaction effect that was highly significant in the field study. Under conditions of low affective conflict, the mean number of coding errors with high consideration and lower structure was significantly lower than with high initiating-structure and lower consideration (5.7 versus 11.4 errors, respectively). Since the coding task is fairly routine and not intrinsically satisfying, having high considerate leadership outperform high initiating-structure is consistent with the path-goal theory. Under conditions of high affective conflict, however, the results are reversed. Subjects assigned to a highly

Table 5. Analysis of Variance for Coding Task

	Affective conflict						
	Low	High		*Source*	*SS*	*DF*	*F*
High consideration	5.7[a]	13.0	9.4	Within cells	654.1	37	
High initiating structure	11.4	6.2	8.9	Leadership	1.8	1	.02
				Conflict	23.4	1	1.32
	8.4	6.2	9.2	Leadership × conflict	344.5	1	22.3*

[a]Numbers represent the mean number of coding errors made by the subjects.
*$p < .001$.

structuring leader committed significantly fewer errors than subjects with the highly considerate leadership.

The ANOVA results for the cross-checking task in which performance is measured by the number of coding errors detected by the subjects revealed no significant main effects or interaction effect. This apparent contradiction might be explained by the nature of the tasks—not in terms of their complexity but in terms of the interaction required of the subjects. The cross-checking task is an interindividual or conjunctive type task in which the subject is not unilaterally responsible for its completion. As a result, he can respond to the induced tension either by becoming more engrossed in the task or by withdrawing and simply letting the confederate read his list of codes. In contrast, the coding task is an individualistic or disjunctive type task in which the subject is unilaterally responsible for the completion. Consequently, he does not readily have the option of withdrawing but can react by becoming more involved in the task, a reaction that is facilitated by a structuring leader.

Implications and Conclusions

The most important result is that the strength of the relationships between the dimensions of leadership style and the criteria of performance and satisfaction seem to be contingent upon the kind of intragroup conflict being experienced by the involved subordinates. Employees who are experiencing stress from affective conflict may desire less structuring and perhaps more considerate leadership. Contrastingly, both the field study and laboratory experiment found that the positive relationship between performance and the structuring dimension of leadership was intensified when high affective conflict was present.

As a result, a group of subordinates afflicted by high interpersonal stress could pose a difficult problem for the manager, for he may be caught between alternative demands. The manager might attempt to respond directly to the needs of his subordinates by trying to relieve the tension from affective conflict with a somewhat less structuring and perhaps more considerate style of leadership. On the other hand, he could overlook his employees' immediate needs and conflicts by adopting a highly structuring style, thereby attempting to ensure and maintain high performance. The evidence from the field study seems to indicate that the first alternative approach may be correlated with employee satisfaction. However, both the field and laboratory studies found that performance was more correlated with the second approach; though it is possible that dissatisfaction might ensue from more rather than less initiating-structure as evidenced by the negative relationship between the structuring discrepancy scores and affective conflict.

If, in fact, it is true that the demands made upon the structuring dimension for high satisfaction and performance are in opposite directions when high affective conflict is present, then the common alternative of simply being both highly considerate and highly structuring may not be an appropriate strategy. Such opposing demands, however, were found only for the structuring dimension and were not found for the consideration dimension. What actually happens, i.e., what leadership style the manager finally decides to adopt in such circumstances, is probably a function of a number of variables, including: the external pressures placed upon the manager for higher and better performance by his superiors; the kind of time pressures that exist; the manager's own attitudes, beliefs, and characteristics; and the relative distribution of power such as more powerful groups and individuals are more likely to influence the leadership to suit their needs.

The rationale for desiring more consideration and less initiating-structure lies in the employee's need to reduce the current interpersonal strain. It seems reasonable that a manager who attempts to meet such needs will most likely enhance performance to the extent that he succeeds in eventually reducing or resolving the affective conflict. Trying to reconcile interpersonal conflicts, however, could be an extremely difficult undertaking. Some recent findings by Katz, Phillips, Cheston, and Potratz (1976) have shown that more of the successful methods for resolving interpersonal conflicts involved "forcing" rather than "problem-solving." In almost all of the cases, the forcing solution included the removal or reassignment of one of the conflicting parties.

Some caution should also be voiced about the alternative of more structuring leadership with high interpersonal stress. It is quite possible that effectiveness is related to initiating-structure under conditions of affective conflict only in the short run. The laboratory experiment, for example, only monitored performance for a very short period of time. Had it continued for a longer period, performances may have started to decline. Furthermore, performance might be facilitated by structuring leadership, but perhaps at the expense of eventual turnover, or similar undesirable consequences. Employees experiencing interpersonal stress will probably try to reduce such pressures and if the leader is unresponsive, some of the employees might decide to withdraw, terminate, rebel, etc. On the other hand, it is also possible that the achievement of high task performance can be a great help in the reduction of interpersonal conflicts. As discussed by Schein (1970) and Farris (1975), task success can be a powerful vehicle for removing conflict between group members and is a significant influence on other important variables such as leadership, satisfaction, and motivation.

Clearly, a leader has a variety of ways to deal with situations of high interpersonal stress. Moreover, each alternative has its own strengths and weaknesses that have to be weighed in each specific setting. In some sense, however, it may be that with consideration and less structure, the leader is trying first to resolve the affective conflict while with the more structuring response, the leader is trying, first, to manage it.

If it is true that structuring leadership helps offset, at least in the short run, the problems emerging from interpersonal conflict that might otherwise interfere with performance, its mediating influence under condition of high task conflict did not appear as beneficial. In the field study, the interaction term between initiating-structure and task conflict was not significantly related to perceived performance. In fact, task conflict remained significantly and negatively related to perceived effectiveness, as shown in Table 4.

In contrast with task conflict, affective conflict was unrelated to performance in the field study once the significant moderating effects of initiating-structure were accounted for. Moreover, the results from the laboratory experiment also showed that performance under high affective conflict was as good as the performance under the low affective conflict treatment. Such findings tend to indicate that situations of high interpersonal stress may not necessarily result in poorer performance than situations of low interpersonal stress.[5]

Since structuring leadership did not significantly mediate the negative relationship between performance and task conflict in the field study, it is possible that under conditions of high task-related stress, structuring leadership may not be as helpful in maintaining high performance as under conditions of high interpersonal stress. If such findings hold true, then the manager of a group with high task conflict would have to resolve the intragroup conflict in order to alleviate the performance distractions. The adoption of a more structuring role might help the immediate needs of the employees (recall that structuring discrepancy was positively correlated with task conflict) but there was no evidence that either leadership dimension influenced performance to a significantly greater degree with high task conflict. Considerably more research is needed to investigate and understand the relationship between various kinds of leadership behaviors and the solving of task-related conflicts.

It also seems likely that employees within the same work group can significantly differ in their individual amounts of task and affective conflict. In the present field study, there was as much variation in the conflict scores within groups as between groups. As a result, the leader could be dealing with subordinates whose needs are substantially different. Some may be experiencing tension and stress; others may not. The demands made upon the leadership role, therefore, might vary from employee to employee. It is possible that with significant intragroup variation, a leader might want to assume different leadership behaviors with different employees according to their particular type and degree of conflict—a kind of individual-leadership match.

---

[5] A similar conclusion was reached by Fiedler (1967). He noted that performance under conditions of high interpersonal stress was as good in quality as under conditions of low interpersonal stress.

If such leadership differentiation tends to be effective, it may be important not only to train managers to be both highly considerate and structuring, but also how to select the most appropriate style of leadership for each individual subordinate and how to modify such leadership behavior as the situation changes for the given employee. To accomplish this, managers might have to learn what kinds of factors and information are important for these decisions. In formulating his approaches, the manager might want to look beyond the kind of task being performed by focusing additionally on the individuals, their interactions, and the kinds of stressful problems and conflicts that confront them. As Schein (1970) points out, ". . . the successful manager must be a good diagnostician and must value a spirit of inquiry."

The analysis presented in this study represents only a small part of what we need to learn about effective leadership. Considerably more research is needed on how one learns about and measures intragroup conflict. Furthermore, the interrelationships among leadership, conflict, and effectiveness should be investigated for different kinds of task dimensions, such as structured-unstructured and conjunctive-disjunctive. Clearly, leadership effectiveness is dependent on both the nature of the group and the nature of the task. Additionally, not only is it important to differentiate between affective and task-related conflict, but it is also important to distinguish between conflict with peers and conflict with supervisors, or more generally, conflict between rank equals and conflict between individuals of unequal rank or status. Finally, it is crucial that we learn more about the management and resolution of intragroup conflict. Most likely, more specific kinds of leadership behavior will have to be defined to investigate these processes. Increased understanding about dealing with intragroup conflict is crucial, for it is often these kinds of problematic situations that provide leaders with their greatest challenge.

REFERENCES

Assael, H. Constructive role of inter-organizational conflict. *Administrative Science Quarterly*, 1969, **14**, 573–582.

Bass, B. M. *Leadership, psychology and organizational behavior.* New York: Harper & Row, 1960.

Campbell, D. T. *Leadership and its effects upon the group.* Research Monograph No. 83, Ohio State University, 1956.

Cattell, R. New concepts for measuring leadership in terms of group syntality. *Human Relations*, 1951, **4**, 161–184.

Corwin, R. G. Patterns of organizational conflict. *Administrative Science Quarterly*, 1969, **14**, 507–520.

Crockett, W. Emergent leaders in small decision-making groups. *Journal of Abnormal and Social Psychology*, 1955, **51**, 378–383.

Dessler, G. A. *A test of the path-goal theory of leadership.* Unpublished doctoral dissertation, Baruch College, City University of New York, 1973.

Downey, H., Sheridan, J., & Slocum, J. Analysis of relationships among leader behavior, subordinate job performance and satisfaction: A path-goal approach. *Academy of Management Journal*, 1975, **18**, 253–262.

Evan, W. Conflict and performance in R&D organizations. *Industrial Management Review*, 1965, **7**, 37–46.

Farris, G. Chickens, eggs and productivity. *Organizational Dynamics*, 1975, (Spring) 2–15.

Fiedler, F. *A theory of leadership effectiveness.* New York: McGraw-Hill, 1967.

Gibb, C. A. The principles and traits of leadership. *Journal of Abnormal and Social Psychology*, 1947, **42**, 267–284.

Green, P., & Rao, V. *Applied multidimensional scaling.* New York: Holt, Rinehart, & Winston, 1972.

Hackman, J. R., & Vidmar, P. Effects of size and task type in group performance and member reactions. *Sociometry*, 1970, **33**, 37–54.

Heider, F. *The psychology of interpersonal relations.* New York: Wiley, 1958.

Hemphill, J. K. *The leader and his group.* Educational Research Bulletin Number 28, Ohio State University, 1955.

House, R. A path-goal theory of leader effectiveness. *Administrative Science Quarterly*, 1971, **16**, 321–338.

House, R., & Dessler, G. The path-goal theory of leadership. In J. G. Hunt & L. L. Larson (Eds.), *Contingency approaches to leadership.* Carbondale, Ill.: Southern Illinois University Press, 1974.

Katz, R. *The effects of group balance on leadership style.* Unpublished doctoral dissertation, University of Pennsylvania, 1974.

Katz, R., Phillips, E., Cheston, R., & Potratz, J. *Methods of conflict resolution—a re-examination.* Unpublished manuscript, M.I.T., 1976.

Kerr, S., Schriescheim, C., Murphy, C., & Stogdill, R. Toward a contingency theory of leadership based on the consideration and initiating structure literature. *Organizational Behavior and Human Performance*, 1974, **12**, 62–82.

Locke, E. A. What is job satisfaction. *Organizational Behavior and Human Performance*, 1969, **4**, 309–336.

Pelz, D. Creative tensions in the research and development climate. *Science*, 1967, **157**, 160–165.

Porter, L. W. Job attitudes in management. *Journal of Applied Psychology*, 1962, **46**, 375–384.

Schein, E. *Organizational psychology.* Englewood Cliffs, N.J.: Prentice-Hall, 1970.

Stinson, J., & Johnson, T. The path-goal theory of leadership: A partial test and suggested refinement. *Academy of Management Journal*, 1975, **18**, 242–252.

Stogdill, R. *Handbook of leadership.* New York: Free Press, 1974.

Torrance, E. P. The behavior of small groups under the stress of conditions of survival. *American Sociological Review*, 1954, **19**, 751–755.

Vroom, V. Leadership. In M. Dunnette (Ed.), *Handbook in industrial and organizational psychology*. Chicago: Rand-McNally, 1976.

Yukl, G. Toward a behavioral theory of leadership. *Organizational Behavior and Human Performance*, 1971, **6**, 411–440.

THE PROCESS OF LEADERSHIP ON THE SHOPFLOOR[1]

Bruce Partridge
The University of Aston in Birmingham

INTRODUCTION

Much of the theory of leadership has been developed from the empirical study of the military, management, and students. Whereas these types of leaders have been heavily researched, others, such as politicians and trade union leaders, have been relatively neglected (Stogdill, 1974a). The result of this imbalance has been an implicit assumption about the nature of leadership authority. A central theme of leadership literature has been how to legitimize the explicit exercise of authority and control (Stogdill, 1974b); that is, authority and control which is overt and recognized, as it is within the military and in management. But is leadership theory derived from such studies relevant for areas where this authority is challenged or at least is uncertain?

[1] This paper arises from a research project on workplace industrial relations supervised by Professor Ray Loveridge and financed by the Social Science Research Council.

Other current themes in the literature see leadership as an aspect of role differentiation (Newcomb, Turner & Converse, 1966), as the initiation and maintenance of role structure (Stogdill, 1959), as well as the clarification of path-goals (Evans, 1970; House, 1971). The assumption behind such approaches is how to improve the task performance of the leader's group; but what is the implication when the leader's main objective is not improving task performance but in challenging the task, its performance, or its rate of pay?

Stogdill (1974b) has criticized leadership theory as being unable to integrate explanations of the emergence of leadership in initially unstructured groups, of the maintenance of leadership once a role structure has been developed and stabilized, of the relation of leader personality and behavior to follower and group response, and finally of the conditions under which specific patterns of leader personality and behavior were effective.

The purpose of this study is not to attempt such an integration, but more modestly to cast some light upon these processes from the relatively unusual perspective of a shopfloor leader, the shop steward. In the British context of workplace industrial relations, the steward faces a complex role set of the union which authorizes him, management which recognizes him, and his constituency which elects him (Clegg, 1972; Goodman & Whittingham, 1973). Role theory usually presupposes a normative consensus which raises the question of whether role analysis can be applied in such conflict situations as collective bargaining (Preiss & Ehrlich, 1966). The role of the steward is perhaps more easily understood by focusing on its formal nature, being a role that involves skills of communication and interaction rather than technical expertise. The steward has few, if any, sanctions which he can use against his members or to reward them. Furthermore, his members do not have to accept the steward's recommendation; at any time, they can ignore him or recall his credentials and elect someone else to represent them.

The Problems of Shopfloor Leadership

This study highlights the process of leadership on the shopfloor with some examples taken from a diary study of shop stewards in a drop forgings plant in the United Kingdom. The stewards kept a diary of their activities for one day per week over a ten-week period. The days selected each week were varied so as to collect a typical time profile. The day after the diary entries, the steward was interviewed in depth about the issues and activities of the day before with the emphasis of exploring the meaning and purpose of the steward's behavior as he himself saw it, i.e., the interview was based on an Action Approach (Silverman, 1970).

The main concern of these stewards was the ambiguity and uncertainty inherent in their role, and in particular what the values, beliefs, and opinions of their members were. This is typical of the British shop steward (McCarthy & Parker, 1968). Typical responses to questions about the problems and/or difficulties of being a steward were: "Trying to guess how strongly they feel about it," "You don't know when they're trying it on," "You don't know whether the member has a real grievance or whether he just got out of bed on the wrong side." Likewise, when the stewards were asked why they undertook a particular activity, a frequent response was "To try and get the feeling of the shop." Even the most experienced stewards tended to seek second opinions as to what their members were thinking. The identity of the group as a unit of collective action became problematic for the steward. When the steward progressed a grievance he could not be sure as to who would actively support it and who would not be interested. It is therefore useful to distinguish between the constituency and the workgroup. The constituency is easily identifiable as the unit of election, but the group which is the unit of action may be more variable and less predictable. Indeed, there may be various groups within the constituency.

Hill (1974) has argued that the concept of the workgroup has been overworked, tending to mean all things to all people. The use of the concept is criticized for its lack of precision in both the definition and description: composition, size, and purpose are all left ambiguous. One can also criticize the lack of attention given to the process of group formation. This failure to explore the underlying processes has resulted in a tendency to treat workgroups as universal and equivalents.

The concept of the workgroup becomes even more dubious when one tries to identify and measure it in practice. Brown (1973) argues that the term "the workgroup" is misleading in that it suggests a compactness and distinctiveness which is difficult to empirically validate as groups tend to wax and wane in significance and size. Hyman and Brough (1975) have similarly criticized Reference Group Analysis for exaggerating the coherence and stability of such groups.

When an individual has a grievance, he wants a collectivity with power to support him and progress his grievance. Therefore, he makes use of a collective representative, such as the steward. The steward then has to mobilize commitment for action, or at least a potential commitment, from a collectivity that has some bargaining power. The steward has to legitimize the grievance amongst his members by accessing some system of values and beliefs. In this sense, the grievance can be said to define the group. This process of defining/legitimizing the grievance is simplified if there is one dominant system of values and meanings among the workforce. Obviously, it is made more difficult when there is a variety of value and meaning systems within the workplace.

Given the inherent ambiguity and uncertainty in such a situation, there is an obvious leadership function to be fulfilled in articulating the grievance. This function is demonstrated by some examples from the diary study.

Some Examples of Grievance Definition

The first example concerns a strike in the die shop. The die shop comprises the die shop proper (n = 65 skilled) plus the polishing shop (n = 12 semiskilled). The two shops are a single bargaining unit partly because their work is interdependent but also because each enhances the other's power base (Marchington, 1975). The polishers are responsible both for placing the dies in the forge hammers and for minor repairs of the dies so they have a high disruptive power. But the polishers are also keen to be seen as part of the skilled group in the die shop. The die makers' power is based on their market irreplaceability, as their only link with the rest of production is through the polishers.

The strike was essentially a work allocation dispute between these two shops. One section of skilled workers, the die-sinkers, refused to do a job returned by the semiskilled polishers who thought it was beyond their ability; that is, neither section wanted to do the job. A die-sinker was requested by the superintendent to do the job; he refused and was suspended. The other die-sinkers downed tools immediately.

The die-sinkers saw the grievance in purely personal terms, i.e., the erratic nature of their superintendent. Management also saw the situation as a matter of personalities in that "the die-sinkers were trying it on again." Tension had been building up between this section and their superintendent for two to three months over the question of having days off for exceptional reasons. The polishers saw the situation in terms of the status gap between the two sections, while the steward was concerned about the latent disquiet about reduction of differentials between the skilled and semiskilled which this incident could have brought into the open. That is, there was more than one way of interpreting the facts as to what the grievance was about. This situation could have developed into an intragroup conflict upsetting the basic trade union principle of unity. Part of the problem was that the grievance was immediate—the steward had no time to intervene before the superintendent had made his decision. However, the steward managed to gain control by redefining the grievance: He did not question the substance of the superintendent's decision, but the procedural way in which it had been reached. The steward maintained that the grievance was basically concerned with natural justice in that the member should be represented by his steward prior to suspension. This redefinition maintained shop unity between all the sections and also enabled a quick settlement because management did not have to withdraw support from the superintendent's decision. Although this definition might appear self-evident, in retrospect there was nothing inevitable about the definition. A similar dispute about work allocation had occurred three months earlier between different sections of the maintenance department. The maintenance steward failed to define the issue in such a way as to maintain unity, the department fragmented, and the steward resigned.

The definition maintained only a precarious unity since one section did not attend the shop meeting because they thought it did not concern them. Consequently, they did not down tools with the other sections, although they did go out on strike with the other sections three hours later. This tardiness in stopping work caused dissension in the shop when the work allocation dispute had been settled because this section had been earning money when the others had not. The steward had been too busy seeing management about the suspension to go and see why they had not downed tools. Feeling in the shop grew that this section should forego the money earned while the others had downed tools—or at least be fined. The steward was again in a cleft-stick trying to maintain unity between two factions. The section was going to resist losing any wages and if they would not agree to be fined then management cooperation would be needed to "fine" the recalcitrants. The steward did not want to show the disunity to management nor did he think that management would cooperate. The steward managed to cool the issue by severely reprimanding the section—not for not downing tools, but for not attending the shop meeting.

The definition of the grievance can also vary over time according to the audience to which the definition is addressed, as the following two examples from the finishing shop demonstrate. The finishing shop (n = 90) is a large heterogeneous shop of 12 different semiskilled sections. Many of these workers had been retired from the forges when they found it difficult to maintain piecework earnings because of age or accident.

The first example concerns an individual who, it was felt, was being paid the wrong rate for the job. The individual was semiskilled but the custom and practice had been to pay a skilled rate for that job even if sometimes the occupant was not skilled. Initially, the steward defined the issue in terms of the individual not being paid the customary rate. However, as the grievance was progressed the steward became aware of the Union's District Committee jurisdiction over wage rates within the factory; he realized that there was an overwhelming majority of skilled craftsmen sitting on the District Committee and that they would not be enthusiastic about a semiskilled man being paid a skilled rate. Therefore, the steward redefined the issue in terms of the individual being paid the average bonus of an adjacent section which would have meant his actual earnings were within a few shillings of the skilled rate.

The second example concerns an individual whom management had not upgraded. The shop felt that the individual had been hard done-by and were willing to go on strike. Management resisted the steward's case for upgrading the individual in terms of seniority and experience, and only under the threat of a strike did they give the reason—"He had the wrong attitude." The steward now had a decision: adopt a confrontation strategy by going on strike or redefining the grievance. The steward felt the men would "win" if they went on strike, that is, the individual would be upgraded. But this would be achieved at a high opportunity cost in terms of severing the bargaining relationship between the steward and his superintendent (Walton & McKersie, 1965). There was also the probability that management would demote the individual at the first sign of indiscipline. The steward eventually redefined the issue in terms of whether it was necessary to have two grades for this particular kind of work. The conditions under which it had been decided to have two grades no longer existed as the job had changed. The steward was also aware that if only one was promoted the others who were not might feel aggrieved. The redefinition resulted in a prompt settlement—the lower grade was abolished except for probationary workers and everyone, including the individual with the wrong attitude, was upgraded.

These two examples from the finishing shop also highlight the variable identity of the "group." These two grievances were concurrent: They had much in common and had come to the attention of the steward about the same time. In the second example, the whole shop was ready to go on strike whereas, in the first example, few other workers were interested and none had contemplated action if management did not respond. In fact, the tradition of the shop was one of fragmented action: At times the unit of action had been a section, whereas at other times it had been a combination of sections and/or individuals.

So far, these examples have indicated how successful the stewards were in defining issues and grievances in a manner that was congruent with their members' expectations insofar as the members supported their stewards. However, another example from the same site demonstrates how precarious this achievement is. The electricians, who belong to a different union from the rest of the shopfloor, went on strike. Since the electricians were responsible for starting up the presses in the press shop and for maintaining equipment in the forge, piecework earnings in these two departments were drastically affected by the electricians' action. These two departments saw the issue in very immediate terms—their earnings were being affected in the weeks before Christmas. Consequently, they pressured management to employ outside contractors to keep the plant going and even threatened the electricians with physical violence. The stewards' committee, although they did not support the electricians' action, attempted to maintain plant unity by emphasizing the need for solidarity on the ground of such general union principles as, "Don't blackleg," "Don't use scab labor." The forge and the press shop refused to consider the issue in such terms and demanded action from the stewards' committee. The situation could well have erupted into a protest situation with a consequent disintegration of plant bargaining but for the fortuitous return of the electricians. In this example, the ability of the forge stewards to define the issue is not in question given their undoubted ability in the stewards' committee. What is demonstrated is that the steward cannot define the issue in any way he likes—he has to present the issue in a manner which is congruent with the minimal frame of reference held in common by his members.

In all of these cases, the steward can be seen as crystallizing a range of value beliefs as to the source and nature of the grievance in such a way as to create a focus for commitment.

The Process of Definition

Unfortunately, not enough incidents occurred during the course of study to test any overall pattern. However, these few examples demonstrate some general features about defining and articulating "the grievance." The stewards took into consideration:

1. Which value system to access in order to legitimize the group and so maintain a collective unity and a collective commitment to action;
2. Which part of the management system to utilize in progressing the grievance once it had been defined;
3. How to articulate the grievance so as to minimize opposition from other workgroups and management;
4. How to feed back the results of any bargaining in such a way as to confirm or change the values and beliefs of group members accessed under (1) above so as to develop a group strategy.

By failing to consider any of these four facets, the steward undermines his effectiveness as the group's representative and also the group's effectiveness as a bargaining unit. For example, if the steward neglects the likely reactions and counter definitions of management and/or other workgroups, the result may be incompatible definitions around the bargaining table which could escalate the grievance to a zero-sum bargaining encounter which the steward's group may lose. Similarly, by accessing an inappropriate part of the management system, the steward could confuse the definition of the grievance as far as management is concerned, which may in turn delay the settlement. The steward's effectiveness obviously depends on a satisfactory outcome to the grievance. The outcome may be satisfactory either because of some tangible result, or in the way the steward interprets the outcome for his constituents. That is, the steward or the group comes out of it with honor even if nothing tangible has been achieved. These four facets will now be considered, in turn, in light of the examples discussed above.

Defining the Grievance to Mobilize Appropriate Values

The steward has to define the grievance by reference to some set of values and beliefs. This is made problematic for the steward when there is no prevailing value system, either because different members of his constituency have different values or have the same values but different perspectives of what the grievance is about. The first example above, in the die shop, demonstrates the different perspectives. But even if perspectives were similar, the problem would remain because it is highly doubtful that there is a generalized set of values, beliefs, priorities, against which *all* work experience is measured by the individual, let alone by more than one. Mann (1970) suggests that empirical evidence of apparent inconsistencies in workers' values indicates a dualism of consciousness. However, Mills (1963) implies that values are specific to their context.

Although the values do not cause the grievance, they help to determine the collective action that follows because the saliency of the values determines what they are prepared to do as a collectivity. As Fox (1973) notes, it is not the "odds" in an objective sense that determines behavior; it is the interaction between those odds and the nature and strength of the motivating values. The way in which a grievance is defined expresses these values and so the definition of the grievance is crucial. Although there may be a range of alternative or competing frames of reference, the steward cannot arbitrarily define the grievance and expect his constituents to accept it (e.g., the steward's definition of the electricians' strike was not accepted and the stewards lost control). There is also the possibility that an influential member of the steward's constituency may define the grievance differently. Choosing which values to try and legitimize the grievance is problematic for the steward. With the benefit of hindsight, the definition is a matter of straightforward common sense. But there is nothing self-evident about it. The above example suggests that the group could be considered as a fragile coalition in a perpetual state of being formed. It is suggested here that the group could be considered to exist if and when the values successfully accessed by the steward to legitimate grievances across different contexts are expressed in terms of previous collective experiences. That is, the group is distinguished from the coalition by having a stock of commitment to collective action based on its previous experience of collective action (Loveridge, 1973). In none of the above examples did the stewards feel confident in defining the grievance in such terms. This problem is further discussed in terms of how the steward should feed back the results of the bargaining encounter.

The Choice of Networks

A corollary of defining the grievance is choosing in which part of the management network to progress the grievance. There is a choice since management is not a unitary structure but is comprised of different groups operating in a system of rules, targets, and constraints. These different groups may be based on organization tasks (e.g., a production department) or on political networks either as cliques or cabals (Dalton, 1959; Fletcher, 1973). These groups within management have different perspectives and do not necessarily agree with each other. These groups will tend to react differently to any particular definition of a grievance. Consequently, there is a choice in defining the issue in terms that make it appropriate to access the bargaining procedures at preferred points. In the die shop strike, the grievance was defined in such terms as would make it appropriate to bargain with the Personnel Department rather than the Production Management (i.e., the grievance was defined as a procedural issue rather than a substantive issue). The die shop was not questioning the superintendent's decision but rather whether the procedure by which the decision was implemented was itself fair. If the issue had been defined as a substantive one, then the bargaining would have been between the Production Management and the steward and the outcome might have been very different. The choice is not limited to the formal grievance procedure but depends on the informal understandings between individual managers, supervisors, and stewards as shown in Beynon (1973). The choice of which part of the network to access is not just a question of going to the top, that is, going to the positions which have the authority to make the desired decision, but also includes those who influence the top positions. The definition of the grievance must, however, be appropriate to that part of management.

Minimizing Opposition

The choice of which part of the management network to utilize in progressing the grievance is related to how different parts of management define the grievance. If the steward can persuade management, or a part of management, to accept his definition of the grievance, then his bargaining position is that much easier. If, on the contrary, the definitions of the grievance are mutually incompatible, then bargaining is made more difficult. A careful choice of definition can reduce the conflict. In the example of the finishing shop concerning the upgrading of an individual employee, management and workgroups saw the issue in terms of personality as to whether or not the individual was the right type to be upgraded. Management's definition of the situation was incompatible with that of the workgroup. The grievance escalated and would have resulted in strike action had not the grievance been redefined away from the personality of the individual towards querying the necessity of having two grades on that job. This meant that the respective definitions were no longer incompatible and a solution could be negotiated. The process of conflict resolution can be seen here as one where definitions of the grievance converge. Consequently, the process of grievance resolution must depend on how the grievance is formulated in the first place. If the steward wishes to avoid zero-sum encounter, he must at least ensure that his definition is not incompatible with that of management.

The steward's purpose in trying to define the grievance for management is more than just avoiding incompatible definitions. The purpose is also to limit the choice of action open to management so as to improve the likelihood of a favorable outcome to the steward (Schelling, 1960; Walton & McKersie, 1965).

Developing Group Identity

Part of the problem in understanding values and the role they play in the formation and activation of groups is that it is a dynamic process. Group activation depends, to some extent, on values and beliefs, but at the same time the experience of the group acting together as a collectivity will have some effect on the values and beliefs of the individual members. The steward, in considering how to define the grievance, has to take account of how he will be able to feed back the results of the bargaining with management to his members. Particular meanings in the workplace can then be seen as persisting through their reaffirmation in action or at least through feedback (Silverman, 1970). This feedback by the steward is the mechanism whereby the experience of the group acting together is translated into meaningful terms for its members. The precise experience of that situation obviously varies between individuals, but the steward's feedback can be seen as the way in which a general consensus is achieved either in terms of a commonly experienced "good time" or "bad time" (Gouldner, 1954). Therefore, when a situation containing similar features recurs, each individual will respond in a similar manner in an attempt to repeat or avoid the experience. Thus, the steward must consider the longer term implications when he tries to mobilize support for a particular issue. If the steward can build up a series of good experiences for his members, then the power of that workgroup can be mobilized in terms of previous collective experience (Loveridge, Partridge, Marchington, & Crighton, 1976).

This feedback of the outcome of the grievance by the steward to his members is similar to the educative role usually highlighted in the literature (Beynon, 1973; Goodman & Whittingham, 1973). This feedback emphasizes the role of the steward in maintaining and strengthening the consensus of the collectivity. Generally, the steward has few sanctions that he can personally apply against individuals or cliques within his constituency; consequently the steward has to rely on the feedback process to maintain the consensus. The feedback process is, however, more than just maintaining consensus; it also encompasses a strategy of group action (Sayles, 1958). Thus, the feedback process can reaffirm or modify the choice of industrial action in the future.

The group which has been mobilized to process a grievance faces the same problem of identity as any other interest group, i.e., what happens to the group once its immediate objective has been met. The choice is either disbandonment or finding another objective. The difficulty of the second choice is that there may not be another objective immediately at hand so the feedback process has to include ideally some notion of being ready when the next time or objective comes along.

This discussion of the four facets of grievance definition is not meant to imply that the definition is a simple process; on the contrary, it can be extremely difficult.

In the above examples, the focus has been on the leadership role of the steward with little direct attention given to management. Yet the effectiveness of the steward depends in part on managerial reciprocation. However, management responses on this site were reactive rather than pro-active because of internal political differences within the senior management team, with the result that the stewards' joint committee was more conscious of the need for a negotiating strategy.

DISCUSSION

This study has highlighted aspects of the leadership process on the shopfloor. This type of leader is interesting because he does not operate in a context where his authority is unchallenged, nor does he have sanctions to motivate his constituents. Obvious parallels can be drawn with other types of leaders in similar situations, particularly where decisions cannot be imposed and persuasion is used instead. Power (1973) sees civil servants as defining the issue or problem in such terms that the decisions of their political masters are preempted. Galbraith (1969) sees decisions in business organizations as structured by the technical experts. Indeed, the whole concept of non-decision-making is about how strategic decisions are not challenged because actual grievances are redefined in terms of safe issues (Bachrach & Baratz, 1962).

Likewise the politician can be seen as a power craftsman who assembles packages of bargains that fashion and shape disparate conceptions, ambitions, and aspirations and links them with concrete outcomes. He also manipulates his network so that it is just sufficient, in terms of resources mobilized, to attain the desired outcomes (Power, 1973). These comparisons show the close overlap between the processes of leadership and decision-making. Leadership can be seen, in part, as controlling the process by which decisions are made (Vroom, 1974). They also emphasize the political nature of the leadership and the use of information as a resource in a power game.

There are some obvious connections between this process of grievance definition and recent trends in the leadership literature, in particular with the path-goal approach to leadership where the leadership function is seen as clarifying for followers the kind of behavior or actions that leads to goal accomplishment and valued rewards. The major difference is one of degree: The steward has to cope with a greater degree of uncertainty over a longer time horizon than his managerial counterparts.

The situational favorableness (Fiedler, 1967) for the steward is very limited as regards power and is highly variable as regards task structure and member relations. This variability combined with the lack of suitable criteria of steward or group performance makes it difficult to apply Fiedler's Contingency approach. The process of defining the grievance has obvious parallels with Vroom and Yetton (1973). However, the definition is a process through time rather than a decision at a point in time, which the steward responds to by keeping an open approach, i.e., the steward straddles two distinct leader dimensions.

Grievance definition has obvious similarities with initiating structure where the leader in an instrumental fashion structures his followers' environment by assigning tasks, specifying procedures, clarifying path-goal relationships, etc. But the process of grievance definiton also encompasses social-emotional behavior in providing consideration (i.e., a supportive environment) for his subordinates. Apart from the obvious consideration implicit in progressing an individual's grievance, the steward is also involved in an ongoing situation in providing socio-emotional support in the form of advice, sympathy, and information. The stewards used it as a way of sorting out genuine grievances from "pleas" for consideration, and also as a precaution: Even if they could do nothing else (i.e., they could not legitimize the grievance), they could sympathize. Overall, the consideration behavior was a form of protecting this position vis-a-vis their constituency and facilitating their initiation of role structure.

The major implication for leadership theory from this study of shopfloor leaders is the variability of action or style of leadership. The steward's treatment of a member's grievance varies from one grievance to another. The steward's choice of definition depends, in part, on his ability, his constituents' values, attitudes and beliefs, and the previous experience of those constituents acting together as a collectivity. Other situational variables will include the power of the collectivity and past management reciprocity. Just because the steward is effective in legitimizing a particular grievance is no guarantee that he will be able to legitimize other grievances in the same way.

REFERENCES

Bachrach, P., & Baratz, M. S. Two faces of power. *American Political Science Review*, 1962, **56**, 947–952.

Beynon, H. *Working for Ford*. Harmondsworth: Penguin, 1973.

Brown, W. *Piecework bargaining*. London: Heinemann, 1973.

Clegg, H. A. *The system of industrial relations in Great Britain*. Oxford: Blackwell, 1972.

Dalton, M. *Men who manage*. New York: Wiley, 1959.

Evans, M. G. The effects of supervisory behavior on the path-goal relationship. *Organizational Behavior and Human Performance*, 1970, **5**, May, 277–298.

Fiedler, F. E. *A theory of leadership effectiveness*. New York: McGraw-Hill, 1967.

Fletcher, C. The end of management. In J. Child (Ed.), *Man and organization*. London: George Allen & Unwin, 1973.

Fox, A. Industrial relations: A social critique of pluralist ideology. In J. Child (Ed.), *Man and organization*. London: George Allen & Unwin, 1973.

Galbraith, J. K. *The new industrial state*. Harmondsworth: Penguin, 1969.

Goodman, J. F. B., & Whittingham, T. G. *Shop stewards*. London: Pan, 1973.

Gouldner, A. W. *Wildcat strike*. New York: Harper, 1954.

Hill, S. Norms, groups and power: The sociology of workplace industrial relations. *British Journal of Industrial Relations*, 1974, **12**(2), 213–235.

House, R. J. A path-goal theory of leader effectiveness. *Administrative Science Quarterly*, 1971, **16**(3), 321–338.

Hyman, R., & Brough, I. B. *Social values and industrial relations*. Oxford: Blackwell, 1975.

Loveridge, R. *Member orientations to trade unions*. Paper presented at the meeting of the Industrial Sociology Section of the British Sociological Association, Imperial College, London, April 1973.

Loveridge, R., Partridge, B., Marchington, M., & Crighton, S. *Leadership and commitment in workplace collective bargaining*. Working Paper No. 29, Management Centre, University of Aston, 1976.

Mann, M. The social cohesion of liberal democracy. *American Sociological Review*, 1970, **35**, 423–439.

Marchington, M. *Sources of workgroup power capacity*. Working Paper No. 41, Management Centre, University of Aston, 1975.

McCarthy, W. E. J., & Parker, S. R. *Shop stewards and workshop relations*. Research Paper No. 10, Royal Commission on Trade Unions and Employers Associations. London: HMSO, 1968.

Mills, C. W. *Power, politics and people.* New York: Oxford University Press, 1963.

Newcomb, T. M., Turner, R., & Converse, P. E. *Social psychology.* London: Routledge, 1966.

Power, J. The reticulist function in government: Manipulating networks of communication and influence. *Public Administration,* (Australia), 1973, 32(1), 21–27.

Preiss, J., & Ehrlich, H. *An examination of role theory.* Lincoln, Neb.: University of Nebraska Press, 1966.

Sayles, L. R. *Behavior of industrial work groups.* New York: Wiley, 1958.

Schelling, T. C. *The strategy of conflict.* Cambridge, Mass.: Harvard University Press, 1960.

Silverman, D. *The theory of organizations.* London: Heinemann, 1970.

Stogdill, R. M. *Individual behavior and group achievement.* New York: Oxford University Press, 1959.

Stogdill, R. M. *The handbook of leadership—a survey of theory and research.* New York: Free Press, 1974. (a)

Stogdill, R. M. Historical trends in leadership theory and research. *Journal of Contemporary Business,* 1974, 3(4), 1–17. (b)

Vroom, V. H. Decision making and the leadership process. *Journal of Contemporary Business,* 1974, 3(4), 47–65.

Vroom, V. H., & Yetton, P. W. *Leadership and decision making.* Pittsburgh, Pa.: University of Pittsburgh Press, 1973.

Walton, R. E., & McKersie, R. B. *A behavioral theory of labor negotiations.* New York: McGraw-Hill, 1965.

PART 3

CONSTRAINTS ON DECISION MAKERS

CHARACTERISTICS OF DECISION MAKING AS A FUNCTION OF THE ENVIRONMENT [1]

Peter Suedfeld
The University of British Columbia

The topic of this study is the relationship between information processing and the molar environment going beyond the making of decisions in problem solving situations. Problems are not solved in a cognitive vacuum. Decision making is strongly affected by relevant aspects of the total milieu and of the individual. Regardless of how much problem-specific information the person has available, general characteristics of the situation and pervasive tendencies in his approach to problems will interact strongly with specific conditions in such a way as to affect the final decision. These characteristics and tendencies can be thought of as analogues of background and residual stimuli, respectively, in adaptation level theory (Helson, 1964). They will affect any decision-making or problem-solving activity in which the individual engages. The way in which the person selectively attends to, evaluates, and reacts to

[1] The preparation of this paper, as well as much of the author's research, was supported by Grant # A9589 from the National Research Council of Canada. The author's studies on political and international behavior are being funded by Canada Council Grant S75-0752-R1.

informational input is always played out against this more global and consistent background.

The major factor dealt with in this discussion is one aspect of the environment: affective/cognitive information load. Load is a function of a finite but large number of interacting variables, making up the total input that then influences the behavior of the people in the environment. The *primary focus is on situations of unusually low and unusually high load*, and on the ways in which these situations modify receptivity to information and cognitive strategies in dealing with it.

The construct of environmental load may underlie a number of intervening events; it certainly does affect behavioral outcomes. Load varies from very low to very high, and also includes such subsidiary dimensions as the proportion of the total information that is relevant to a particular problem or decision; the clarity or consistency of relevant information; its complexity, which, in turn, includes both diversity at any given moment and change over time; the clarity and intensity of the information; and a vast number of meaning variables, such as reinforcement value, source, and perceived credibility.

One problem in much of the research in this area has been the attempt to establish *general* levels of underload, overload, and optimal load. This is an attempt that I think is doomed to failure. Underload and overload both connote levels that are different from some optimal level; but it seems impossible to specify a universal optimum. If it is the standard that the subject is most used to, then it clearly differs across individuals and even more across cultures. If it is the level that the individual prefers, the same differences exist, with the addition of temporal changes in the person's mood, health, fatigue, and other personal states. If it is the load at which the individual does his best work, then again all of the previous variables are relevant, with the addition of task variables such as the type of performance required, the resources available, and the other people involved.

Moreover, the mere gross level of environmental stimulation is not related in any simple way to decision making or to any other kind of performance. As has been shown by Glass and Singer (1972) and Frankenhaeuser (e.g., Frankenhaeuser & Gardell, 1973), among others, and in the taxonomies prepared by Sells (1973) and Borrie (1976), one must also consider the duration of high or low information input, the degree of voluntariness with which the subject entered the condition, the extent to which the information in the environment demands a response and to which it facilitates or hinders problem-solving decisions, pre-planning and pre-training for the condition, the emotional tone of the condition, and the degree to which environmental input and its changes can be predicted and controlled by the individual.

Ranging from the Stone Age environment of some isolated tribes to the dynamic, loud, crowded metropolis, today's world offers a wider range of information and stimulus loads than any other in human history. Between the anchor points, we see the life of the hermit, the prospector, the rural settler, the dweller in small towns, and the urbanite; the individual who periodically moves from one to another of these situations; and the person who seeks out different levels of the range available within each environment. The availability of this array is not fully appreciated; if it were, people could seek out milieux that suit their personality, or even their temporary preference. Instead, they remain docilely in informational environments that they find unpleasant and counterproductive, and in many cases suffer serious psychological and physical damage.

Let us look first at situations of low load. At the very end of the continuum is the experimental environment in which much of my own research has taken place, the sensory deprivation chamber. There is a widespread belief that the effect of this extremely low level of input on human decision making is adverse: lowered intellectual competence, disruptive alterations in mood, even pseudo-psychotic experiences such as hallucinations. Actually, the negative picture is misleading. Perceptual processes frequently become more acute in sensory deprivation, while moods are quite often pleasant and relaxed. There is also evidence that while the ability to solve complex cognitive problems decreases, the ability to do simple tasks such as memorization improves (Landon & Suedfeld, 1972; Suedfeld, 1969; Zubek, 1969).

Sensory deprivation also appears to make subjects more open to new experiences (Myers, Murphy, Smith, & Goffard, 1966), which makes it feasible to use the procedure to improve the subject's self-esteem (e.g., Gibby & Adams, 1961) and to perform other therapeutic functions. Important among these is the chance that the sensorially deprived subject has to think about serious personal problems, to consider both new and old information relating to the problem, to gain control over aspects of his own behavior that had taken on an autonomous and undesired power—including smoking and overeating—and to make appropriate and ·beneficial decisions (Borrie, in preparation; Suedfeld, 1975b; Suedfeld & Best, in press).

Among less extreme situations we find the condition of individuals who are socially isolated for a long period of time: prisoners, castaways, solitary sailors and fliers (Rasmussen, 1973). These individuals frequently suffer not only solitude, but also danger, disease or injury, deprivation, and uncertainty as to their fate (see Sells, 1973). It is possible to cope with such situations effectively by generating internal stimulation and information, thus maintaining a reasonably normal total information load. Individuals who are able to take advantage of improved recall to enjoy unusually vivid memories, or who can relax and let themselves float in fantasy without worrying about maintaining cognitive control, or who can set up and solve hypothetical future problems that they might encounter when the experience is over, tend by these techniques to solve the real problem of adjusting to the current environment (Bone, 1957; Deaton & Richlin, in press; Suedfeld, 1974; Suedfeld, Ramirez, & Clyne, in preparation).

Some amount of withdrawal from the environment may be beneficial in helping the individual to survive (Schein, 1961). For example, isolated American prisoners of war in North Vietnam achieved detachment from immediate stressors by thinking about their lives before and after captivity, evoking the vivid memories that low-load environments make possible, fantasizing, and devising routines to keep themselves fit for normal life (Deaton & Richlin, in press). On the other hand, extreme withdrawal can lead to the death of the victim through the lack of sufficient effort to maintain his strength and health (Bettelheim, 1958).

Let us next look at workers in monotonous and/or isolated environments. This includes radar observers, submarine crew members, and assembly line operators, among others. Vigilance is improved in sensory deprivation (Myers et al., 1966); but during long periods of duty, the number of faulty decisions increases. In confined groups, even when they are compatible and highly motivated, there is increasing withdrawal from each other and from the outside world, along with the growth of interpersonal conflict and isolation as time goes on (Smith, 1969). Interestingly, intellectual functioning is not damaged; any impairment that does occur seems to be on routine tasks, with the subjects responding at the accustomed levels of efficiency on tasks that are challenging and interesting.

The other, more common, example is that of the worker performing routine, repetitive tasks in an unglamourous setting. It is clear that many workers in such jobs experience a great deal of boredom and resultant adverse effects (e.g., Caplan, Cobb, French, Van Harrison, & Pinneau, 1975; Gardell, 1971; Kornhauser, 1965). In these situations, few, if any, decisions worthy of the name are made. In fact, that is one reason why they are so monotonous and uninteresting (Bolinder & Oström, 1971). Younger workers, more used to high and changing stimulation, are the most susceptible to boredom on the job (Stagner, 1975). To remedy this situation, one must provide compensatory enrichment. Some of the techniques used in more extreme environments—varied cuisine, shorter shifts, stimulating off-duty facilities—might be worth investigating in this respect. At the same time, they might also lessen the occurrence of deliberate vandalism both by reducing the causes of such behavior and by evoking favorable Hawthorne effects.

Boredom can cause a dangerous or disruptive search for stimulation. Prisoners taunt and provoke their guards even when such behavior would result in serious punishment, just to generate some excitement. Similarly, self-injurious behavior, ostensible suicide attempts, and the breaking of various prison regulations are undertaken merely in order to obtain a change of scenery, a trip to the hospital, or a few days in court (Suedfeld et al., in preparation).

In one major theory, sociopathic behavior is interpreted as an attempt to rectify chronic understimulation (Quay, 1965). Instead of attempting to incarcerate and/or "treat" the psychopath, society might do better by making available to him environments that are high enough in stimulation load to make him comfortable. Many such opportunities now require unusual talents, coordination, skill, training, or money; but there is an increasing number of very exciting individual sports that do not demand the repetitiveness of team practice, and in which individuals with even moderate funds and physical skills can participate. The recent freeing by a guerilla team of a number of American youths held on drug charges in Mexico and the constant recruiting of mercenaries may exemplify other possibilities (Suedfeld & Landon, in press).

As our environment has become ever more information-satiating, increasing numbers of people have been turning to activities such as meditation, relaxation training, weekend retreats, return to the soil movements, and camping trips to obtain some time-out and to regain serenity by giving the information processing mechanisms a rest (Suedfeld, 1974). Even the extreme case, sensory deprivation, is losing its negative aura. People are beginning to recognize its therapeutic possibilities, and there are growing numbers of volunteers who want to go into the chamber for some period of time, without any particular problem that they want to solve and without payment, just to escape overstimulation. I may add that mothers of young children are prominent among this group.

In gradually overcoming our culture-bound biases, we are now beginning not only to appreciate the beauties of low load, but also to recognize the adverse aspects of very high load. Those accurate prophets, the writers of science fiction, strongly agree that we are facing a generally increasing level of stimulus overload in general and informational overload in particular. They predict a consequent increase in stress, time pressures, interpersonal and societal conflict, alienation, and social breakdown. Several writers couple these developments with widespread boredom as meaningful work is taken over by machines and becomes less and less available to the average individual. Psychological research certainly supports the results of the projected outcomes (Suedfeld & Ward, 1976).

The relatively high portion of the load continuum is easier to adapt to in the short run than low stimulation, but probably takes a greater toll in the final analysis (see, e.g., Insel & Moos, 1974; Lipowski, 1971; Toffler, 1970). There is evidence that individuals with various kinds of behavioral problems, including alcoholics and schizophrenics, are stressed by what the rest of us consider normal levels of stimulation. As a result, they tend to seek out and enjoy lower levels of input (Harris, 1959; Rank & Suedfeld, in press; Suedfeld & Roy, 1975). A variety of psychosomatic ills, such as heart disease, hypertension, and ulcers, also seem to be linked to overload although others appear to result from monotony (e.g., Caplan et al., 1975; Viskum, 1975). Frankenhaeuser and her coworkers have investigated this phenomenon in detail, and have linked both high and low environmental load with a variety of negative outcomes (e.g., Frankenhaeuser & Johansson, 1974).

Laboratory research on extremely high stimulation levels has demonstrated that high-load situations are in fact generally aversive, and that they lead the subject to work fairly hard in order to avoid further input (Ludwig, 1971). There are also cognitive disorganizations and impairment similar to those found in sensory deprivation, but no studies have as yet looked at complex decision making during multimodal overstimulation (for a review, see Borrie, 1976). Two particular kinds of high load have been more intensely studied, and their effects can perhaps be generalized. These are the situations of high-intensity noise and high levels of crowding or density.

High noise levels can cause actual physiological damage (Kryter, 1970). They also impair cognitive processes including memorization, the recognition of errors in written material, children's ability to learn, and group problem-solving. There is a startling similarity to the effects of low-load environments: "Adverse effects are more likely with 'complex' tasks, and facilitatory effects with 'simple' tasks" (Hockey, 1969, p. 245). As mentioned previously, factors such as the predictability and controllability of the noise interact with intensity and other physical dimensions, so that the relationship is not a simple one.

Data on the effects of crowding have aroused considerable controversy. Freedman, one of the pioneer investigators in this area, has denied that significant adverse effects on cognitive or social behavior result from crowding, and has taken the opportunity to praise the city as an exciting and efficient human environment (e.g., 1975). On the other hand, his work has been criticized for its definition of crowding as mere density (i.e., reduced space per person) by researchers who feel that crowding in real life involves many other variables including odors, heat, restriction of movement and communication, and high levels of bodily and eye contact (Epstein, 1974).

Research based on the latter model has found that crowding improves simple task performance (although no deterioration of complex performance was found), decreases group cohesiveness among men and increases it among women, makes men more and women less competitive in a game situation, and decreases the likelihood of contributions to charity (Epstein, Aiello, & Karlin, 1976; Saegert, Mackintosh, & West, 1975). Population density is positively and significantly related to a number of indicators of pathology including death rate, male deaths from heat disease, admissions to hospital, and a group of measures of social maladaptation (Levy & Herzog, 1974). As in the case of noise, cognitive factors are important: Levels of crowding that are seen as comfortable and appropriate in one situation are evaluated as stressful in another (Desor, 1972).

Simulation studies of decision making in the conceptual complexity framework (see chapter 13) have demonstrated the adverse effects of both low and high information loads. The relationship between information load and decision-making complexity is curvilinear, with informational and personality variables playing a role in specifying the details of the function. Decision making under high load tends to become stereotyped, characterized by the reduction of information search, the selective use of information, and increasingly stimulus-bound reactions. Holsti (1972) has demonstrated that national leaders follow this pattern when they perceive that decisions have to be made under conditions of high load and external pressure. Unless careful steps are taken, the decisions become hurried and restricted to a smaller range of possibilities than necessary (see also Janis, 1972).

We have recently completed a number of studies on communication complexity and the resolution of international crises (Suedfeld & Tetlock, 1976). The complexity score reflects the degree to which the communicator expresses flexibility, the consideration of alternative points of view in solving problems, a willingness to consider the motivations and goals of his opponent as legitimate even if he disagrees with them, and the ability to organize a diversity of decisions, perspectives, and desires into some coherent pattern.

In one study, we compared communications from leaders of the major participants in the European international crisis leading to the First World War with those of American and Soviet leaders during the Cuban missile crisis of 1962. Complexity increased significantly from an early to a later phase during 1962, and both began and remained at a relatively low level in 1914. The implication is that a deliberate attempt to maintain high levels of decision-making complexity in the face of intense environmental stress and load, which was a feature of John F. Kennedy's approach during the Cuban crisis (Holsti, 1972), was successful in resolving the situation without resorting to war.

In a second study, we compared crises that occurred within a given historical period. Communications during the 1911 Moroccan crisis, which was resolved peacefully, were considerably higher in complexity than were those sent before the outbreak of World War I. Similarly, for three US-USSR confrontations of the mid-20th century (the Berlin blockade of 1948, the beginning of the Korean War in 1950, and the Cuban missile crisis in 1962), we found significantly lower complexity in the situation that eventually led to war than in the two peacefully resolved conflicts. Relatively high complexity in 1962 as compared to 1948 reflected some other relevant parameter. This may have been the general easing of Cold War tension, or different information-processing characteristics of the leaders involved in those two events.

Where does this leave us? Clearly, both low and high environmental information load affect problem solving and decision making. It is probably inappropriate to talk about suboptimal and superoptimal loads in general, since this usage glosses over important differences among situations. Some decisions can and should be made quickly, after consideration of a restricted amount of data, while others should be made slowly and only after processing all available information; some can be made most effectively by relying upon well-learned and efficiently performed habit patterns, while others call for the generation of novel and sometimes even bizarre approaches; some must be linked with an array of other decisions made by a number of people, while others can stand alone. There is no reason to expect that any one particular environment will be optimal for all of these, and a number of other, parameters of decision making. Perhaps what we need is a more individualized attempt to match the appropriate kind of environment to the kind of decision that must be made in it, and even to the personalities of the decision-makers. This may require a paradigm shift of the kind that Harré and Secord (1972) have recently advocated for social psychology, with its emphasis on individual cases and on the meaning of events to the participants in those events; lacking that, a more intense study of crosscultural and historical comparisons might give us at least the beginning of a taxonomic matrix.

REFERENCES

Bettelheim, B. Individual and mass behavior in extreme situations. In E. E. Maccoby, T. M. Newcomb, & E. L. Hartley (Eds.), *Reading in social psychology* (3rd ed). New York: Holt, 1958.

Bolinder, E., & Oström, D. *Stress in Swedish work places.* Stockholm: Prisma, 1971.

Bone, E. *Seven years' solitary.* New York: Harcourt, Brace, 1957.

Borrie, R. A. *A conceptual model of sensory overload.* Unpublished manuscript, The University of British Columbia, 1976.

Borrie, R. A. *Sensory deprivation and therapeutic messages used with behavioral techniques in a weight control program.* Doctoral dissertation, The University of British Columbia, in preparation.

Caplan, R. D., Cobb, S., French, J. R. P., Jr., Van Harrison, R., & Pinneau, S. R., Jr. *Job demands and worker health.* Washington, D.C.: Department of Health, Education and Welfare, 1975.

Deaton, J. E., & Richlin, M. Coping activities in solitary confinement of U.S. Navy POWs in Vietnam. *Journal of Applied Social Psychology,* 1977, in press.

Desor, J. A. Toward a psychological theory of crowding. *Journal of Personality and Social Psychology*, 1972, 21, 79–83.

Epstein, Y. M. *The effects of crowding: A conjoint approach.* Unpublished manuscript, Rutgers University, 1974.

Epstein, Y. M., Aiello, J., & Karlin, R. An applied research perspective on crowding. In P. Suedfeld & J. A. Russell (Gen. Eds.), *The behavioral basis of design.* L. M. Ward, C. Coren, A. Gruft, & J. C. Collins (Eds.), *Book 1, Selected papers, EDRA-7.* Stroudsburg, Pennsylvania: Dowden, Hutchinson, & Ross, 1976. (Abstract)

Frankenhaeuser, M., & Gardell, B. *Underload and overload in working life: A multidisciplinary approach.* Unpublished manuscript, University of Stockholm, 1973.

Frankenhaeuser, M., & Johansson, G. *On the psychophysiological consequences of understimulation and overstimulation.* Reports from the Psychological Laboratories, University of Stockholm, Supplement No. 25, August 1974.

Freedman, J. L. *Crowding and behavior.* San Francisco: Freeman, 1975.

Gardell, B. Alienation and mental health in the modern industrial environment. In L. Levi (Ed.), *Society, stress and disease (Vol. 1): The psychosocial environment and psychosomatic diseases.* London: Oxford University Press, 1971.

Gibby, K. G., & Adams, H. B. Receptiveness of psychiatric patients to verbal communication: An increase following partial sensory and social isolation. *Archives of General Psychiatry*, 1961, 5, 366–370.

Glass, D. C., & Singer, J. E. *Urban stress.* New York: Academic Press, 1972.

Harré, R., & Secord, P. F. *The explanation of social behavior.* Totowa, N.J.: Rowman & Littlefield, 1972.

Harris, A. Sensory deprivation and schizophrenia. *Journal of Mental Science*, 1959, 105, 235–237.

Helson, H. *Adaptation level theory: An experimental and systematic approach to behavior.* New York: Harper & Row, 1964.

Hockey, R. Noise and efficiency: The visual task. *New Scientist*, 1969, 42, 244–246.

Holsti, O. R. *Crisis, escalation, war.* Montreal: McGill-Queen's University Press, 1972.

Insel, P. M., & Moos, R. H. (Eds.), *Health and the social environment.* Lexington, Mass.: Heath, 1974.

Janis, I. L. *Victims of groupthink.* New York: Houghton Mifflin, 1972.

Kornhauser, A. *Mental health of the industrial worker.* New York: Wiley, 1965.

Kryter, K. D. *The effects of noise on man.* New York: Academic Press, 1970.

Landon, P. B., & Suedfeld, P. Complex cognitive performance and sensory deprivation: Completing the U-curve. *Perceptual and Motor Skills*, 1972, 34, 601–602.

Levy, L., & Herzog, A. N. Effects of population density and crowding on health and social adaptation in the Netherlands. *Journal of Health and Social Behavior*, 1974, 15, 228–240.

Lipowski, J. A. Surfeit of attractive information inputs: A hallmark of our environment. *Behavioral Science*, 1971, **16**, 467–471.

Ludwig, A. M. Self-regulation of the sensory environment. *Archives of General Psychiatry*, 1971, **25**, 413–418.

Myers, T. I., Murphy, D. B., Smith, S., & Goffard, S. J. *Experimental studies of sensory deprivation and social isolation* (HumRRO Tech. Rep. 66-8). Washington, D.C.: George Washington University, June 1966.

Quay, H. C. Psychopathic personality as pathological stimulation-seeking. *American Journal of Psychiatry*, 1965, **122**, 180–183.

Rank, D. S., & Suedfeld, P. Positive reactions of alcoholic men to sensory deprivation. *International Journal of the Addictions*, 1977, in press.

Rasmussen, J. (Ed.), *Man in isolation and confinement*. Chicago: Aldine, 1973.

Saegert, S., Mackintosh, B., & West, S. Two studies of crowding in urban public spaces. *Environment and Behavior*, 1975, **7**, 159–184.

Schein, E. H. *Coercive persuasion*. New York: Norton, 1961.

Schroder, H. M., Driver, M. J., & Streufert, S. *Human information processing*. New York: Holt, Rinehart & Winston, 1967.

Sells, S. B. The taxonomy of man in enclosed space. In J. Rasmussen (Ed.), *Man in isolation and confinement*. Chicago: Aldine, 1973.

Smith, S. Studies of small groups in confinement. In J. P. Zubek (Ed.), *Sensory deprivation: Fifteen years of research*. New York: Appleton-Century-Crofts, 1969.

Stagner, R. Boredom on the assembly line: Age and personality variables. *Industrial Gerontology*, 1975, **2**, 23–44.

Suedfeld, P. Changes in intellectual performance and in susceptibility to influence. In J. P. Zubek (Ed.), *Sensory deprivation: Fifteen years of research*. New York: Appleton-Century-Crofts, 1969.

Suedfeld, P. Social isolation: A case for interdisciplinary research. *Canadian Psychologist*, 1974, **15**, 1–15.

Suedfeld, P. The benefits of boredom: Sensory deprivation reconsidered. *American Scientist*, 1975, **63**, 60–69. (a)

Suedfeld, P. The clinical relevance of reduced sensory stimulation. *Canadian Psychological Review*, 1975, **16**, 88–103. (b)

Suedfeld, P., & Best, J. A. Satiation and sensory deprivation combined in smoking therapy: Some case studies and unexpected side-effects. *International Journal of the Addictions*, 1977, in press.

Suedfeld, P., & Landon, P. B. Approaches to treatment. In R. D. Hare & D. Schalling (Eds.), *Psychopathic behavior*. New York: Wiley, in press.

Suedfeld, P., Ramirez, C., & Clyne, D. *The effects of involuntary social isolation on prison inmates*. Unpublished manuscript, The University of British Columbia, in preparation.

Suedfeld, P., & Rank, A. D. Revolutionary leaders: Long-term success as a function of changes in conceptual complexity. *Journal of Personality and Social Psychology*, 1976, **34**, 169–178.

Suedfeld, P., & Roy, C. Using social isolation to change the behavior of disruptive inmates. *International Journal of Offender Therapy and Comparative Criminology*, 1975, **19**, 90–99.

Suedfeld, P., & Tetlock, P. *Integrative complexity of communications in international crisis.* Unpublished manuscript, The University of British Columbia, 1976.

Suedfeld, P., & Ward, L. M. Dark trends: Psychology, science fiction, and the ominous consensus. *Futures*, 1976, **8**, 22–39.

Toffler, A. *Future shock.* New York: Random House, 1970.

Viskum, K. Mind and ulcer. *Acta Psychiatrica Scandinavia*, 1975, **51**, 182–200.

White, R. W. Strategies of adaptation: An attempt at systematic description. In G. V. Coelho, D. A. Hamburg, & J. E. Adams (Eds.), *Coping and adaptation.* New York: Basic Books, 1974.

Zubek, J. P. (Ed.), *Sensory deprivation: Fifteen years of research.* New York: Appleton-Century-Crofts, 1969.

THE HUMAN COMPONENT IN THE DECISION-MAKING SITUATION [1]

Siegfried Streufert
Universität Bielefeld

Organizations must make decisions. The more competitive their relevant environment, the more complex the world with which they have to deal, and the more rapidly their environment changes over time, the higher the quality and quantity their decision making has to be. Without a sufficient number of high quality decisions, most organizations operating in a complex and less than stable environment would soon be as unadaptive as some national bureaucracies already are.

Organizational decisions are made by individuals or groups of individuals. When these persons are dealing with a decision-making problem, they are aided by their special skills and their experience, but they are subject to their own limitations as well. In addition, the quality and quantity of their decisions are influenced by the characteristics and constraints of the environment with which they are faced. This theoretical study deals with predictions of decision making on the basis of individuals' or a group's capacity [1]

[1] Specifically, one particular kind of capacity: the multidimensional processing of information. The ability to make strategic decisions in complex settings depends among other factors widely on integrative multidimensionality.

to make decisions, and on the basis of the aiding and hindering effects of the environment. It is based on the complexity theory of Streufert and Streufert (1977).

The theoretical propositions of Streufert and Streufert (1977), as well as those which shall be made here, are, in part, the result of many years of research and are, in another part, based on previous complexity theory (e.g., Driver & Streufert, 1966, 1969; Schroder, Driver, & Streufert, 1967; Streufert, 1970). I am not going to discuss the data we have collected on complexity in this work. The interested reader can find them in the literature (cf. the review of complexity in Chapter 2 of Streufert & Streufert, 1977). However, it may be useful to spend a small amount of time on the more general underlying theory.

Complexity theory deals with the potentially perceived dimensionality of stimulus material, with the cognitive structure of the perceiving organism, and with the dimensionality of his responses to stimulation. Complexity theorists (e.g., Driver & Streufert, 1966, 1969; Schroder et al., 1967; Streufert, 1970) have attempted to explain behavior, for example decision making, as an interaction between a particular group of "personality" variables (ability, style or preference of multidimensional information processing) and certain environmental variables which have been loosely subsumed under the term "stress effects."

Standard complexity theory follows the logic of its name: It is interested in situations which themselves are complex, in persons who are capable of multidimensional information processing, and in the integrative dimensionality of decisions made by persons who are multidimensional enough to "qualify." In this focus, previous forms of complexity theory find their own limits: Much human behavior is not multidimensional. Many persons have little capacity to engage in multidimensional information processing, even though the environment in which they operate provides ample opportunity to perceive and act upon their informational input on more than one dimension. But about those persons who do not fall into the "complexity framework," i.e., many people in most situations, the earlier forms of complexity theory have little to say. To predict the behavior of these persons in most situations, the theory is not very useful. To put it more bluntly: The complexity theory of Schroder, Driver, and Streufert (1967) has limited potential for applications. Nonetheless, it has been shown to have *some*, and it would be unwise to throw out the baby with the bath, particularly if newer forms of complexity theory may eliminate this shortcoming.

What appears needed is a larger theoretical framework, one which includes some of the predictions of previous theory, but also goes beyond that to include predictions based on unidimensional information processing with the same interest as predictions based on multidimensional information processing.

Such a theory has been proposed by Streufert and Streufert (1977). It is the purpose of this report to extend that theory to decision-making situations.

A further difference of current theory (including the view proposed here) from the earlier statements of Schroder, Driver, and Streufert lies in an additional focus. While that theory concerned itself primarily with stimulus and person characteristics, the current theory also focusses on response characteristics; for the purposes of this report, on two quite divergent kinds of decision-making responses which have been repeatedly observed in a number of decision-making simulations, i.e., integrative and respondent decision making.

Before explaining the meaning of these terms and beginning with the discussion of the current theoretical views, it is probably useful to state the limits within which this theory is expected to have meaning. In Chapter 12, Suedfeld has discussed environmental effects on behavior including decision making. Suedfeld's focus was on *total* evironmental input, including not only the task related information but also background information, the setting, and so forth. In this study, all stimulus variables which are not task related will fall under the heading "all other things being equal" (i.e., we will assume a medium level of stimulation, one that may be normal for a decision-making task). It is probably true that most decision-making groups or individuals function in a *somewhat* conducive environment, an environment that is (in the sense of complexity theory formulations) neither inherently depriving nor overloading. For that matter, the decision maker might even be able to "adjust" his environment (for example, by telling his secretary that he wants no calls to get through to him, by asking for coffee, etc.).

With a task environment that provides a normal or average level of ecological stimulation, moderate levels of deprivation or overload are often due to task relevant stimuli. It is specifically these task information effects with which we are here concerned, in contrast to the wider range of stimuli discussed by Suedfeld. In the views of Suedfeld, deprivation and overload refers to much more extreme conditions. Nonetheless, the reader shall find some interesting similarities between the views developed by Suedfeld and the view presented here. Let me clarify the distinctions, or for that matter, the similarities, a little further. Both Peter Suedfeld and I are concerned with the degree to which the decision maker is exposed—or exposes himself—to information. However, the minimum information load levels in Suedfeld's work are much lower, and the maximum levels are probably higher than those considered or measured in our work. In other words, a graphic representation of my theoretical statements should fit within the middle range of a graphic representation of Suedfeld's theory. The attentive reader will note that the two views are not contradictory within that range.

Theory

Let us assume that we want to describe and predict the behavior of a *task oriented decision maker* or a task oriented decision-making group. I am intentionally not making a distinction between individuals and groups in the realm of this research area, since we have rarely, if ever, obtained differences among them. But we will assume task orientation, and we will assume that the task as such is of the decision-making, not the problem-solving type[2]—regardless of whether it is responded to in that fashion by our subjects.

Information—Presence and Absence

Let us begin with the stimulus situation. For the decision makers, task information can vary from the extremely low level where it is relatively absent to the extremely high level where it appears to be relatively infinite. I would predict that:

> (1) In the absence of information, the decision maker(s) will seek relevant information, or (if relevant information is not available) will obtain irrelevant information and/or will generate (often irrelevant) information as a basis for responses.
> (2) Response levels to self-sought or self-generated information will not be high, and they will decrease with increasing levels of externally provided information (see Fig. 1). Most of the responses will be unrelated to each other or to any strategy.

They may often appear similar to responses in problem-solving tasks.

In most cases, decision makers find that externally provided information is available to them, even if some, much, or all of it is not particularly useful (i.e., relevant). However, information seems to have "value" in our societies (cf. Brock, 1969). Even persons who already have too much information to handle tend to ask for more information, but tend to disregard much of it when it arrives. Nonetheless, even useless information appears to have *some* effect on decision making. I would suggest that:

> (3) In the presence of information, decision makers tend to respond to information (i.e., utilize it in their decisions) whether the information is relevant or not relevant.

[2] In problem-solving situations, a (usually single) correct solution to a problem must be found. In a decision-making situation, there is no correct solution. Rather, the task force must explore the potential alternatives and select a course of actions according to their own frame of reference.

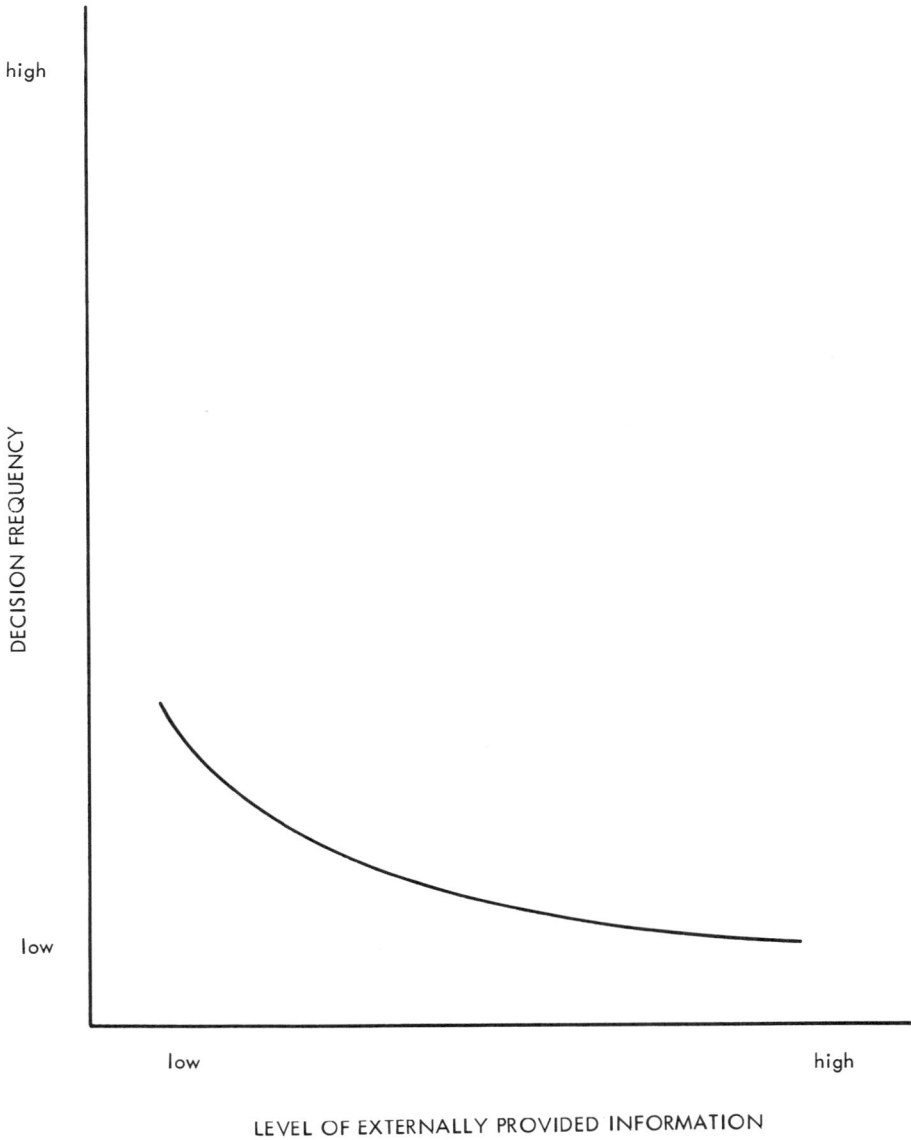

Fig. 1. Effects of externally provided information on the frequency of decisions based on sought or self-generated information.

This does not mean that obviously relevant information will not have a larger effect on decisions than obviously irrelevant information. However, particularly in situations where little or no relevant information is available, irrelevant information does have considerable influence on decision making. But even when fairly large amounts of relevant information are externally provided, irrelevant information does retain some effect. Often decision makers feel that the very presence of information suggests that something about it must be meaningful for the situation in which they are operating.

Kinds of Decision Making

While one can describe human decision making in a number of ways, one particular distinction appears especially useful to me. I would propose that:

(4) Information processing and the resulting decision making in response to externally provided information proceeds along two specific curves, relating stimulus characteristics to response frequencies of each of two information-processing methods (or decision categories). Either or both responses (or decision categories) may occur.

(a) Simple one-to-one responding, relating information input directly to decision output. This form of response often shows great similarity to the responses observed in many problem-solving tasks, and may also have similarity to what Suedfeld has discussed as performance of simple tasks. We have called this kind of behavior *respondent decision making*. Typically, only one response is associated with each stimulus.

(b) Integrated responding where several perceptually related information items are tied into one or more decisions which may have multiple purposes and may be part of a strategic sequence of decisions. Here the behavior of individuals or groups suggests a decision-making orientation which goes considerably beyond the search for the right answer to an immediate problem. Behavior of this nature in Suedfeld's approach would probably fall within the complex task function, and would be related to his data on national decision making in crisis situations (e.g., Suedfeld & Rank, 1976).

For both respondent and strategic integrated decision making, there is a maximum level of decisions that can be reached by the decision maker(s), i.e., a maximum *number* of decisions per unit time. Beyond this maximum ability level (at least for that specific task), one cannot go. That maximum level should be considerably higher for respondent than for integrated decision making (see Fig. 2).

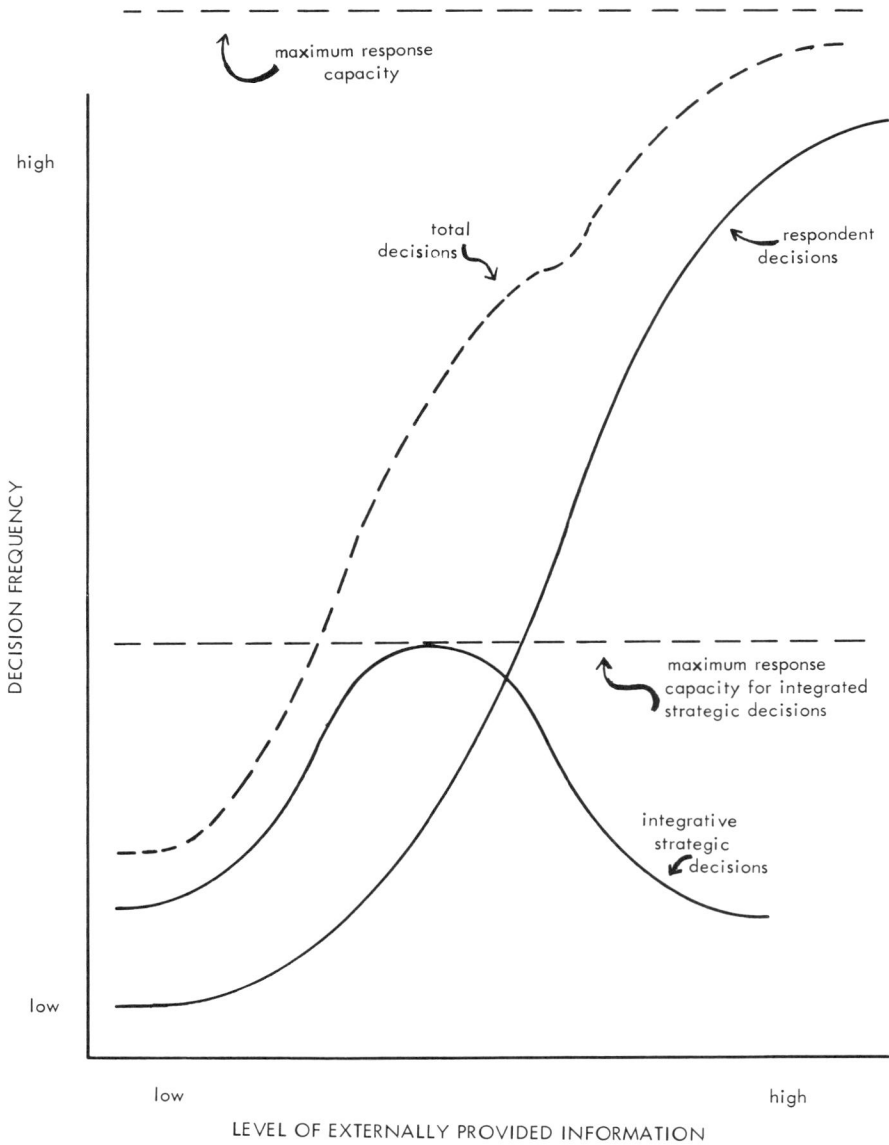

Fig. 2. Effects of externally provided information on the frequency of respondent and integrative strategic decisions.

Where is this maximum level obtained? Previous complexity theory has talked about an *optimal* level on an "environmental complexity" dimension (see below) where the maximum decision output (for integrated strategic decisions) is reached. No optimum was defined for respondent (or any other kind of) decisions, since the Schroder et al. (1967) theory considered those responses to be of lesser quality and consequently of little importance. Certainly such maximum, or, for that matter, optimal levels on the "environmental complexity" dimension could be considered for more than one decision measure. But is it meaningful to do that, for example, for the measure of respondent decision making?

Defining the location of any point, including an optimum, on a loosely defined dimension is difficult, if not impossible. The Schroder et al. theory defined "environmental complexity" very loosely. It included in the environmental complexity concept such diverse phenomena as information load (number of information items per unit time), success (eucity), failure (noxity), and more. In addition, other factors may have an influence, even if we (in contrast to Suedfeld) include only task relevant or task related stimuli in that supposedly summative concept, e.g., information relevance, information importance, etc.

In an attempt to identify and resolve the problems of our previous theoretical approach, we have attempted to measure separately the effects of a number of these variables on decision making (e.g., Streufert, 1970, 1972; Streufert & Schroder, 1965; Streufert, Streufert, & Castore, 1969; S. C. Streufert, 1973). It turns out that each of these variables tends to provide reliable (even on a cross-cultural basis) sources of prediction for task oriented decision making. Some of the variables even produce reliable optima.[3] And it appears that some of their interactions—something that might come close to the old "environmental complexity" concept—might be reasonably accounted for by the information-load concept alone. More about that will be said later on. But are these so-called optimum points on the stimulus variables really optima, or are they merely points where maximum levels of particular repsonses—to which no particular value should be attached—do occur?

---

[3]Some writers have questioned the usefulness of optimality formulations. Suedfeld (in Chapter 12), for example, suggests that a generalized optimum may turn out to have little meaning and may be "doomed to failure." Nevertheless, it has been shown that there are reliable psychological and physiological limits to perceptual and response capacity [e.g., Miller's (1956) magic number seven]. If the particular response in question is, for some reason, a desirable response (to more or less the exclusion of other responses), then its maximum possible level may well be produced by an environment that may be termed "optimal" in this sense. Consequently, I am proposing various "optimal environmental stimulus levels" relevant to various response characteristics on specified tasks (e.g., decision-making categories in complex decision-making tasks).

Whether any maximum response level can indeed be identified as produced by an optimum environmental stimulus level can be determined only after we decide whether the kind of decision making with which we are dealing is worthwhile. Clearly, respondent decisions are quite different from integrated strategic decisions. Which form of decision is better must depend on the task requirements. If the task tends toward problem solving or if momentary demands in a task (which typically is of decision-making nature) require immediate action without allowing time for integrative activity, then respondent decision making would, without question, be more appropriate. Integrative strategic perceptions and decisions—even if high in quality or quantity—are of little use when a correct decision has to be made immediately to avoid impending disaster. On the other hand, respondent decision making does not help when a well trained response to a set of information items has become inappropriate because of some small change in the information pattern. Ideally, one should match the best kind of decision making to each situation.[4] To be able to do that, it would be useful to understand when respondent and when integrative strategic decision making might be expected. I propose that, all other things being equal,

> (5) Task-oriented decision makers will attempt to make integrated strategic decisions when:
>> (a) certain pre-conditions are given (e.g., the information received is relevant, the situation permits multidimensional responding, etc.);
>> (b) individual or group capacity for integrative decision making exists; and
>> (c) the information which is externally provided does not exceed certain intermediate levels (e.g., too much information per unit time).

On the other hand,

> (6) Decision makers will tend to make respondent decision when
>> (a) pre-conditions for multidimensional decision making are not given (e.g., when there is no relevant information, decision makers lack the capacity, etc.);
>> (b) when information items and the relevant decisions cannot be related among each other;
>> (c) information-processing requirements are beyond the maximum level for the specific decision maker(s) (e.g., when they

---

[4] Another example of divergent appropriateness to an (experimental) set of tasks will be given below.

received more information per unit time than they can integratively handle).

Statements (5) and (6) may require some elaboration. One might initially state that an organism (here a decision maker) will tend to respond to information (if relevant or perceived as at least partially relevant) in some fashion. If one kind of response is impossible, the decision makers will necessarily resort to another kind of response. In other words,

(7) Decision makers will tend to respond to information in an inappropriate way (when they cannot respond appropriately) rather than not respond at all. This applies as well for multiple decisions in response to a single informative stimulus.

(8) Given the capacity for integrative responding and given the opportunity (e.g., excessive time without new information), an appropriate respondent decision in response to an item of information will often be followed by inappropriate integrative decisions.

The inverse is equally the case:

(9) Given limitations on integrated responses (decisions) (e.g., inability to respond integratively because of time limitations), the information will be translated into potentially inappropriate respondent decisions. It should be remembered, however, that many respondent decisions are not inappropriate.

(10) Decision makers will respond appropriately to information best handled by integrated decision making as long as the incoming information (quantity, kind, etc.) does not exceed their ability level, and as long as they have not yet reached the maximum number of integrated decisions they can make per unit time.

(11) Decision makers will respond appropriately to information best handled in respondent fashion when either no potential for integrative responding is inherent in the information or when their ability level to handle information in an integrated strategic fashion has been exceeded.

Some readers may have drawn a further conclusion from these arguments which must logically follow from the previous ones:

(12) Given the capacity of the decision makers to respond integratively, and given the potential of integrated strategic responding to the information and to the decision-making situation, the decision makers will tend to respond integratively rather than in

respondent fashion, unless the information which must be handled exceeds their ability to respond integratively. Beyond that point, integrative decisions will begin to decrease, and respondent decisions will begin to increase, until the maximum respondent response level of the decision makers has been reached. At this level, the respondent decisions will stabilize at a constant level.

I would not deny the possibility of a break-down even in respondent decision making if externally provided information reaches excessively high levels.

The tendency toward integrative responding that I have postulated probably has some similarity to the observations by Suedfeld that prisoners in solitary confinement, particularly those who are able to use their imagination in association with the development of relative detachment from their situation, are able to best survive. Here may be a trend toward more "normal" responding, i.e., more integrative responding, even if the stimuli are self-generated.

Total Decision Responses

We have so far spoken of two different kinds of decisions. Certainly one could single out other decision forms that might occur *in response to stimuli from the task environment*, yet these decisions can be grouped under respondent and integrative strategic decision making as well. Summing these two decision types, we should then obtain the total number of decisions made in response to information provided in the environment. When we plot total number of decisions against externally provided information, we should obtain the typical input to output curve which is indicated by the dotted line in Figure 2.

However, as stated at the beginning of this study, there are other decisions which are *not produced via external stimulus effects*: responses to self-generated (usually cognitive) stimulation and information-search responses. If we would add these responses into the total curve presented in Figure 2 (remember that proposition 1 suggested a decrease of such responses with increasing externally produced information), we would obtain less of a slope in the input to output curve, but the general shape of the curve would not be modified.

One of the important differences between the current view and that of Schroder et al. (1967) should probably be stated again. From the present viewpoint, no form of decision making is considered superior to any other. The situation should determine which one is most useful. The contrast between the simulated decision-making situations of Kennedy and Streufert might serve as a useful example.

Kennedy (1971) placed subjects in a stock market situation in which they could win and lose money by purchasing and selling stocks. The increase and decline in stock values was experimentally controlled. Subjects were provided with several sources of prediction for the progress of stocks on the market. Only one of the sources made moderately accurate predictions. Other sources made random predictions. Subjects who learned to base their purchasing and selling decisions via respondent decision making on the one moderately correct source made money. Others who attempted to find ways of integrating the predictions from various sources lost money.

Streufert (e.g., 1970) and associates placed subjects into an experimental simulation representing a complex decision-making task. Strategic decision making was most appropriate in the solution of a problem. Only those subjects who were able to integrate various decisions from diverse decision areas into an overall planned strategic sequence were successful. Subjects who merely responded to incoming information in a one-to-one fashion were unable to progress toward a solution of the problem.

For each of the situations, a different decision category was most appropriate. To make a choice among decision categories, each task situation would have to be analyzed carefully before an appropriate selection of the best possible decision response could be made.

Information Variables

The theoretical formulations of Schroder, Driver, and Streufert were considering "environmental complexity" as a series of variables which would define information in some joint fashion. How they would add, or even potentially interact, was not stated. In some way, a specific level of information load (quantity of information per unit time) would combine with failure, success and other potential variables to produce an effect on complex responding. It would appear useful to try to consider how these variables would add to or interact with each other.

Information characteristics, in many cases, imply more than just the stated information, particularly at the level of the perceiver. Multiple perceptions of environmental stimuli may be produced in interaction with previously received or stored information, attitudes, etc.[5] Multiple perceptions may suggest multiple actions. Similar effects may be produced by success and failure content of information. All other things being equal, then,

> (13) Information characteristics other than the quantity per unit
> time of information received by a decision maker adds or subtracts

[5] I would like to disclaim any predictions for emotions generated by information. Certainly there are important emotional effects (cf. Streufert & Streufert, 1977). But they cannot be easily handled in limited space. Consequently, we will (unhappily) ignore them in this work.

from the information load to the degree to which increased or decreased information processing is required.

For example, failure information adds information load, since it typically requires at least two responses to a single item of information:

(a) repairing the damage created by the failure;
(b) remaking a decision that had been unsuccessful.

The effects of information containing success elements are much more complicated. Decision-making groups typically expect success at some level. As a result, success information is—unless it comes in extreme quantities—often considered as "neutral" information by decision makers, which merely calls for the next action in a planned sequence of responses, eliminating any direct success effects (i.e., it may be identical to information load produced by neutral information quantity per unit time). With "final" or "excessive" success, however, effective information load is often decreased. No further action appears necessary. The problem has been solved or is resolving itself.

There are other, related variables. Recent analysis of the effects of externally induced information "importance" suggests that focusing the attention of decision makers on some relevant information by labeling it "important," while other equally relevant information is not labeled, adds to load: More decisions need to be made in response to these items. Both the decision curves for respondent decision making and for integrated decision making show the expected effects.

Personality Variables

Differences between individual decision makers or between homogeneous groups of decision makers have been researched with considerable frequency—without great surprises. I see no need to go into great detail about personality predictions in this chapter, since most of the predictions that could be made here are discussed in detail by Streufert and Streufert (1977). It may merely be useful to state where that theory differs from previous views in regard to decision-making situations.

The complexity theory of Schroder, Driver, and Streufert (1967) assumed that a different maximum response capacity for integrative responses to stimulation for what Schroder et al. called persons of "complex" conceptual structure (more multidimensional information processors) as opposed to what Schroder et al. called persons of "simple" conceptual structure (more unidimensional information processors) should be obtained. Repeated data analysis has supported that proposition. The theory also proposed that these maxima should occur at different levels of environmental input. It has been difficult, if not impossible, to establish the correctness of that prediction. The current view drops this prediction. The uniformity with which one item of information per 3-min time period produces maximal integrative responding across persons and groups (always assuming a normal background stimulus situation) suggests as much of a physiological (rather than style) characteristic as the magic number seven might be. If it is a physiological characteristic of human responding, then meaningful individual differences tend to be less likely.

Further, it may be necessary to limit the optima for "complex responding" proposed by Schroder et al. specifically to *integrative* responses (as has been done in this work). Another form of multidimensional responding, i.e., differentiation,[6] increases with externally produced information, and either shows a decrease postulated in U-shaped functions *much later or not at all.*

Previous forms of complexity theory did not make predictions for other than integrative decision making. I propose that

(14) Persons of more unidimensional conceptual structure will exceed persons of more multidimensional structure in the number of respondent decisions made at all levels of externally provided information.

There are two potential reasons for this view:

(a) Respondent decision making is a more typical style of persons with more unidimensional conceptual structure. Consequently, this kind of decision is made more easily and more comfortably by these persons than by persons with more multidimensional conceptual structure; and
(b) Persons with more multidimensional structure would show a greater strain toward integrative decision making, resulting in time loss, thereby reducing the time that could be used for respondent decision making (even at information levels where meaningful integrative decision making is not possible).

Finally, it is possible to predict differences between individuals with more multidimensional and more unidimensional conceptual structure for behavior under conditions of low levels of environmentally provided information. I would propose that:

(15) Persons with more unidimensional conceptual structure should exceed persons with more multidimensional conceptual

---

[6]While Streufert and Streufert (1977) deal in detail with both differentiative and integrative responding, we will not dwell on differentiative decision making in any detail. Differentiation does not aid very much (except as a pre-condition for integrative decision making) in strategic decision-making behavior and tends to lead (by itself) to respondent decision making.

structure in the search for information or the generation of information (see proposition 1) as long as externally provided information is quite low. At moderately low information levels or moderate information levels, the reverse should hold. However, for both groups, information search decisions and decisions based on self-generated information should decrease with increasing externally provided information.

The rationale for this prediction is derived from previously predicted response preferences. At quite low loads, persons of more unidimensional conceptual structure require more information for respondent decision making. As more externally provided information is added, the need for self-generated information or information search is decreased. On the other hand, decision makers with more multidimensional conceptual structure can reuse obtained or self-generated information in various integrated decision sequences, so that their total need for information at quite low levels of externally provided information is somewhat less than for their more unidimensional counterparts.

As externally provided information input increases toward more moderate levels, that information can be integrated with other—previously received or stored—information. Even at moderate or at moderately high levels of externally provided input, there is a continuing (though slightly decreasing) need for additional information which would likely be obtained by search activities, since that specific information may be needed (in association with externally provided information) for integrative decision making. Consequently, information search by more multidimensional decision makers should decrease more slowly with increasing information load and should reach a greater downward slope only when the maximum level of integrative decision making has been surpassed.

SUMMARY AND IMPLICATIONS

The theoretical statements proposed here are directly concerned with decision making in complex settings, the kind of settings that occur every day in organizations. I have not dealt with the content of decisions (i.e., what decisions are made on what specific dimensions), but rather with the structure of decision making (i.e., what *kind* of decision may be made), and the fit of decision structure to task requirements. For example, the situation in which the organizational decision maker should best follow a long-term strategy involving several matched, but different decisions in a sequence of time, in contrast to a situation where he has to make a decision rapidly, independent of strategy, but respondent to immediate information, would require a quite different decision process. Ideally, environmental situation and decision maker(s) should be matched to produce the—for any present purpose—optimal decision. The theoretical propositions of this study have shown what environments—and to some degree what persons—are likely to produce specific decision categories. The theoretical propositions then allow for (at least experimental, and possibly applied) selection of the right environmental/person decision making combination to produce the desired optimal decision characteristics.

REFERENCES

Brock, T. C. Implications of commodity theory for value change. In A. Greenwald (Ed.), *Psychological foundations of attitudes.* New York: Academic Press, 1969, pp. 243–275.

Driver, M. J., & Streufert, S. *Group composition, input load and group information processing.* Institute for Research in the Behavioral, Economic and Management Sciences, Purdue University, Institute Paper No. 142, 1966.

Driver, M. J., & Streufert, S. Integrative complexity: An approach to individuals and groups as information processing systems. *Administrative Science Quarterly,* 1969, **14**, 272–285.

Kennedy, J. L. The systems approach: A preliminary exploratory study of the relation between team composition and financial performance in business games. *Journal of Applied Psychology,* 1971, **55**, 46–49.

Miller, G. A. The magical number seven plus or minus two: Some limits on our capacity to process information. *Psychological Review,* 1956, **63**, 81–97.

Schroder, H. M., Driver, M. J., & Streufert, S. *Human information processing.* New York: Holt, Rinehart & Winston, 1967.

Streufert, S. Complexity and complex decision making: Convergence between differentiation and integration approaches to the prediction of task performance. *Journal of Experimental Social Psychology,* 1970, **6**, 494–509.

Streufert, S. Success and response rate in complex decision making. *Journal of Experimental Social Psychology,* 1972, **8**, 389–403.

Streufert, S., & Schroder, H. M. Conceptual structure, environmental complexity and task performance. *Journal of Experimental Research in Personality,* 1965, **1**, 132–137.

Streufert, S., & Streufert, S. C. *Behavior in the Complex Environment.* Washington, D.C.: V. H. Winston & Sons, 1977, in press.

Streufert, S., Streufert, S. C., & Castore, C. H. Complexity, increasing failure and decision making. *Journal of Experimental Research in Personality,* 1969, **3**, 293–300.

Streufert, S. C. Effects of information relevance on decision making in complex environments. *Memory and Cognition,* 1973, **1**, 224–228.

Suedfeld, P., & Rank, A. D. Revolutionary leaders: Long term success as a function of changes in conceptual complexity. *Journal of Personality and Social Psychology,* 1976, **34**, 169–178.

INFORMATIONAL AND STRUCTURAL DETERMINANTS OF DECISION-MAKER SATISFACTION[1]

L. L. Cummings
University of Wisconsin

Michael J. O'Connell[2]
United States Air Force Academy

George P. Huber
University of Wisconsin

THEORETICAL PERSPECTIVES

Organizational environments have been investigated using three perspectives: (1) the objective environment as it exists outside the organization, (2) exchanges between organizations and the associated interorganizational relationships, and (3) the perceived environment as viewed by organizational participants.

These three perspectives on organizational environment are conceptually distinct and certainly imply different procedures for operationalization and measurement. Table 1 presents what we consider to be representative conceptual and empirical papers depicting organizational environments within this classification system.

[1] This research was supported in part by the Air Force Office of Scientific Research, the University of Wisconsin Engineering Experiment Station, and the Wisconsin Alumni Research Foundation.

[2] On active duty in the U.S. Air Force. The views expressed in this study do not necessarily reflect those of the U.S. Air Force.

Table 1. Classification of Environmental Research by Perspectives Toward Organizational Environments

Conceptual	Empirical
Objective environment	
Dill (1958)	Burns & Stalker (1959)
Thompson (1967)	Chandler (1962)
Lawrence & Lorsch (1967)	Dill (1958)
Emery & Trist (1965)	Lawrence & Lorsch (1967)
Terreberry (1968)	Duncan (1972)
Duncan (1972)	Tosi, Aldag, & Storey (1973)
Jurkovich (1974)	
Interorganizational exchanges and relationships	
Levine & White (1961)	Meier (1965)
White, Levine & Vlasak (1973)	Baty, Evan & Rothernel (1971)
Litwak & Hylton (1962)	Aiken & Hage (1968)
Litwak & Rothman (1970)	Warren, Burgunder, Newton &
Clark (1965)	Rose (1973)
Lefton & Rosengren (1966)	Turk (1973)
Lefton (1973)	Pfeffer (1972a, 1972b, 1973)
Guetzkow (1966)	Pfeffer & Leblebici (1973)
Evan (1966)	
Dill (1958, 1962)	
Terreberry (1968)	
Perceived environment	
Dill (1958, 1962)	Lawrence & Lorsch (1967)
Weick (1969)	Khandwalla (1972)
Child (1972)	Duncan (1972)
Silverman (1970)	Downey, Hellriegel, & Slocum
Duncan (1972)	(1975)
Starbuck (1976)	

Because of the considerable ambiguity and the variety of conceptualizations of organizational environment and because of our desire for an integrating framework for our work, the model presented in Figure 1 was developed.

Organizational environment and organizational structure are depicted as the factors influencing both decision processes and decision-maker effects as dependent variables. Organizational environment is conceptualized as informational inputs. Two dimensions of informational inputs are given particular emphasis: (1) the *load* of information impacting the organization and its decision makers, and (2) the *specificity* of that information. Organizational

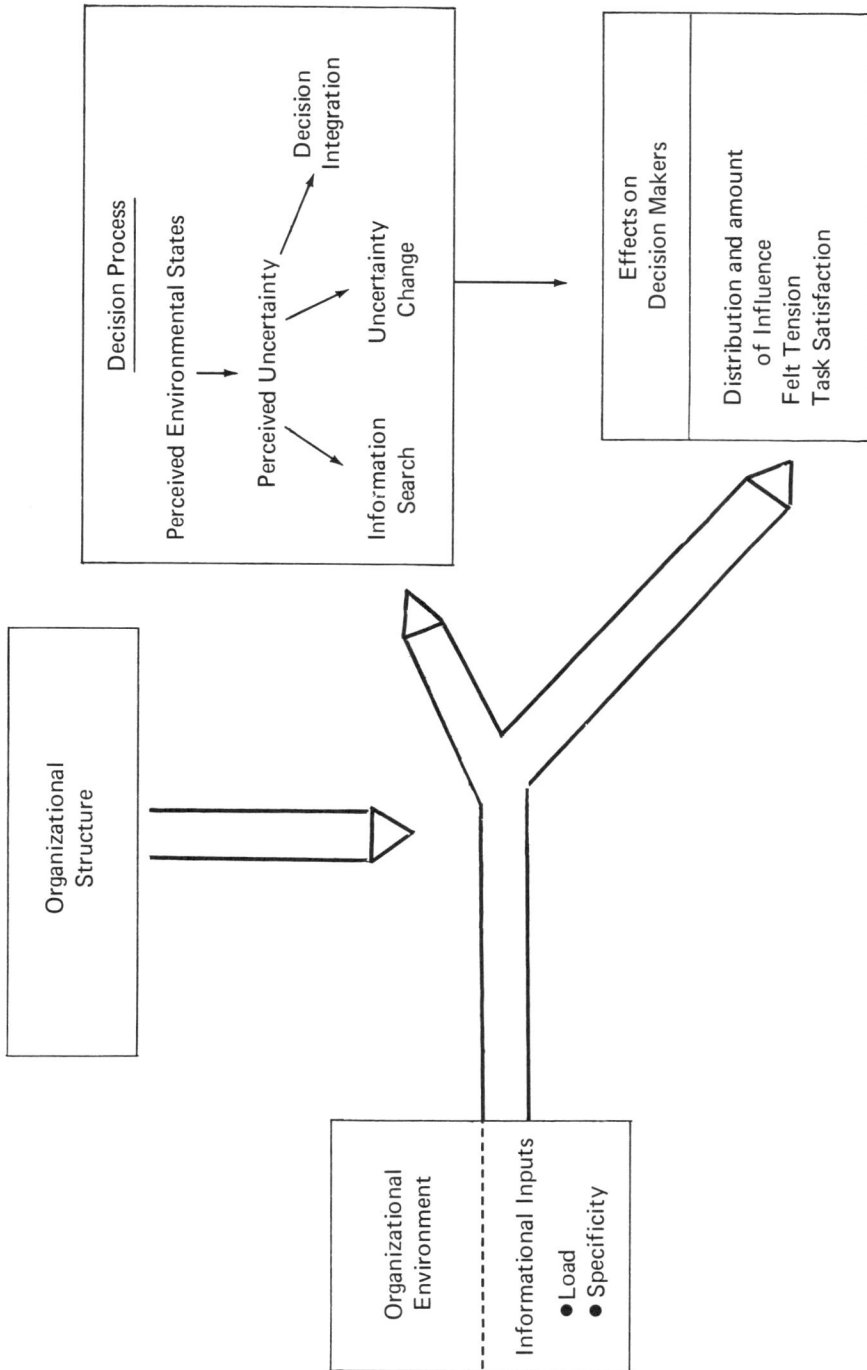

Fig. 1. Schematic model of variables and their relationships.

233

structure is conceived as impacting both decision processes and decision-maker reactions through two roles. First, the impact of information from the environment may be filtered or influenced by the nature of the organizational structure through which it passes in reaching the decision maker. Second, several small group communication network studies lead us to expect that organizational structure may exert a direct impact on decision processes and decision-maker reactions.

The major decision process variables in the model are information search, uncertainty change, and decision integration (linkages among decisions in a systematic pattern). Environment and structure are seen as influencing these through the decision-maker's perception of the number and diversity of environmental states and the perception of uncertainty.

Decision-maker reactions included in the model are (1) perceptions of the distribution and amount of influence among members of a decision-making group, (2) the tension experienced by the decision maker, and (3) the satisfaction with the task experienced by the decision maker. This study focuses upon decision-maker satisfaction.

HYPOTHESES

In this section we will develop the specific hypotheses guiding the study. We also provide the rationale linking environment and structure to perceptions of task satisfaction.

Hypothesis No. 1 Task satisfaction will be higher at moderate information load levels than at either very low or high load levels.

While satisfaction has been widely studied in both the small group and organizational psychology literature, the effects of information load on task satisfaction have not been studied directly. At low levels, group members will demonstrate a need for more information requests through their higher information seeking and the lack of forthcoming information will contribute to their dissatisfaction. At high load levels, the great influx of information and the group's inability to integrate and cope with all the information also should lead to dissatisfaction. Kahn, Wolfe, Quinn, Snoek, and Rosenthal (1964) found that role overload was associated with dissatisfaction. Sales' (1970) analysis of the effects of role over- and underload showed that satisfaction was lower under the objective overload condition. His experiment did not provide for a moderate load condition, so no support can be drawn from his findings as to the curvilinear relationship postulated in Hypothesis 1.

Hypothesis No. 2 Task satisfaction will be higher when information specificity is high.

Several counteracting forces may act on the subjects. In another study (Huber, O'Connell, & Cummings, 1975) we have found that at least for one measure of uncertainty high specificity information led to more uncertainty. This would suggest that high specificity information might produce less satisfaction insofar as uncertainty is a source of dissatisfaction. On the other hand, Shaw (1964) reviews several studies where noisy information, information that tends to be irrelevant or ambiguous, contributed to dissatisfaction. In this research, information that was perceived to be nonspecific also was perceived to be irrelevant ($r = .496$, $p < .005$). The proposition stated here is based on the assumption that the perceived irrelevancy of low specificity information contributes more to dissatisfaction than feelings of uncertainty caused by high specificity information.

Hypothesis No. 3 Loosely structured groups will be relatively more satisfied under low load conditions and tightly structured groups will be more satisfied under high load conditions.

Shaw (1964), in analyzing a number of earlier studies, found that for both simple and complex problems, loosely structured groups reported higher satisfaction than did tightly structured groups. We expect this finding to be replicated at low and perhaps moderate load levels but to be reversed at high load levels. As we will report momentarily, for 3 of the 12 satisfaction factors, satisfaction is relatively low at high load levels; but this proposition implies that in comparing the two structures, satisfaction will be lower for the loosely structured group. The high load will inhibit the loosely structured group's ability to integrate decisions and will generate a feeling of confusion and, perhaps, helplessness. The tightly structured group will be better able to cope with the high load. Mulder's (1959) findings that the more centralized decision structure performed faster, with higher quality, and more efficiently gives some support to this proposition insofar as high performance leads to satisfaction.

Hypothesis No. 4 The central decision maker in the tightly structured group will express higher satisfaction than the boundary spanning members and the differential will be greatest at high load levels.

This proposition relates only to the tightly structured group. Trow's (1957) study of the relationship between autonomy and satisfaction as well as Shaw's (1964) review of communication nets support the general expected relationship. People in leadership positions who have decision-making responsibility generally derive more satisfaction than subordinates. That the two deputies could only make recommendations and had no assurance that the director would act in accordance with their wishes should prove frustrating and dissatisfying. The latter portion of this proposition indicates that the director should experience relatively more satisfaction than the deputies as the information load increases. At high load levels the role of the deputies as buffers shielding the central decision maker should be more critical. The higher information input will be directly experienced by the deputies who should express more dissatisfaction as the load increases.

METHOD

Experiment Setting

To rigorously control the objective environment, a laboratory simulation was chosen in which three-man teams played a Vietnam-type war game under closely controlled conditions. This simulation, called the tactical and negotiations game, was developed by Streufert and has been used extensively by him and his colleagues (Schroder, Driver, & Streufert, 1967; Streufert & Castore, 1971; Streufert, Castore, & Kliger, 1967; Streufert, Kliger, Castore, & Driver, 1967).

Streufert and Castore give a brief description of a recent experiment using the TNG.

> Each of the . . . decision-making teams was given the task of directing the military, economic, intelligence, and negotiation activities of a small underdeveloped nation called "Shamba" which was plagued by an internal revolution. Subjects read a manual on historical, economic, and military information about this nation. The time required for reading the manual was approximately 2 hours. After reading the manual, subjects were told that they would be permitted to make decisions on military, economic, intelligence, and negotiation characteristics within the limits of their resources. Decisions were made on forms provided for this purpose and handed to the experimenters. Subjects were informed that they were playing the Tactical and Negotiation Game against another team, and that the game would continue for a number of periods of indeterminate length until the issues of the "Shamba conflict" were resolved. The experimenters would serve as judges, assisted by a computer, and information on the outcome of subjects' decisions would be fed back to them as soon as available (Streufert & Castore, 1971, pp. 129–130).

Subjects, in fact, play against a predetermined program controlled by the experimenter. Each playing period is 30 min in length and simulates 6 months in game time. In the experiment reported here, subjects played for three game

Table 2. Number of Information Inputs

Game period	Load level		
	Low	Medium	High
1	5	10	21
2	6	12	22
3	5	10	21
	—	—	—
	16	32	64

periods with the total exercise taking approximately five hours to complete. Streufert and Castore (1971), and our own post-experiment questionnaire (O'Connell, 1974), indicate considerable involvement and little skepticism on the part of the subjects. Two groups of subjects participated in the experiment, 72 ROTC students at two large state universities and 72 cadets at the USAF Academy.[3] The subjects were debriefed at the conclusion of the experiment.

Experimental Design

Information concerning the objective environment of the three-man teams varied on two dimensions, load and specificity. Information load was controlled at *three* levels, low (16 input messages over the 3 game periods), medium (32 input messages), and high (64 input messages). *Information specificity* was controlled at *two* levels, low and high. Tables 2 and 3 provide the operationalization of these two variables.

To understand how perceptions might be affected by the internal structure of the decision unit, half the teams played the game as loosely structured groups and half as tightly structured groups. In the loosely structured groups, subjects were instructed to interact freely as coequals and to attempt to reach group consensus in the formation of decisions. In the tightly structured groups, a two-level hierarchy was established by the experimenter's appointing a team leader who was instructed to formulate all the teams' decisions using inputs and recommendations from the other two team members as he saw fit. His role was accentuated by his being seated at the front of the room and by the other two team members being allowed to communicate to him only in

---

[3]ROTC students participated as part of their military training and received compensatory time off from their normal ROTC classes. AFA cadets participated as volunteers. Additional details concerning this research setting and design can be found in O'Connell (1974).

Table 3. Examples of Low and High Specificity Messages

Low specificity	High specificity
Military	
Carrier based airplanes patrolling in Western Shamba sighted and attacked an enemy truck convoy. Damage determined.	Two carrier based F-2's on a routine patrol from NG-2A sighted and attacked an enemy truck convoy in sector G-3. Five trucks were completely destroyed, two partially damaged.
Intelligence	
J.S. reports that the enemy may be planning a large attack on a major transportation route in central Shamba.	J.S. has heard discussions indicating plans for a major enemy offensive somewhere along the railroad between Mckosam and Savin. He was not sure where enemy staging area for this operation is, but the equipment moving across the Ondulu River recently indicates it might be the swamp in sector J-6.

writing and not with each other at all. The leader communicated verbally to the two subordinates. Each subordinate was assigned specific responsibilities for processing incoming information, i.e., he acted as a boundary spanner. One of the boundary spanners received messages concerned with military and intelligence activity while the other received messages dealing with negotiation and economic matters.

The above treatment of the independent variables resulted in a 3 × 2 × 2 factorial design. To control for the effect of the two subject populations, ROTC versus AF Academy students, an additional two-level subject factor was included in the analysis. Using this augmented 3 × 2 × 2 × 2 design, two ROTC teams or two AF Academy teams were assigned to each of the 24 cells. Additionally, to control for the three different positions in each group, a three-level group member position factor was included, making the final design for purpose of analyses of variance 3 × 2 × 2 × 2 × 3.

Measurement of Task Satisfaction

Self-reports of the decision makers were used to measure this variable. At the end of the game, following a procedure suggested by Scott (1967), semantic differential scales were used to measure satisfaction. This procedure,

Table 4. Summary of 12 Task Satisfaction Components

Task satisfaction factor	Sample of adjectives loading highly on this component
ME PLAYING THIS GAME	
I "General Vigor"	Optimistic, alert, efficient, eager spirited, liked, lively, refreshed, effective, ethusiastic
II "Personal Stability"	Relaxed, calm, patient
III "General Affective Tone"	Motivated, informed, free, satisfied, unhampered, clear
IV "Self-Control"	Deliberate, consistent, wise
THE GAME	
I "Intrinsic Game Worth"	Good, interesting, pleasant, attractive, valuable, meaningful, varied, important, positive, broad, exciting, superior
II "Task Complexity"	Complex, difficult, unusual
III "Task Stability"	Structured, stable
IV "Task Clarity"	Explicit, clear, permanent
OUR GROUP PLAYING THIS GAME	
I "Group Harmony"	Sociable, happy, vigorous, pleasant harmonious, cooperative, helpful
II "Group Diligence"	Stable, careful, unemotional
III "Group Evaluation"	Contented, informed, free, efficient, satisfied, educated, wise, successful
IV "Group Complexity"	Complex

also used by Scott and Rowland (1970), Cherrington, Reitz, and Scott (1971), and Hamner and Harnett (1974), recognizes that satisfaction is probably a multidimensional construct and assumes that satisfaction is an "intraorganismic condition or process" and that "there are discriminable aspects of the work surroundings to which the individual differentially reacts" (Scott, 1967). Feelings about three concepts ("Me Playing this Game," "The Game," and "Our Group Playing this Game") were assessed using sets of 26, 20, and 20 bipolar adjectives, respectively.

A principal component analysis was used to reduce the dimensionality of the data. This procedure was applied to responses to each set of adjectives,

Table 5. Average Task Satisfaction Factor Scores for Three Information Load Levels

Task satisfaction measure	Information load			F ratio
	Low	Medium	High	
Me Play IV "Self-Control"	.018	.361	−.380	7.06***
Our Group II "Group Diligence"	.066	.212	−.278	2.93*
Our Group III "Group Evaluation"	−.195	.025	.170	1.76 ($p < .25$)
Our Group IV "Group Complexity"	.176	.142	−.318	3.59**

*$p < .10$.
**$p < .05$.
***$p < .01$.

scored on a 7-point scale with 7 indicating the more positive or preferred end of the scale. For each of the three analyses, components whose eigenvalues were greater than one were orthogonally rotated using the varimax criterion to identify those key adjective pairs that characterize each component. Using this criterion, 4 components were identified for each task satisfaction factor for a total of 12 different components of task satisfaction. Descriptions of the 12 satisfaction components are given in Table 4.

RESULTS

The results are presented in sequence by hypothesis. Repeating, Hypothesis No. 1 predicted that "task satisfaction will be higher at moderate information load levels than at either very low or very high load levels." The analysis of variance of the 12 task satisfaction measures showed significant main effects for load for 3 of the 12 measures, "self control," "group diligence," and "group complexity." For one additional measure, "group evaluation," load was marginally significant ($p < .25$). As shown in Table 5, only the satisfaction scores for "self control" and "group diligence" follow the pattern predicted by Hypothesis No. 1. The "group evaluation" scores are directly related to load while the "group complexity" scores are inversely related to load. Hypothesis No. 1 is supported only for ROTC subjects using the "general vigor" measure and AFA subjects using the "group evaluation" measure. There was a slight tendency toward the inverted U-curve relationship

Table 6. Average Task Satisfaction Factor Scores by Information Specificity

Task satisfaction measure	Information specificity		F ratio
	Low	High	
Me Play III "General Affective Tone"	−.203	.363	6.02**
Game IV "Task Clarity"	−.181	.181	4.17**
Our Group I "Group Harmony"	.214	−.214	6.97**
Our Group III "Group Evaluation"	−.156	.156	3.73*

$*p < .10.$
$**p < .05.$

for groups receiving high specificity information using the "intrinsic game worth" measure and for groups receiving low specificity information using the "group harmony" measure. Overall, the data do not provide strong support for Hypothesis No. 1.

Hypothesis No. 2 predicted that "task satisfaction will be higher when information specificity is high." Information specificity produced a significant main effect on the four task satisfaction measures identified in Table 6 which shows average task satisfaction scores for the respective task satisfaction factors. The scores on task satisfaction factors, "general affective tone," "task clarity," and "group evaluation," support Hypothesis No. 2. Individuals who felt that their group played in a pleasant, cooperative, and helpful manner, i.e., "group harmony," tended to be in groups receiving low specificity information. This suggests that groups with low specificity information had an easier time resolving any differences of opinion or interpretation and is consistent with one of our earlier findings that low specificity information can lead to more perceived certainty (Huber et al., 1975).

Hypothesis No. 3 predicted that "loosely structured groups will be relatively more satisfied under low load conditions and tightly structured groups will be more satisfied under high load conditions." Of the 12 task satisfaction components, only "general affective tone" (Me Play III) showed a significant load-group structure interaction. This interaction is shown in Figure 2 and is supportive of the relationship predicted in Hypothesis No. 3. While

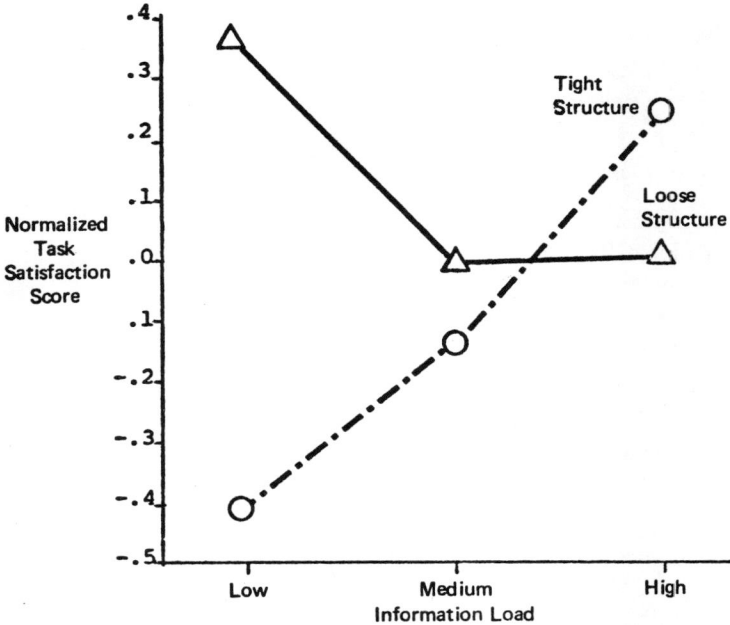

Fig. 2. Interactive effect of information load and group structure on "general affective tone"—Me Play III.

the tightly structured group expressed much lower satisfaction at low information loads, subjects in this structure expressed more satisfaction than those in loosely structured groups at high information loads.

Hypothesis No. 4 predicted that "the central decision maker in the tightly structured group will express higher satisfaction than the boundary spanning members and the differential will be greatest at high load levels." Table 7 summarizes task satisfaction scores for the 12 task satisfaction measures. The last three columns of this table show the comparative differences between the director's satisfaction and the average deputy's satisfaction. Positive differences indicate the director expressed more satisfaction than the deputies and, therefore, would be supportive of the first portion of Hypothesis No. 4. Only at high information loads is there a slight tendency for Hypothesis No. 4 to be supported with 6 of the 12 satisfaction measures showing differences in the expected direction. For medium and low information loads, the data tend to be in the opposite direction.

Comparing low load levels with high load levels, the differences in scores across information loads become less negative or more positive for nine of the twelve satisfaction measures showing general support for the relationship predicted in the second portion of Hypothesis No. 4.

Table 7. Task Satisfaction for Tightly Structured Groups by Group Member and Information Load

Task satisfaction measure	Information load									Comparative differences in task satisfaction (Director-Deputies' Ave.)		
	Low			Medium			High			Low	Medium	High
	Dir.	Dep. B	Dep. C	Dir.	Dep. B	Dep. C	Dir.	Dep. B	Dep. C			
Me Play I "General Vigor"	-.37	.32	.21	-.01	.32	-.17	-.20	.00	.16	-.63	-.08	-.28
Me Play II "Personal Stability"	-.31	.42	.60	-.67	.66	-.22	-.40	.10	-.48	-.82	-.89	-.21
Me Play III "General Affective Tone"	-.32	-.41	-.52	-.59	.31	-.26	.61	.13	-.06	.15	-.62	.57
Me Play IV "Self-Control"	-.24	.10	.31	.41	1.14	.53	.07	-.04	-.37	-.44	-.42	.27
Game I "Intrinsic Game Worth"	-.39	.18	-.21	-.06	.33	-.03	.00	-.04	-.15	-.37	-.21	.09
Game II "Task Complexity"	.50	-.09	.45	-.11	-.33	.12	-.45	-.52	.02	.32	-.01	-.20
Game III "Task Stability"	-.48	.09	.64	-.46	.51	.41	-.03	-.06	-.31	-.84	-.92	.15
Game IV "Task Clarity"	-.03	-.10	-.25	-.20	.18	-.03	-.07	.13	-.19	.15	-.27	-.04
Our Group I "Group Harmony"	-.33	-.43	-.01	.17	.21	-.04	.14	-.02	-.22	-.11	.09	.26
Our Group II "Group Diligence"	-.31	.25	.45	.36	.40	.35	.02	.27	-.19	-.66	-.02	-.02
Our Group III "Group Evaluation"	-.57	-.31	-.32	-.28	.34	-.07	.32	.03	-.06	-.26	-.42	.30
Our Group IV "Group Complexity"	.07	.58	.49	.00	.30	.22	-.85	-.29	-.21	-.46	-.26	-.60

243

DISCUSSION AND CONCLUSIONS

The general tenor of much of the findings reported here suggests caution concerning current prescriptions toward decentralized organizational forms, loose structures, and generally less hierarchical designs. Our data indicate that conditions exist under which hierarchy and structure yield satisfaction. Environments imposing high information loads on decision makers and requiring the processing of highly specific information (and thereby many bits of information) seem to yield positive results when filtered (or simplified) by structure.

Even more strikingly, our data show the tremendous complexity of the causal network impacting decision-maker satisfaction. Interactions are predominant in our findings. This is all the more noteworthy when considering the simplicity of our experimental setting relative to the typical organizational milieu within which decisions are made.

These complexities are illustrated not only by the research reported here but also by other studies from this research program (O'Connell, Cummings, & Huber, 1976; O'Connell & Cummings, in press). The influence exercised by the group, felt tension, and task satisfaction of the group members were affected by the independent variables in several different ways. The higher average influence exercised by the tightly structured group was due mainly to the high influence attributed to the director. The role prescriptions and division of labor in this group were intended to give the director the ability to influence the group and, in fact, he was perceived as so doing. While average influence in the group can be increased by giving lower participants more power, the common approach of power equalization proponents, group influence also can be increased by modifying the responsibilities and authority of the leader. The relative advantages of these two approaches have not been fully addressed in the literature.

Information inputs affected felt tension and task satisfaction in a number of ways. Under low specificity conditions, higher loads led to higher "generalized tension" but high specificity information dampened the adverse effect of high loads on "generalized tension." A similar pattern was observed for "intrinsic game worth" and "group harmony" measures, suggesting that some of the adverse effects of high information load can be offset if information specificity is improved. However, as noted below, particularly for loosely structured groups, high specificity information may have a detrimental impact.

Tightly structured groups experienced less "role overload tension" and less "role ambiguity tension," indicating that the division of labor and detailed role prescriptions in these groups had beneficial effects. Consistent with this is the fact that members of the tightly structured groups perceived themselves as having more self-control and their group as being more diligent. In a task oriented atmosphere such as that imposed by this game, the bureaucratic characteristics of hierarchy of authority, division of labor, and formalized role prescriptions can have a functional effect on participants.

Whereas there were few interactive effects of information load and group structure on attributed influence, felt tension, and task satisfaction, information specificity and group structure interacted in a very consistent manner on these variables. High specificity information worked in a positive manner on tightly structured groups while it tended to inhibit and frustrate members of loosely structured groups. Compared to tightly structured groups receiving high specificity information, members of loosely structured groups in this same information condition attributed less influence to the group in the first two decision phases, experienced more "generalized" and "information deprivation tension," tended to perceive themselves as having less "self control," tended to perceive the game as being more complex, and to perceive their group as working less diligently. Evidently, the specific information covering a variety of environmental situations, together with the freely interacting nature of the loosely structured group, caused members of this group to become more argumentative and more doubtful of what was happening in the environment.

That groups receiving high specificity information felt less "group harmony" than groups receiving low specificity information is supportive of this interpretation. High specificity information may be detrimental to the processes of groups engaged in a complex task unless the group has developed procedures and forms for interpreting and integrating the information. High specificity information may give an illusion of thoroughness and completeness, but in an atmosphere of open discussion and questioning, very specific information may only highlight the fact that other necessary information is lacking. High specificity information in answering some questions may generate other questions for which answers are unavailable. In the loosely structured group, the open communication channels and free sharing of interpretations of the specific information may have the effect of increasing information load within the group. The higher information load and the fact that many questions are unanswered may contribute to the group's frustration and lead to more negative evaluations of its own performance.

Task satisfaction is clearly a complex phenomenon. Treating satisfaction as a multidimensional construct complicated the analysis and findings, but such an approach seems necessary in light of the fact that the various hypotheses were differentially supported across the 12 satisfaction measures. Simple statements about the effects of the informational environment and decision unit structure on decision makers' affective responses are clearly not possible. This research indicates that the effects of environment and structure depend on which dimension of satisfaction one assesses; which feature of the informational environment, load or specificity, one manipulates; the interactive pattern of the environment and decision unit structure; and the population form which the decision makers are chosen.

REFERENCES

Aiken, M., & Hage, J. Organizational interdependence and intraorganizational structure. *American Sociological Review*, 1968, **33**, 912–930.

Baty, G. B., Evan, W. M., & Rothernel, T. W. Personnel flows as interorganizational relations. *Administrative Science Quarterly*, 1971, **16**, 430–443.

Burns, T., & Stalker, G. M. *The management of innovation.* London: Tavistock, 1959.

Chandler, A. D. *Strategy and structure.* Cambridge, Mass.: M.I.T. Press, 1962.

Cherrington, D. J., Reitz, H. J., & Scott, W. E. Effects of contingent and noncontingent reward on the relationship between satisfaction and task performance. *Journal of Applied Psychology*, 1971, **55**, 531–536.

Child, J. Organizational structure, environment and performance: The role of strategic choice. *Sociology*, 1972, **6**, 1–22. (a)

Child, J. Organizational structure and strategies of control: A replication of the Aston study. *Administrative Science Quarterly*, 1972, **17**, 163–177. (b)

Clark, B. R. Interorganizational patterns in education. *Administrative Science Quarterly*, 1965, **10**, 224–237.

Dill, W. R. Environment as an influence on managerial autonomy. *Administrative Science Quarterly*, 1958, **2**, 409–443.

Dill, W. R. The impact of environment on organizational development. In S. Mailick & E. H. Van Ness (Eds.), *Concepts and issues in administrative behavior.* Englewood Cliffs, N.J.: Prentice-Hall, 1962.

Downey, H. K., Hellriegel, D. H., & Slocum, J. W. Environmental uncertainty: The construct and its application. *Administrative Science Quarterly*, 1975, **20**, 613–629.

Duncan, R. B. Characteristics of organizational environments and perceived environmental uncertainty. *Administrative Science Quarterly*, 1972, **17**, 313–327.

Emery, F. E., & Trist, E. L. The causal texture of organizational environments. *Human Relations*, 1965, **18**, 21–32.

Evan, W. M. The organization-set: Toward a theory of interorganizational relations. In J. D. Thompson (Ed.), *Approaches to organization design.* Pittsburgh: University of Pittsburgh Press, 1966.

Guetzkow, H. Relations among organizations. In R. V. Bowers (Ed.), *Studies on behavior in organizations.* Athens, Ga.: University of Georgia Press, 1966.

Hamner, W. C., & Harnett, D. L. Goal setting, performance, and satisfaction in an interdependent task. *Organizational Behavior and Human Performance*, 1974, **12**, 217–230.

Huber, G. P., O'Connell, M. J., & Cummings, L. L. Perceived environmental uncertainty: Effects of information and structure. *Academy of Management Journal*, 1975, **18**, 725–740.

Jurkovich, R. A core typology of organizational environments. *Administrative Science Quarterly*, 1974, **19**, 380–394.

Kahn, R. L., Wolfe, D. M., Quinn, R. P., Snoek, J. D., & Rosenthal, R. A. *Organizational stress: Studies in role conflict and ambiguity.* New York: Wiley, 1964.

Khandwalla, P. N. *Uncertainty and the "optimal" design of organizations.* Paper presented at the 19th International Meeting of The Institute of Management Science, Houston, April, 1972.

Lawrence, P. R., & Lorsch, J. W. *Organization and environment.* Boston: Graduate School of Business Administration, Harvard University, 1967.

Lefton, M. Client characteristics and organizational functioning: An interorganizational focus. In A. R. Negandhi (Ed.), *Modern organizational theory.* Kent, Ohio: Kent State University Press, 1973.

Lefton, M., & Rosengren, W. R. Organizations and clients: Lateral and longitudinal dimensions. *American Sociological Review*, 1966, **31**, 802–810.

Levine, S., & White, P. E. Exchange as a conceptual framework for the study of interorganizational relationships. *Administrative Science Quarterly*, 1961, **5**, 583–601.

Litwak, E., & Hylton, L. F. Interorganizational analysis. *Administrative Science Quarterly*, 1962, **6**, 305–415.

Litwak, E., & Rothman, J. Towards the theory and practice of coordination between formal organizations. In W. R. Rosengren & M. Lefton (Eds.), *Organizations and clients.* Columbus, Ohio: Charles E. Merrill, 1970.

Meier, R. L. Information input overload: Features of growth in communications-oriented institutions. In F. Massarik & P. Ratoosh (Eds.), *Mathematical explorations in behavioral science.* Homewood, Ill.: Richard D. Irwin, 1965.

Mulder, M. Power and satisfaction in task oriented groups. *Acta Psychologica*, 1959, **16**, 178–225.

O'Connell, M. J. *Environmental influence on organizational decision making.* Doctoral dissertation, University of Wisconsin-Madison, 1974.

O'Connell, M. J., Cummings, L. L. The moderating effects of environment and structure on the satisfaction-tension-influence network. *Organizational Behavior and Human Performance*, in press.

O'Connell, M. J., Cummings, L. L., & Huber, G. P. The effects of environmental information and decision unit structure on felt tension. *Journal of Applied Psychology*, 1976, **61**, 493–500.

Pfeffer, J. Merger as a response to organizational interdependence. *Administrative Science Quarterly*, 1972, **17**, 382–394. (a)

Pfeffer, J. Size and composition of corporate boards of directors: The organization and its environment. *Administrative Science Quarterly*, 1972, **17**, 218–228. (b)

Pfeffer, J. Size, composition, and function of hospital boards of directors: A study of organization-environment linkage. *Administrative Science Quarterly*, 1973, **18**, 349–364.

Pfeffer, J., & Leblebici, H. Executive recruitment and the development of interfirm organizations. *Administrative Science Quarterly*, 1973, **18**, 449–461.

Sales, S. M. Some effects of role overload and role underload. *Organizational Behavior and Human Performance*, 1970, **5**, 592–608.

Schroder, H. M., Driver, M. J., & Streufert, S. *Human information processing.* New York: Holt, Rhinehart & Winston, 1967.

Scott, W. E. The development of semantic differential scales as measures of "morale." *Personnel Psychology*, 1967, **20**, 179–198.

Scott, W. G., & Rowland, K. M. The generality and significance of semantic differential scales as measures of "morale." *Organizational Behavior and Human Performance*, 1970, **5**, 576–591.

Shaw, M. E. Communication networks. In L. Berkowitz (Ed.), *Advances in experimental social psychology* (Vol. 1). New York: Academic Press, 1964.

Silverman, D. *The theory of organizations.* New York: Basic Books, 1970.

Starbuck, W. H. Organizations and their environments. In M. D. Dunnette (Ed.), *Handbook of industrial and organizational psychology.* Chicago: Rand McNally, 1976.

Streufert, S., & Castore, C. H. Information search and the effects of failure: A test of complexity theory. *Journal of Experimental Social Psychology*, 1971, **7**, 125–143.

Streufert, S., Castore, C. H., & Kliger, S. C. *A tactical and negotiations game: Rationale, method, and analysis* (ONR Tech. Rep. No. 1). New Brunswick, N.J.: Rutgers University, 1967. (Clearinghouse, Springfield, Va.)

Streufert, S., Kliger, S. C., Castore, C. H., & Driver, M. J. Tactical and negotiations game for analysis of decision integration across decision areas. *Psychological Reports*, 1967, **20**, 155–157.

Terreberry, S. M. The evolution of organizational environments. *Administrative Science Quarterly*, 1968, **12**, 590–613. (a)

Terreberry, S. M. *The organization of environments* (Doctoral dissertation, University of Michigan, 1968). (University Microfilm No. 69-12254. (b)

Thompson, J. D. *Organizations in action.* New York: McGraw-Hill, 1967.

Tosi, H., Aldag, R., & Storey, R. Comment on the Lawrence and Lorsch reply. *Administrative Science Quarterly*, 1973, **18**, 397–398. (a)

Tosi, H., Aldag, R., & Storey, R. On the measurement of the environment: An assessment of the Lawrence and Lorsch environmental uncertainty questionnaire. *Administrative Science Quarterly*, 1973, **18**, 27–36. (b)

Trow, D. B. Autonomy and job satisfaction in task-oriented groups. *Journal of Abnormal and Social Psychology*, 1957, **54**, 204–209.

Turk, H. Comparative urban structure from an interorganizational perspective. *Administrative Science Quarterly*, 1973, **18**, 37–55.

Warren, R. L., Burgunder, A. F., Newton, J. W., & Rose, S. M. The interaction of community decision organizations: Some conceptual considerations and empirical findings. In A. R. Negandhi (Ed.), *Modern organizational theory.* Kent, Ohio: Kent State University Press, 1973.

Weick, K. E. *The social psychology of organizing.* Reading, Mass.: Addison-Wesley, 1969.

White, P. E., Levine, S., & Vlasak, G. J. Exchange as a conceptual framework for understanding interorganizational relationships: Applications to nonprofit organizations. In A. R. Negandhi (Ed.), *Modern organizational theory.* Kent, Ohio: Kent State University Press, 1973.

THE EFFECTS OF TASK CONDITIONS ON SUBJECTIVE JUDGEMENTS [1]

Lee Roy Beach, Terence R. Mitchell and
Bruce Drake
University of Washington

It seems that there is an increased emphasis on research in real-world organizations and with it an increased scorn for laboratory research. This is disturbing because we think that the laboratory remains a valid setting for examining a large number of questions that are important to organizational psychology. Certainly it is true that in many cases the laboratory has been a Procrustean bed and that the results of many studies have little generalizability. But it also is true that for subtle questions the laboratory, used with caution, provides the precision of control that is necessary to adequately answer the questions. The three experiments described in this study represent three different questions that, we think, are best approached in the laboratory before real-world studies are undertaken. The thesis central

[1] This research was supported by Office of Naval Research Contract N00014-76-C-0193. The authors wish to thank Ms. Joyce Prothero, Ms. Marcia Deaton, and Ms. Olga Crocker for their help in conducting these experiments, and Dr. Norman Anderson, Dr. James Shanteau, and Mr. L. Clark Johnson for their help in conducting the data analyses.

to all three is that a variety of environmental variables can interfere with the judgment processes that precede decision making and that as a result the judgments may be inaccurate and the judge may lack confidence in them and be reluctant to rely upon them. Furthermore, the degree to which the judgments influence the final decision may influence the judge's evaluation of the task.

The first experiment involves the effects of information relevance and source credibility on assessed subjective probabilities. The second involves the effects of the structure of the information and the judge's ability to control the rate at which the information is received on the accuracy of proportion estimates and on the judge's confidence in them. The third experiment involves the effects of horizontal and vertical power in group judgment making on satisfaction with participating in the task.

EXPERIMENT 1

The first study examines how people utilize information to revise their subjective probabilities when the information source, and therefore the information itself, is not wholly credibile or reliable. Previous research has focused on the degree to which revisions of subjective probabilities conform to the prescriptions of the Bayesian Hierarchical Inference model, the normative model for revising prior opinion in light of the implications of new data when the implications have been discounted to allow for the lack of credibility of the source (Gettys & Wilke, 1969; Peterson, 1973; Schum & DuCharme, 1971).

Formally, the Bayesian model begins with prior opinion being represented as a ratio of the probability that the hypothesis in question is true to the probability that it is not. After observation of a datum (information), this prior probability ratio is multiplied by a discounted likelihood ratio which incorporates the probability that the datum is accurate and what it means for the hypothesis if it is and the probability that the datum is not accurate and the implication for the hypothesis of that.

Research comparing unaided subjective probability revision with the Bayesian model indicates that while people clearly discount noncredible information, the Bayesian model is not a good description of what they are doing. Attempts to produce more descriptive alternative models (Gettys, Kelly, & Peterson, 1973; Snapper & Fryback, 1971) have retained the basic Bayesian assumption of a multiplicative discounting mechanism as a fundamental part of the model. It is plausible to suppose that instead of the discounting process being multiplicative, it is subtractive. That is, people reduce either the likelihood ratio or the posterior probability ratio by merely subtracting some amount that reflects the degree of noncredibility of the information. The purpose of the present research was to examine the adequacy of the multiplicative discounting mechanism and, if it is adequate, to see if source credibility is the multiplicative discounting factor as suggested by Gettys, Kelly, and Peterson (1973) and Snapper and Fryback (1971).

Participants were asked to evaluate hypothetical job candidates and assess the "probability of success" on a particular job for each candidate. Each candidate for a particular job was described as having some personality trait or characteristic that has been assessed by an outside agency. This trait varied in its relevance to the job and the agencies varied in their credibility, where the latter was defined as the percentage of times in the past that the source had provided accurate information. Relevance and credibility are variables that have previously been shown to be important in opinion revision research (e.g., Choo, 1964; Hill, 1963; Hovland, Janis & Kelley, 1966).

Method

Experimental materials consisted of hypothetical "referral reports" in which applicants for one of three jobs (Driver Education Teacher, Journalist, or Social Worker) were described as having an attribute that was of one of three degrees of relevance (high, medium, or low) to job performance. The referral reports supposedly came from personnel agencies (sources) that had differing degrees of credibility as a result of their past records of accurate evaluations (100%, 75%, 50%, 25%). The 3 jobs × 3 relevance levels × 4 credibility levels = 36 hypothetical referral reports, 1 for each of 36 hypothetical applicants. Each report constituted a page in a booklet that was given to each participant in the experiment; the pages of each booklet were scrambled to control for presentation order effects.

The three levels of relevance of the applicant attributes for each job were: for the Driver Education Teacher, (high) Perceptual accuracy—speed and depth perception, (medium) Ability to solve abstract theoretical problems, and (low) Artistic ability; for the Journalist, (high) Verbal ability, (medium) Arithmetic ability, and (low) Musical ability; for the Social Worker, (high) Sensitivity and compassion, (medium) Memory—especially for numbers, and (low) Knowledge of art history. The hypothetical applicants all were given favorable evaluations in the reports in order to hold favorableness constant.

Selection of the attributes and specification of the relevance levels were determined before the experiment. Twenty persons (from the same population as the experimental participants) used 5-point scales to rate a large number of personal attributes in terms of their importance for performance of each of the three jobs. The three attributes that received the greatest level of agreement about being of high, medium, and low importance (relevance) for a job were selected for use in the experiment.

Participants read each referral report and estimated the probability that the applicant would succeed in the job. Estimates were made by marking a 100-point scale that was printed on the page below each report. The instructions explained that .0 on the scale meant that the applicant definitely would fail, 1.00 meant that he or she definitely would succeed, .50 meant that one really could not tell one way or the other, and that in-between numbers meant in-between degrees of certainty of success or failure. Thirty-four college students participated.

On the basis of the attitude change literature, it was expected that the less relevant the information was to the occupations in question, the more it would be discounted and that the assessed probability of success of the applicant would decrease as a function of decreased relevance. And, on the basis of both the attitude change literature and the decision literature, it was expected that, for each level of relevance of the information, assessed probability would decrease as a function of decreased source credibility.

The first test consists of seeing whether discounting is subtractive or multiplicative using Anderson's (1971) analytic techniques. These involve both graphing the data for visual inspection and subjecting them to analyses of variance. If discounting is subtractive, the visual inspection should show parallel lines. The main effects of the analysis of variance should be significant but the relevant interaction should be nonsignificant. If discounting is multiplicative, the visual inspection should show converging or diverging lines. The main effects of the analysis of variance should be significant, the relevant interaction also should be significant, and the bilinear component of the interaction should comprise virtually all of the interaction sum of squares.

If discounting proves to be multiplicative, the next step is to see if source credibility is the multiplicative discounting factor. A test of this is afforded by the fact that for some of the hypothetical applicants the sources were represented as 100% credible. Participants' probability assessments for these cases can be regarded as a revision of some unknown prior opinion using some unknown but undiscounted likelihood to obtain the known (the observed assessments) undiscounted posterior opinions. Then, when source credibility is 75%, 50%, or 25%, the observed assessments should be 75%, 50%, or 25% of what they are for 100%. So, for a given level of relevance, knowing the mean observed assessment for when the source is 100% reliable makes it possible to compute what the assessment ought to be for the other three levels of reliability if source credibility is the discounting factor.

Results

In Figure 1, for each job the mean probability assessments are plotted against source credibility for each level of information relevance. If the

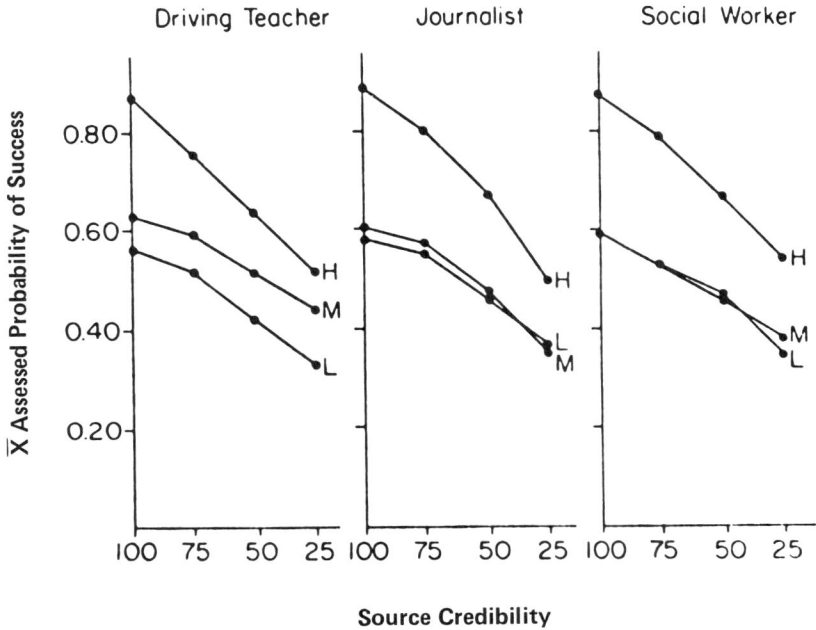

Fig. 1. Mean assessed probability of success as a function of source credibility for high (H), medium (M), and low (L) information relevance for each of three occupations.

influence of the information on assessed probability decreases with decreasing relevance, the curves for the low relevance information should be lowest, and the medium relevance curve should be between the other two—which is indeed the obtained order, although there are small differences in the heights of the curves for the different jobs. If information is discounted as a function of source credibility, the curves should decline from left to right, which they do.

If discounting due to source credibility is subtractive, the curves should be parallel and if it is multiplicative, the curves should converge from left to right; they appear to converge but it is difficult to tell merely by visual inspection.

The assessments were subjected to a 3 X 3 X 4 (jobs X relevance X source credibility) analysis of variance. There was no significant main effect for jobs, $F(2,66) = .148$, but then none was expected. There was a significant jobs X relevance interaction, $F(4,132) = 4.83$, $p < .001$, resulting from the experimenters' failure to make the three levels of relevance precisely the same for all three jobs (Fig. 1); the interaction is of no substantive interest.

The important results are the significant main effects of relevance, $F(2,66)$ = 87.31, $p < .001$, source credibility, $F(3,99)$ = 82.43, $p < .001$, and the relevance $\times$ source credibility interaction, $F(6,198)$ = 8.43, $p < .001$.

The main effect for relevance confirms that the differences in the elevations of the curves in Figure 1 are statistically significant, which means that information has less impact as its relevance decreases. The main effect for source credibility confirms that the differences in the left-to-right decreases of the curves in Figure 1 are statistically significant, which means that information is discounted more as its source's credibility decreases. The significant relevance $\times$ source credibility interaction confirms that the curves in both figures are not parallel, which strongly suggests that discounting is multiplicative, not substractive.

Further analysis of the relevance $\times$ source credibility interaction, using Shanteau's (1976) program for determining the multiplicative (bilinear) component of interactions in factorial designs, revealed that the bilinear sum of squares accounted for 92% of the interaction sum of squares. While there is as yet no adequate test to see if the residual 8% is statistically significant for the design that was used here, it is so small that its significance would be of little interest anyway. The point is that the interaction can be almost completely accounted for by its bilinear component, which means that discounting is multiplicative.

Having eliminated the subtractive model, we turn to the question of whether discounting is merely the result of multiplying the likelihood ratio by source credibility. To do this the participants' probability assessments were converted to ratios and averaged across jobs for each of the three levels of relevance and each of the four levels of source credibility. These means are the observed data that are connected by the solid lines in Figure 2. Then, for each level of relevance, the mean assessment for 100% credible sources was multiplied by .75, .50, and .25; these are the predicted points connected by the dashed lines in Figure 2. If discounting consists merely of multiplying the likelihood ratio (or even the ratio of posterior probabilities) by the credibility of the source, the two sets of points should correspond for each level of relevance. They do not; the obtained curves should all be straight but the curve for the high relevance information clearly is not and the other two clearly have the wrong slopes.

EXPERIMENT 2

The purpose of the second experiment was to see if a judge's confidence in a judgment is influenced by the "orderliness" of the information upon which the judgment is based and whether being unable to control the rate of flow of

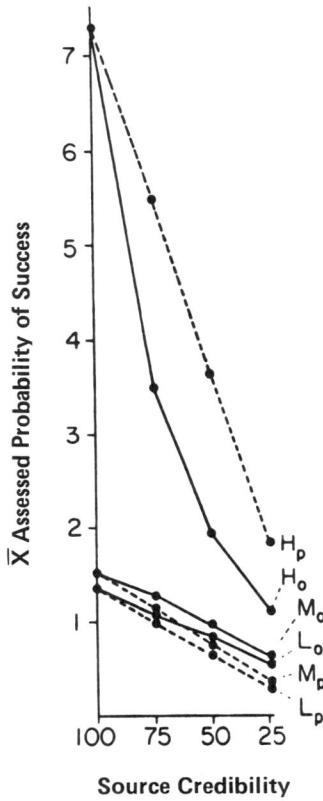

Fig. 2. Predicted (p) and observed (o) mean ratios of assessed probabilities of success as a function of source credibility for high (H), medium (M), and low (L) information relevance.

the information decreases confidence. Information in this case consisted of series of random binary events, yeses and noes.

Much has been said about the effects of perceived randomness, or lack of it, upon behavior, especially in the context of probability learning and the gambler's fallacy (e.g., Alberoni, 1962; Jarvik, 1951; Tune, 1964). In general, humans tend to impose perceptual order on random events and may thereby distort the information content of the events in question, usually by adding more structure than actually exists. This suggests that even for series for which the proportions of different kinds of events are equal, long runs of one kind of event might exert an overlarge impact on the observer and lead to overconfidence in his or her subsequent assessment and to greater satisfaction than might be warranted.

In the same vein, if the observer controls the pace at which the information is received, he has time to digest it and to consider its implications. But, if the information comes at an erratic pace, over which he has no control, no such rumination is possible. It seems reasonable, therefore, to expect both confidence in, and satisfaction with, subsequent judgments to be lower when no control exists than when it does.

For the purposes of this study, orderliness in a series of binary events is defined as the number of times that an event in the series is not the same kind of event as the one it follows. That is, if the series were 011010001 its orderliness index would be 5 because there are 5 changes from 1 to 0 or 0 to 1. To make this work for the experiment, all series were 20 events in length, total alternation (i.e., 010101010101) was eliminated as a possibility, and the strings were 60%, 65%, or 70% one event.

Method

Experimental materials consisted of three scenarios in each of which a person was described as procuring a random sample of 20 people's opinions about a topic—each opinion was merely a yes or a no. One scenario involved a sampling of one employee from each of the 20 different departments of a large business in order to estimate the overall proportion of employees who would contribute to a fund to buy a gift for a college. Participants in the experiment saw the 20 opinions sequentially in the form of 35mm slides that each contained either yes or no and the department to which the employee belonged; 70% were yes. The second scenario involved sampling to determine the proportion of students who would support a levy on tuition to support consumer research at a university. Each of the 20 slides contained either a yes or a no and the polled student's name; 60% were yes. The third scenario involved a business that had the option of buying 1000 lbs. of ostrich feathers. To test the market for ostrich feathers, the business sampled 20 of the many firms that customarily use feathers (for costumes and clothing) to see what proportion could be expected to buy at least one pound of feathers. The 20 slides contained each polled firm's name and its yes or no answer; 65% were yes.

The procedure consisted of having the participants read a scenario and then see the sequence of 20 yeses and noes. Next, they estimated the percentage of yeses in the sequence by marking a 100-point scale (they were asked not to count yeses during the sequence). Then they marked the scale twice more, once to the left of the proportion estimation and once to the right of it. These marks were to delimit the range within which they felt confident that the true proportion lay. This is called an equivalence interval (EI) and it is similar in conception to a statistical confidence interval except that no probability level is specified. The EI is a fairly sensitive measure of the confidence of judges in the accuracy of their own or someone else's judgments (Beach, Beach, Carter, & Barclay, 1974; Beach & Solak, 1969; Laestadius, 1970). In addition to marking this scale, the participants marked 100-point scales to indicate how satisfied they were with their judgment and how orderly the sequence had seemed to them.

One half of the participants controlled the rate of appearance of the 20 slides for each scenario by pressing the change control on the projector whenever they were ready for the next slide. The other half were yoked to the first half; while a participant in the first group was going through the slides, a tape cassette recorded the sound of the projector changing slides. Then when the yoked member of the second group was shown the slides, the experimenter merely listened to the tape through an earphone and changed the slide whenever the tape indicated that the first person had changed. In this way, each person in the second (no-control) group got exactly the same exposure to the slides as did his or her counterpart in the first group, but he or she did not control the rate nor the duration of presentation.

Seventy-two business school students participated in the experiment, 36 in each group (control vs. no control).

Results

To control for individual differences in the use of the response scales, each participant's responses were z-transformed using his or her own mean response and standard deviation. Then a two-way analysis of variance for repeated measures was performed on EI (three levels of orderliness and two levels of control of information flow). This showed significant effects on EI of orderliness ($F = 3.3$, $df = 2,140$, $p = .04$) and of the interaction between orderliness and control ($F = 3.1$, $df = 2,140$, $p = .05$).

Closer examination of the data showed that the interaction was due to the effect of orderliness being solely in the group that could control the information flow. Analyses of variance on the two groups separately revealed a strong effect of orderliness on EIs in the control condition ($F = 6.9$, $df = 2,70$, $p < .001$) and no effect in the no-control condition ($F = 0$). This result can be seen by looking at the mean z-transformed EIs for each level of orderliness for each group in Table 1.

Table 1. Mean Z-Transformed EIs for the Group that Controlled Information Flow (C) and the Group that Did Not (NC) for the Three Levels of Orderliness (H = 6, M = 9, L = 12)

Control	Orderliness		
	H	M	L
C	−.439	.078	.359
NC	−.024	.043	−.018

Note. — Negative numbers indicate small EIs and positive numbers indicate large EIs.

EXPERIMENT 3

The first two experiments dealt primarily with the effects of information variables on judgments. The third experiment is addressed to more explicitly situational factors—the effects of different kinds of influence one has in determining the outcome of a group judgment on satisfaction with the task.

The preponderance of interest about the effects of a group member's power or influence has focused on power within the structure of the group itself. However, there is a neglected, collateral variable that also can have an effect. This is the degree to which the member's group has power when a number of groups all contribute to the final judgment, a common occurrence in organizations. We call the former influence "vertical power" and the latter "horizontal power." The purpose of this experiment was to examine the relative contribution of vertical and horizontal power to satisfaction in a simulated work situation.

Method

One hundred and fifty-one marketing students were asked to rate nine sporting goods products in terms of market potential. Each group was composed of three people, a leader and two followers. Although the task was done separately, the three judgments were weighted, according to one of three power distributions, and combined to form a group judgment. This group judgment was in turn weighted, according to one of four power distributions, and combined with the score generated by a (fictitious) group of engineering students to give an overall decision. Thus, there were three levels of (within group) vertical power and four levels of (between group) horizontal power. Students from an introductory marketing course were assigned the role of "members" and students from an intermediate course were "leaders." Overall, there were 45 leaders and 106 members.

Participants were informed that the study was being conducted by a number of the marketing and engineering faculty in conjunction with the "GMA Research Co." in order to explore the feasibility of using student input to improve new product evaluations. This involved evaluating sporting goods products currently being considered by firms who were clients of GMA.

Participants were told that the nine new products were to be evaluated by 6-person teams composed of two 3-person subgroups. One subgroup, composed of engineering students, was to evaluate the products on a production-cost basis. The other subgroup, composed of the marketing students, was to evaluate the market potential of the products. Moreover, they were told that due to time and room constraints it was not possible to schedule the engineering and marketing student evaluations at the same place, but the two subgroup ratings would be combined later in the day to form an overall team rating of the products. Thus, the experimental sessions included only marketing subgroups. In fact, no engineering students took part in the study.

Six criteria were specified for evaluating each product idea and a brief statement was provided to give information about each product. The participants rated the product on each of the criteria, using 10-point scales, in terms of the market potential of the product. The group leader calculated the marketing subgroup's rating by weighting the three individual ratings. Vertical power was defined as these individual weights. Participants were told that the weights represented their individual contribution to the marketing subgroup, this contribution being based on their training rather than on their ability to persuade others. Since the leader had more training (in an upper level course) than the other two members (who were from the introductory course), the leader was always given more influence than the two members, each of whom was assigned equal weights. There were three vertical power distributions:

Distribution 1: Leader   = .40
                  Member one = .30
                  Member two = .30

Distribution 2: Leader   = .60
                  Member one = .20
                  Member two = .20

Distribution 3: Leader   = .80
                  Member one = .10
                  Member two = .10

A similar weighting procedure was used to combine the two subgroup ratings, horizontal power. However a different explanation was given to justify the difference in the power distribution between marketing and engineering subgroups. The differences in these weights were explained on the basis of product characteristics:

> Each of the client firms was asked to indicate the relative amount of influence it gave to marketing and engineering information in the initial evaluation of new product ideas. In general, these firms believed, on the basis of the materials and processes involved, that the engineering groups should be given more/less influence.

Whether reference was made to "more" or to "less" influence for the engineering subgroup depended on the particular horizontal power distribution being implemented in that session:

Distribution 1:   Marketing subgroup   = .80
                   Engineering subgroup = .20

Distribution 2:   Marketing subgroup   = .60
                   Engineering subgroup = .40

Distribution 3:   Marketing subgroup   = .40
                   Engineering subgroup = .60

Distribution 4:   Marketing subgroup   = .20
                   Engineering subgroup = .80

After the groups finished rating the nine products, each participant was given a questionnaire to complete. One question was aimed at subtly assaying satisfaction with the task by asking the number of hours the participants would be willing to commit to further product evaluation. Three additional questions were more straightforward: (1) How satisfied are you with your personal influence within your marketing subgroup? (2) How satisfied are you with your marketing subgroup's influence within your combined marketing-engineering team? (3) How satisfied are you with your overall influence in your combined marketing-engineering team?

Results

It was predicted that satisfaction with the task would increase as both vertical and horizontal power increased. Turning to the question about willingness to commit themselves to further work, the results are mixed. Using an analysis of variance, there was a marginal effect of horizontal power on time commitment of members ($F = 2.51$, $df = 3,127$, $p < .06$). That is, as group power increased, the participants indicated that they would be willing to spend an average of from 1.31 up to 2.08 additional hours rating the products. Vertical power also was marginally related to time commitment ($F =$

2.08, df = 5,127, $p < .07$) with time commitment going from an average of 1.50 up to 2.73 additional hours on the task as vertical power increased.

The question about satisfaction with individual influence within the group showed significant effects only for vertical power (F = 10.41, df = 5,127, $p < .01$) but the effect of horizontal power was negligible, while satisfaction with the subgroup's influence on the overall decision was influenced only by horizontal power (F = 28.64, df = 3,127, $p < .01$) and vertical power had no effect. And, for satisfaction with individual influence on the overall decision, both vertical power (F = 23.32, df = 5,127, $p < .01$) and horizontal power (F = 7.42, df = 3,127, $p < .01$) had significant effects.

CONCLUSIONS

These experiments all involve questions that could not have been adequately examined in real-world settings; the conditions for their examination do not arise with sufficient regularity. It is the case, however, that one must be wary of accepting their results until they have been checked outside the laboratory.

All three of these experiments demonstrate that judges are influenced by environmental conditions that affect the real or perceived quality of the information they receive (experiments 1 and 2) and the impact of their judgments (experiment 3). The first experiment shows that information relevance and source credibility influenced judgments about probability: Information has less influence when it is less relevant and it is discounted when source credibility decreases. Discounting is a multiplicative process, a conclusion supported by research in other contexts by Shanteau and Anderson (1972) and by Birnbaum, Wong, and Wong (1976), but it is not merely a matter of multiplying by source credibility as suggested by Gettys et al. (1973) and Snapper and Fryback (1971). Unfortunately, it is likely that discounting is situation specific and nothing more generalizable can be said about it than that it is multiplicative.

The second experiment showed that when judges control information flow, the orderliness in a series of binary events influences their confidence in their proportion estimates. This suggests that information should be carefully summarized instead of viewed sequentially, if the disorder in the series is not to have an adverse influence on confidence; if summarization is not possible, the judge should be in control of the reception of information rather than receiving it passively, although the judge may resist relying on his or her estimates because of low confidence.

The third experiment suggests that judges are sensitive both to their vertical power and to their horizontal power in multi-group judgment tasks and that their satisfaction with the degree to which they influence the final judgment is affected by both kinds of power. More research needs to be done to investigate the relative effects of the two kinds of power on judge satisfaction.

REFERENCES

Alberoni, F. Contribution to the study of subjective probability. *Journal of General Psychology*, 1962, **66**, 241–264.

Anderson, N. H. Integration theory and attitude change. *Psychological Review*, 1971, **78**, 171–206.

Beach, L. R., Beach, B. H., Carter, W. B., & Barclay, S. Five studies of subjective equivalence. *Organizational Behavior and Human Performance*, 1974, **12**, 351–371.

Beach, L. R., & Solak, F. Subjective judgments of acceptable error. *Organizational Behavior and Human Performance*, 1969, **4**, 242–251.

Birnbaum, M. H., Wong, R., & Wong, L. K. Combining information from sources that vary in credibility. *Memory and Cognition*, 1976, **4**, 330–336.

Choo, T. Communicator credibility and communication discrepancy as determinants of opinion change. *Journal of Social Psychology*, 1964, **64**, 65–76.

Gettys, C. F., Kelly, C., & Peterson, C. R. The best guess hypothesis in multistage inference. *Organizational Behavior and Human Performance*, 1973, **10**, 364–373.

Gettys, C. F., & Wilke, T. A. The application of Bayes' theorem when the true data state is unknown. *Organizational Behavior and Human Performance*, 1969, **4**, 125–141.

Hill, A. H. Credibility, discrepancy and latitude of communication as dimensions of dissonance influencing attitude change. *Australian Journal of Psychology*, 1963, **15**, 124–132.

Hovland, C. I., Janis, I. L., & Kelley, H. H. A summary of experimental studies of opinion change. In M. Jahoda & N. Warren (Eds.), *Attitudes*. Baltimore: Penguin, 1966, 139–151.

Jarvik, M. E. Probability learning and a negative recency effect in a serial anticipation of alternative symbols. *Journal of Experimental Psychology*, 1951, **41**, 291–297.

Laestadius, J. E. Tolerance for errors in intuitive mean estimations. *Organizational Behavior and Human Performance*, 1970, **5**, 121–124.

Peterson, C. R. Introduction to special issue on hierarchical inference. *Organizational Behavior and Human Performance*, 1973, **10**, 315–317.

Schum, D. A., & DuCharme, W. M. Comments on the relationship between the impact and the reliability of evidence. *Organizational Behavior and Human Performance*, 1971, **6**, 111–131.

Shanteau, J. *Polylin: A fortran program for analysis of multiplicative trend components of interactions in a factorial design*. Kansas State University Psychology Report No. 76-4, 1976.

Shanteau, J., & Anderson, N. H. Integration theory applied to judgments of the value of information. *Journal of Experimental Psychology*, 1972, **92**, 266–275.

Snapper, K., & Fryback, D. G. Inferences based on unreliable reports. *Journal of Experimental Psychology*, 1971, **87**, 401–404.

Tune, G. S. Response preferences: A review of some relevant literature. *Psychological Bulletin*, 1964, **61**, 286–302.

DECISION MAKING AND DECISION IMPLEMENTATION IN GROUPS AND ORGANIZATIONS

Carl H. Castore
Purdue University

When a group or organization must choose among alternatives (goals, policies, personnel, etc.), the following process typically transpires:

(a) The alternatives are defined.

(b) Information about the alternatives is gathered. This may result in some redefinition of the alternatives coupled with further information search.

(c) The group members evaluate the alternatives in light of their anticipated relationship to desired outcomes.

(d) The group reaches a decision or selects an alternative by means of some process which combines individual group members' preferences into a group preference.

(e) The actions seen as necessary to implement the decision are organized and undertaken.

(f) Feedback is received about the extent to which the actions undertaken are achieving the desired outcome(s). On the basis of such feedback, groups may decide to maintain their existing course, to explore alternative approaches to implementing the decision, to reconsider the decision, to reformulate the alternatives and begin the process again, or some combination of these.

Within this sequence of events, the process of decision making, selecting a group choice, is but one step in a more general process that is calculated to bring about some desired future state of affairs. Nonetheless, it is a particularly visible and important step in that it constitutes the primary link between the essentially cognitive judgmental processes exercised by individuals and group processes associated with the implementation of the decision. Indeed, some measure of this visibility and importance is seen in the tendency to equate the adequacy of decisions with the effectiveness of the implementation activities.

A variety of factors have been related to various aspects of this decision making-implementation process. The definition of alternatives and subsequent information search activities may be influenced by a number of environmental constraints, such as the time available to make decisions, the availability of particular alternatives, the cost of information, the degree of uncertainty associated with the outcomes anticipated, etc. Various personality characteristics, risk/uncertainty tolerance, the persons' abilities and training relative to information processing, and the goals of the persons involved may further affect choice definition and search processes (cf. Driver & Streufert, 1969; Schroder, Driver, & Streufert, 1967; Streufert, 1977; Suedfeld, 1977). In addition, research by Streufert and his associates (e.g., Streufert & Castore, 1971; Streufert, Suedfeld, & Driver, 1965) as well as by researchers in the Bayesian tradition indicate that characteristics of the available data itself (e.g., complexity, redundancy, reliability, perceived problem relevance, whether it is positive or negative with regard to the hypothesis under consideration) impact on these definitional and search processes (e.g., Ackoff, 1967; Beach, 1977; Ebert, 1972; Moskowitz, 1972; Slovic & Lichtenstein, 1971). It should be noted that most of this research has focused on the information acquisition phase of the decision process. The question of how alternatives are defined and developed has either been of only tangential interest, or it has been ignored altogether. However, the possible extent of the impact of this initial phase on all succeeding steps in the decision process is suggested by recent findings reported by Plott (1976) and Fiorino (1976) as well as the case studies on crisis decision making developed by Janis (1972). In both the laboratory and case studies, the initial definition and development of alternatives were major determinants of the subsequent search, evaluation, and choice phases of the decision process.

The evaluation of alternatives will also be influenced by a number of environmental and individual factors, characteristics of the data itself, and the results of the two preceding steps. The degree of influence which these factors have on the evaluation of alternatives may be largely determined by the nature of the individual judgmental process involved at this stage. Naylor (1977) has suggested that the judgmental processes in decision making may be

Table 1. Types of Judgment Contexts

	Type of judgmental response	
	Statement of preference	Description of alternatives
Criterion present	Selection of subordinates Promotion decisions (I)	Medical diagnoses Weather forecasting (II)
Criterion absent	Political candidate selection by voters Decision by an editor to publish a book (III)	Predicting energy needs 30 years hence Interpretation of photos from Mars (IV)

classified as one of four distinct types, depending upon whether or not a criterion is available to gauge the accuracy of the judgments and whether an individual's judgment is a statement of preference or is descriptive. (In preference judgments, an individual is stating his tastes, his preference for some entity in preference to another, or his indifference between them. In a descriptive judgment, an individual is indicating how much of some attribute an entity appears to possess.) This four-fold categorization and an example of each type of judgment context are indicated in Table 1.

Cells I and II of Table 1 contain situations in which a "correct answer" is either definable in an actuarial sense, or is knowable within a relatively short period of time. Both laboratory tests and subsequent physical developments can confirm a medical diagnosis based on reported and observed symptoms, the weather man merely waits a day or so, and there are performance standards available to let an employer know how accurate his choice was. In contrast, in the contexts typifying Cell III, the preference judgments are based primarily on affective reactions (like-dislike). Such judgments are reflections of personal opinion and are not subject to the same types of verification as those in Cells I and II. The two instances which typify Cell IV reflect situations in which an objective criterion will at some time probably be available. However, the decision maker has no basis for developing actuarial criteria in such contexts, and he has little hope of obtaining access to objective or actuarial criteria in the near future to use in revising his judgments.

Individual values and beliefs, as well as group influences on these, would then be expected to have their greatest effects on judgmental responses in criterion-absent situations, as in Cells III and IV. Alternatively, those characteristics of the environment, individuals, and the data itself which would affect an individual's ability to accurately process information should then have their most pronounced effects on evaluative responses in criteria-present situations, as in Cells I and II. Some support for these contentions may be gleaned from a consideration of the research on group problem solving reviewed by Kelley and Thibaut (1969) and McGrath and Altman (1966). At the same time, it is also apparent that most of the research on group decision making stemming from either the group dynamics tradition or the Bayesian and regression traditions has been conducted in problem solving contexts primarily prototypic of Cell II and to a lesser extent of Cell I. Conversely, findings recently reported by Vroom and Yetton (1973) indicate that many of the decision situations faced by upper level managers, and from these managers' reports their most difficult decisions, are more typical of those found in Cells III and IV.

The judgment context should also have a major effect on the actual decision-making process and its outcome. If a group is attempting to reach a common descriptive judgment when criteria are available (Cell II), as in most problem solving situations, the major focus of the interaction is (or should be) on achieving the most accurate judgment possible within the constraints of time, information quality, group member abilities, and other available resources. In most instances, interaction in this context will lead to a convergence of individual judgments (Moscovici & Zavalloni, 1969). Kelley and Thibaut (1969) have detailed the extent to which characteristics of the judgment task itself, other environmental factors, characteristics of the information available, and group member abilities will further affect group judgments in such contexts. Different decision procedures and communication networks will impact on the outcome of the decision process in this instance to the extent that they facilitate or inhibit the communication and acceptance of the judgments most closely in accord with the criteria (cf. Collins & Raven, 1969; Smoke & Zajonc, 1962).

It might be reasonably anticipated that the effectiveness of the implementation of such decisions would follow rather directly from the adequacy of the decision itself, and the extent to which those responsible for the implementation concur in the decision's adequacy. Indeed, there is some support for this supposition in the literature on participative decision making (Lowin, 1968) and in the aforementioned research by Vroom and Yetton (1973). In the same fashion, the response to feedback concerning decision adequacy in this context should lead to appropriate (when necessary) corrective steps. And, to the extent that individual need satisfaction is related to the formal achievement of the group, group member relations and cohesion should be positively related to decision quality. However, it should be noted that much of the foregoing is speculative. There is little direct evidence available on the nature of the interrelationships among aspects of the decision-making process, the effectiveness of implementation activities, and the response to feedback in such problem-solving contexts.

When a group is attempting to agree on a preference judgment in the absence of criteria (Cell III), the process appears to differ in several important respects from that just described. The task facing the group in this case is the reconciliation of conflicting opinions in a manner conducive to further effective group functioning. In this instance the focus of the decision process is (or should be) on reaching a group decision which is maximally representative of group member preferences. The effects of information characteristics on the decision process in this situation may be quite different from that observed in problem solving contexts. To the extent that the group members disagree about the relative desirability of alternative outcomes (low goal agreement), greater certainty that particular decisions will yield particular outcomes could lead to greater disagreement, more difficulty in reaching decisions, and the hardening of the view of disagreeing factions within a group (Castore, in press; Cummings, O'Connell, & Huber, 1977). Paradoxically, less reliable information could potentially facilitate agreement in such a situation. To the extent that there is some initial moderate level of goal agreement among group members, greater certainty of agreement between actions and outcomes could also increase the ease in reaching decisions, and even lead to the polarization (or radicalization) of groups' positions (Castore, in press; Moscovici & Zavalloni, 1969).

From the vantage of formal theory, the diversity of group member goal preferences is a major obstacle to the definition of a mathematically representative group decision (i.e., one giving equal weight to each person's preferences), regardless of the actual mechanism used to arrive at the decision (Arrow, 1963; Black, 1958). Recently, Castore (1976a; 1976b; in press) and Castore and Murnighan (in press) found that individual perceptions of the representativeness of group decisions and individual satisfaction with such decisions decreased as the diversity of group member goal preferences increased. These perceptions were in general agreement with the mathematical representativeness of the decisions reached. However, decisions in which the groups attempted to take strength of preference into account were generally viewed as less representative and yielded lower individual satisfaction with their outcomes. In addition, individuals in the majority faction of a group tended to view the decisions as more representative and were more satisfied with them than were individuals in the minority factions. The decisions reached by the groups tended to be of comparable representativeness regardless of the actual process used to reach them (benevolent dictatorship; majority rule with formal voting; discussion to majority consensus; and unanimity). Nonetheless, group members were more favorably disposed toward the decisions reached by one of the majoritarian processes. Finally, the participants in these studies were generally willing to put more money or effort into the implementation of their groups' decisions when: (a) They were members of the majority faction within the group; (b) the groups had initially high goal agreement; and (c) the decisions were made by majoritarian procedures rather than by unanimity or autocratic procedures.

There is little basis, at present, from which to speculate about the effects of different communication networks on decision processes in this context. Presumably, to the extent that a communication network is particularly conducive to authoritarian or majoritarian decision processes, the effect of the network would be expected to closely parallel that for the corresponding decision process. On the whole, it must be noted that beyond the studies by Castore (1976a, 1976b), Vroom and Yetton (1973), and a collection of papers edited by Lieberman (1971), relatively little is known about the parameters which affect decision making and decision implementation when the decisions reflect statements of preference in the absence of criteria. That which is known suggests that decisions in this context and their implementation are greatly influenced by the values and goals of the individual group members.

Virtually no group decision research exists which has used a decision context prototypic of Cell IV, descriptive judgments with no criteria available; and Cell I, preference judgments with criteria available. The former (Cell IV) is the context which much of the research on the effectiveness of the Delphi technique has nominally been concerned with. However, an examination of the judgment problems actually used in the research indicates that tasks were used in which criteria were immediately available from an almanac or other such source. Further, some of the decision participants may have had some partial knowledge (conscious or unconscious) of the actual values they were estimating in these tasks inasmuch as they were experts in the subject matter areas from which the problems were drawn.

The data on individual decision making in the Cell I context suggest that the accuracy of the group decision will be influenced by those factors previously mentioned as influencing the accuracy of decisions in a Cell II context. In addition, other factors, such as the level of goal agreement among group members, would be expected to have an impact. Also, the objective data available would seem amenable to more or less self-serving interpretations by individual group members depending upon the importance of the choice. Finally, normative pressures, such as social comparison processes (cf. Sulls & Miller, in press), would be expected to play a major role in the formation of judgments in Cells I, III, and IV. The extent to which such normative pressures would influence the judgments should be dependent primarily upon the intensity of individual preferences and/or the clarity of the criteria. To the extent that such processes were instrumental in the making of group judgments in these three contexts, they would be expected to play a similar role in the implementation of such decisions and in the responsiveness of groups to feedback concerning decision adequacy.

From the preceding brief synopsis, it is readily apparent that the bulk of the research on group decision making and implementation to date has focused on the information search, information evaluation, and decision-making steps in the process. Most of this research has used tasks in which the group has been required to reach descriptive judgments with criteria available, essentially a problem-solving context. In contrast, very little attention has been directed toward decision making in a relatively criteria-free context, which appears to be more typical of that facing many organizational decision makers. Also, virtually no attention has been given to three central phases in the decision process: the selection of alternatives to be considered, the implementation of the decision once reached, and the reaction of the group to feedback. All of these phases are important to a comprehensive understanding of the relationship between organizational decision processes and performance effectiveness. On a related issue, there are a number of methodological problems which appear to crosscut a great deal of decision-making research. Central to these is the need for a better quantification of the constructs of information quality, quantity, complexity, and reliability in a manner that would permit the same measures to be easily used in both the laboratory and field.

Finally, it is apparent that much more work is necessary which focuses on the entire decision process from development of alternatives for consideration through the implementation and feedback phases in both controlled simulation studies (e.g., Streufert, 1977) and quantitative case studies drawn from a variety of contexts (e.g., Janis, 1972; Vroom & Yetton, 1973). This work is necessary for the development of better descriptive models; for the identification of the parameters which influence the overall process; and for a more comprehensive understanding of the interrelationships among the aspects of the decision-making and implementation process.

REFERENCES

Ackoff, R. L. Management misinformation systems. *Management Science*, 1967, **14**, B-147–156.

Arrow, K. W. *Social choice and individual values* (2nd ed.). New York: Wiley, 1963.

Beach, L., & Mitchell, T. Subjective uncertainty in decision making. In B. T. King, S. Streufert, & F. E. Fielder (Eds.), *Managerial control and organizational democracy*. Washington, D.C.: V. H. Winston & Sons, 1977.

Black, D. *The theory of committees and elections*. Cambridge, U.K.: Cambridge University Press, 1958.

Castore, C. H. *Individual reactions to majoritarian processes*. Paper presented at the meeting of the American Political Science Association, Chicago, Ill., 1976. (a)

Castore, C. H. *Individual support of group decisions.* Paper presented at the Interamerican Congress of Psychology, Miami, Fla., 1976. (b)

Castore, C. H. Determination of group member support for majority rule decisions. *Journal of Personality and Social Psychology*, in press.

Castore, C. H., & Murnighan, J. K. Determinants of support for group decisions. *Organizational Behavior and Human Performance*, in press.

Collins, B. E., & Raven, B. H. Group structure: Attraction, coalitions, communication, and power. In G. Lindzey & E. Aronson (Eds.), *Handbook of social psychology* (Vol. IV) (2nd ed.). Reading, Mass.: Addison-Wesley, 1969.

Cummings, L., O'Connell, M., & Huber, G. Information and structural determinants of decision-maker satisfaction. In B. T. King, S. Streufert, & F. E. Fiedler (Eds.), *Managerial control and organizational democracy.* Washington, D.C.: V. H. Winston & Sons, 1977.

Driver, M. J., & Streufert, S. Integrative complexity: An approach to indivduals and groups as information processing systems. *Administrative Science Quarterly*, 1969, **14**, 272–285.

Ebert, R. J. Environmental structure and programmed decision effectiveness. *Management Science*, 1972, **19**, 435–445.

Fiorino, M. *Electoral systems: An experimental approach.* Paper presented at the meeting of the American Political Science Association, Chicago, Ill., 1976.

Janis, I. *Victims of groupthink.* Boston: Houghton-Mifflin, 1972.

Kelley, H. H., & Thibaut, J. W. Group problem solving. In G. Lindzey & E. Aronson (Eds.), *Handbook of social psychology* (Vol. IV) (2nd ed.). Reading, Mass.: Addison-Wesley, 1969.

Lieberman, B. (Ed.). *Social choice.* New York: Gordon & Breach, 1971.

Lowin, A. Participative decision making: A model, literature critique, and prescriptions for research. *Organizational Behavior and Human Performance*, 1968, **3**, 68–106.

McGrath, J., & Altman, I. *Small group research.* New York: Holt, Rinehart, & Winston, 1966.

Moscovici, S., & Zavalloni, M. The group as a polarizer of attitudes. *Journal of Personality and Social Psychology*, 1969, **12**, 125–135.

Moskowitz, H. The value of information in aggregate production planning—a behavioral experiment. *AIIE Transactions*, 1972, **4**, 290–297.

Naylor, J. C., Pritchard, R., & Ilgen, D. *A theory of organizational behavior.* Unpublished manuscript, Lafayette, Ind.: Purdue University, 1977.

Plott, C. R. *The correction of market externalities: An experimental study.* Paper presented at the meeting of the American Political Science Association, Chicago, Ill., 1976.

Schroder, H. M., Driver, M. J., & Streufert, S. *Human information processing.* New York: Holt, Rinehart, & Winston, 1967.

Slovic, P., & Lichtenstein, S. Comparison of Bayesian and regression approaches to the study of information processing in judgment. *Organizational Behavior and Human Performance*, 1971, **6**, 649–744.

Smoke, W. B., & Zajonc, R. B. On the reliability of group judgments and decisions. In J. H. Criswell, H. Solomon, & P. Suppes (Eds.), *Mathematical methods in small group processes.* Stanford, Ca.: Stanford University Press, 1962.

Streufert, S. Decisions and stress: The limits of the human component in the decision making situation. In B. T. King, S. Streufert, & F. E. Fiedler (Eds.), *Managerial control and organizational democracy.* Washington, D.C.: V. H. Winston & Sons, 1977.

Streufert, S., & Castore, C. H. Information search and the effects of failure: A test of complexity theory. *Journal of Experimental Social Psychology*, 1971, 7, 125–143.

Streufert, S., Suedfeld, P., & Driver, M. J. Conceptual structure, information search, and information utilization. *Journal of Personality and Social Psychology*, 1965, 2, 736–740.

Suedfeld, P. Characteristics of decision making as a function of the environment. In B. T. King, S. Streufert, & F. E. Fiedler (Eds.), *Managerial control and organizational democracy.* Washington, D.C.: V. H. Winston & Sons, 1977.

Sulls, J., & Miller, R. (Eds.). *Theoretical and empirical perspectives on social comparison theory.* Washington, D.C.: Hemisphere, in press.

Vroom, V. H., & Yetton, P. W. *Leadership behavior on standardized cases* (Tech. Rep. No. 3). New Haven, Conn.: Yale University, 1973.

AUTHOR INDEX

277

SUBJECT INDEX